Cocolat

ALICE MEDRICH

Cocolat

Extraordinary Chocolate Desserts

Photographs by Patricia Brabant

- - -

Photo Styling by Sara Slavin

- - -

Design by Jacqueline Jones

WARNER BOOKS

A Time Warner Company

Warner Books, Inc.,
666 Fifth Avenue,
New York, NY 10103

Ⓦ A Time Warner Company

Printed in the United States of America
First printing: October 1990
10 9 8 7 6 5 4 3 2 1

Library of Congress Cataloging-in-Publication Data
Medrich, Alice.
    Cocolat / by Alice Medrich.
        p. cm.
    ISBN 0-446-51419-5
        1. Cookery (Chocolate)   2. Desserts.   3. Cocolat (Shop)
I. Title.
TX767.C5M43   1990
641.6'374—дc20   90-31611
                                    CIP

Book design: Jacqueline Jones
Design assistance and mechanical production:
Deborah Shubert and Suzanne Skugstad,
Jacqueline Jones Design
Photography: Patricia Brabant
Illustration: Donnie Cameron
Stylist: Sara Slavin
Food Stylist: Alice Medrich

For Elliott

Acknowledgments

I owe my greatest thanks, love, and appreciation to my husband, Elliott, who not only insisted that I could write a book, but persisted in believing. Moral support is one thing, but this man also entered every single one of my recipe drafts into the computer so that they would be at my fingertips for editing and rewriting. He brought me cold beer and roasted garlic chicken for dinner, and he took care of 2½-month-old Lucy before, during, and after work and weekends so that I could meet my deadlines.

The staff at Cocolat put up with my preoccupation and carried on so splendidly that I never felt guilty, only encouraged. I thank Carol Viliani and Susan Merrill-Chun, Albert Abrams, Christine Blaine, Molly Wantuch, and Mort Miller especially, for helping to make it possible for me to work, have a baby, and finish a book during the same year.

Cynthia Traina, of Traina Public Relations, taught me to appreciate some of my own accomplishments and encouraged many others to do so as well.

Patricia Brabant, whose photography and often art direction make this book so special, was a joy and an encouraging accomplice. Sara Slavin's prop styling and collaboration, and her artist's eye were inspirational to me. The two of them brought my fantasy to life on the page and allowed me to learn food styling "on the job." I can't say how much pleasure this activity brought me. I was sad when it was over and we had to give up our Friday shoot days, even if some of them were long and hard.

Thanks to Jacqueline Jones for designing a beautiful book around my desserts and recipes, and for being extraordinarily patient and lovely to work with.

Donnie Cameron's beautiful illustrations made this book complete and I thank her for working so agreeably around my erratic schedule.

My editor, Liv Blumer, was enthusiastic and encouraging — even when I was terrified and late. I appreciate her hard work, eye for detail, good suggestions, and her patience with a first-time author having a first baby in the middle of it all.

I tip my hat to Bob Miller, formerly at Warner Books, who called me out of the blue to ask if I wanted to write a book. Jane Dystal, my agent, made a deal and held my hand.

Warmest thanks to Charlotte Combe (Charlotte Combe Cooking School), Mary Risley (Tante Marie's Cooking School), and Jack Lirio (Jack Lirio Cooking School), who invited me to teach and taught me that I had something to offer others.

My grandmother, Mabel, taught me that "quality is quality" and "plain is best." My parents, Bea and Herman Abrams, gave me all of the intangibles, including high standards, and especially the belief that I could do it my way.

Victoria Wise bought my first chocolate truffles and cakes for her wonderful Pig-by-the-Tail Charcuterie in Berkeley, and served as a powerful role model for Cocolat's beginning.

Libby Medrich, sculptor and mother-in-law, lent me money to open my first store. I thank her also for bragging about me shamelessly.

Edith McClure stood by me and added something very special to Cocolat in the early years.

Jan Weimer wrote the first feature article about Cocolat for the San Francisco Chronicle in 1977. When we later became friends, Jan helped me choreograph the opening party for my second store. It was Jan who said, "I'll take care of the guest list . . . all you have to do is invent 25 different kinds of chocolate truffles." Jan later asked me to write for Bon Appétit magazine, when she was food editor there, and has continued to encourage and inspire me to do things I never thought I could!

I cherish the memory of special lessons and time given me by Marguerite La Pierre and Camille Cadier in Paris. M. and Mme. Désiré Valentin and their children welcomed me into their home in Rheims and allowed me to see and experience work in a French pâtisserie. Fernande Lestelle, landlady and friend, helped make Paris our home away from home. She began the Cocolat story by giving me my first truffle — and the recipe!

Paris, December 1972.

I am sitting at Madame Lestelle's dining room table, helping her with holiday chores. I have no idea how this afternoon will shape my life. At 73 years of age she is sharp and energetic. In England, the United States, or Scandinavia, we might have been preparing fruits and nuts for Christmas puddings or fruitcakes, or rolling and cutting Christmas cookies. But this is France. We are making fresh homemade chocolate truffles—bite-size morsels of smooth, rich, and intensely bittersweet chocolate, dusted with cocoa—which she will later wrap and deliver to relatives and friends. I am encouraged to taste the fruits of our labors. The first bite is a revelation. ▪ ▪ ▪

This was no mere chocolate kiss or piece of sweet fudge. That truffle was something beyond candy and much closer to an "adult" chocolate dessert. I had never tasted anything so sublimely chocolate. To this day, I refuse to use the word "candy" to describe a real chocolate truffle—made only with chocolate, butter, and eggs or fresh cream. I regret that the chocolate truffle "idea" has become so popular that hundreds of mundane chocolate candies are now called truffles simply because they are chocolate. ▪ ▪ ▪

In one kaleidoscope of a year in France, I surely tasted and enjoyed thousands of wonderful foods, including extraordinary desserts and pastries of every description. Two bites in particular made a profound impression on me. Madame Lestelle's chocolate truffle was one. The second was a simple, rather homey chocolate cake. I tasted it first in a cooking class, then reproduced it in my own cranky oven on the rue Copernic. ▪ ▪ ▪

These two chocolate moments characterized everything that is awesome to me about food in France: that the simplest things are often the most sophisticated, the most elegant, and best of all, the most delicious. The French seem always to know this, despite the dizzy altitudes of haute cuisine. Both the truffle and the cake were superb because each tasted exactly of its few, but excellent ingredients. Chocolate, the star ingredient, could be appreciated for all its rich, almost earthy and sensual qualities because it had not been overwhelmed by sugar. ▪ ▪ ▪

My grandmother's conviction was always "plain is best, dear." Eating and cooking in France won me decidedly to her point of view, and it shaped my philosophy about my own desserts, my business, and so many other things in my life. ▪ ▪ ▪

My husband, Elliott, and I returned to Berkeley the following year, and I entered the graduate program in Business Administration with no idea what I really wanted to do. ▪ ▪ ▪

At the same time, and just for fun, I "perfected" Madame Lestelle's truffle recipe using American ingredients. A French delicatessen (charcuterie) had opened in our Berkeley neighborhood during our year abroad. They had beautiful pâtés and sausages in abundance, but no dessert and no chocolate. I stepped in, timidly, with my truffles two weeks before Christmas Day. To my astonishment, a deal was quickly made for just as many bite-size, cocoa-dusted, French chocolate truffles as I could make. I became the "Truffle Lady." Very soon thereafter, I undertook to make an even softer and creamier truffle—dipped in melted chocolate. ▪ ▪ ▪

Attempting—on my own—to perfect the dipping method, I lost control of the size of the truffle. The result was an alarmingly large, luscious, soft-centered chocolate, the likes of which no Frenchman had ever seen. By the time I realized that the truffles were much too large, my clientele was totally hooked and there was no going back. The large "American Chocolate Truffle" was born by accident in my kitchen. Unfamiliar with the bite-size French "original," many consider the larger truffle to be the standard! - - -

From chocolate truffles I ventured to chocolate desserts. The following year I combined a vacation in France with a week-long *stage* at the Ecole Lenôtre—the most prestigious pastry school in France. By the end of the week I was exhausted— but more challenged and exhilarated than ever. I saw and heard things that I didn't entirely understand at the time, but somehow they entered my subconscious. Like a time capsule, the lessons from Lenôtre have served me over several years. "Oh, so that's what it meant—now I get it." Magically, one by one, things have become crystal clear just when I needed them. - - -

I was having a ball with my tiny dessert business and it grew to capacity in my home kitchen. Meanwhile, business school didn't speak to my heart. I couldn't imagine myself in a corporate environment, and I didn't recognize myself among the students around me. When my husband couldn't reach casually into the refrigerator for a cold drink without toppling a precarious tower of cookie sheets, and I couldn't find a head of lettuce behind bowls of buttercream and chocolate truffles, it was time for a change. My friends at the charcuterie said, "Get serious, open a shop of your own." My business school advisor said, "Get serious, this idea will never work." I took the advice that I wanted to hear and left business school to start my own business "for real." - - -

I quickly learned that no banker would lend money for an untested scheme like mine. Professional bakers said I couldn't possibly spend so much on the ingredients for one cake and still make any money. Suppliers and equipment dealers were convinced I didn't know what I was doing. ▪ ▪ ▪

I used our own savings and a loan from my mother-in-law, a combined total of $14,000. I scrounged for used bakery equipment; I patched and painted walls (if you can work with a spatula and buttercream, you can do it with a putty knife and plaster); and I built tables to save money. ▪ ▪ ▪

In 1976, three years after returning from Paris, I opened a dessert shop in Berkeley, California. I chose the name COCOLAT—a whimsical word, not actually French—to suggest chocolate in all its simple and elegant splendor. I specialized in European desserts—chocolate tortes, chocolate layer cakes, and chocolate mousses. Chocolate truffles—not yet a household word in America—were a cornerstone of the menu. Today there are seven Cocolat stores, and Cocolat products are distributed nationally. Locally, Cocolat stores continue to be a mecca for serious dessert and chocolate lovers. ▪ ▪ ▪

On opening day, we sold every dessert and truffle in the house in three incredible hours. I cannot explain how or why I knew that a chocolate store—not a traditional candy store or a regular bakery, but something halfway between, yet quite different from both—would be successful. ▪ ▪ ▪

Americans then were familiar with bakeries and candy stores, but a chocolate dessert shop was unique. Commercially prepared desserts were not made with top-quality ingredients and did not address a clientele with sophisticated tastes. At

Cocolat I used the best sweet butter, fresh eggs, sipping-quality liqueurs, pure extracts, and freshly roasted nuts. I sought an audience who would appreciate desserts less sweet and more flavorful than the American classics, and who would respond to a more "adult" chocolate experience. ▪ ▪ ▪

I wanted to make and sell desserts that my customers did not make themselves, and that they might otherwise taste only in the very finest pastry shops and restaurants of Europe, or in the kitchens of European grandmothers. I wanted to create a store-bought dessert that the most knowledgeable and discriminating cook could serve with pride. Over the years, my most cherished compliment has been "I am a great cook, but I can't make desserts as well as Cocolat!" ▪ ▪ ▪

I also wanted to share the aesthetic qualities of the European desserts that I admired. The visual elegance and simplicity of French desserts opened my eyes. I appreciated the impressive understatement of decoration, the cleverness with which some desserts were constructed so that additional decoration was unnecessary. Dramatic special effects—ruffles of chocolate, halos of spun sugar, perfect chocolate glazes, and elegant script—were so striking that a simple dessert became a work of art. I came away inspired by the "design," as well as the taste of these desserts. I turned away from the fussy, frilly style of American bakery decoration and aspired to a cleaner, more tailored effect, punctuated here and there by striking special effects. This is now very much the Cocolat signature. To it I brought my preference for desserts with clear, intense flavors and subtle textures, desserts in which sweetness enhances instead of dominates the principal flavors—whether chocolate, or lemon, or almond, or vanilla. ▪ ▪ ▪

For 14 years, Cocolat has been the expression of my creative energies, a laboratory for my culinary and artistic ideas. The greatest fun of creating a new kind of business is the absence of rules and preconceived notions about what it ought to be or how things should be done. I have enjoyed the tremendous thrill of introducing the public to new and different tastes. Since I made the rules, I could stretch them and allow them to grow and change. The original inspiration was French, but I have always dabbled with whatever desserts captured my interest—whether Austrian, Italian, American, or my own creations. By now, Cocolat has become very much its own category—neither strictly European nor wholly American. ▪ ▪ ▪

This collection of desserts includes those recipes for which Cocolat is renowned, as well as some developed for my own home entertaining and special occasions, and desserts created especially for this book. This book is a very personal statement. These are the desserts that I love. I do not pretend to summarize the entire world of desserts or represent any kind of cross section or encyclopedia. I am biased in that most—but not all—of my favorites are chocolate. In keeping with the spirit of Cocolat, you will find a small collection of nonchocolate gems scattered throughout this otherwise very chocolatey book. ▪ ▪ ▪

I am a self-trained pastry chef and an eager and passionate problem solver. As a result, I do not stick to traditional techniques if I can find an easier way to do something well. I love to make complicated or difficult procedures simpler. ▪ ▪ ▪

Over the years, I have found that pastry and chocolate techniques are closely related to those of other crafts. Inspiration comes from many sources and I love to borrow tricks. Italianate paper marbling patterns can be applied to freshly poured chocolate glaze to finish an elegant bittersweet chocolate torte. Fashion and couture offer shapes and ideas for the creation of glamorous chocolate ruffles. I love to use texture to create visual interest. I consult art and design books. I make stencils and use repetitive patterns to maximize graphic effects. The creative possibilities are endlessly challenging. ▪ ▪ ▪

Dessert is the lasting impression of a meal or gathering. The stellar reputation of many a host or hostess is built around fabulous-tasting desserts. A dessert that is as beautiful to see as it is to taste casts the chef as a maker of fantasies. And why not? Sweet dreams and bon appétit.

Ingredients

Almost all of the ingredients I use for baking are straightforward and non-exotic. This makes shopping easy, as most everything can be purchased in a good supermarket. Even the better brands of chocolate are offered in some supermarkets, as are imported specialties, nuts in bulk, and even organic produce. Keep an eye out for freshness and quality. You may enjoy becoming an expert by trying some of the different brands of chocolate and taste-testing the different sweet butters and whipping creams, if more than one brand is offered in your area.

If your neighborhood market stocks only the bare essentials, you may have to seek out one or two specialty shops or use some of the mail-order sources listed in Resources, page 197.

Butter

Sweet (unsalted) butter is best for most all pastry and dessert recipes. Chocolate desserts made with regular (salted) butter are much too salty to be pleasing. Where salt is needed in a recipe, I prefer to add the needed amount rather than be stuck with the amount already in the butter. Sweet butter has a lower water content and a fresher flavor than regular butter. It spoils quickly, so it is frequently sold from the freezer case at the supermarket. Sniff it carefully before using it; it should smell sweet and fresh. If you like to keep some on hand for spur-of-the-moment dessert projects, store your own supply in the freezer.

Chestnuts

As much as I adore eating fresh-roasted chestnuts, I use canned chestnuts for dessert making. Sweetened Chestnut Purée, also called Chestnut Paste or Chestnut Spread, is available in cans imported from France in the gourmet section of super-markets, and, of course, in specialty stores. Do not confuse it with unsweetened purée.

For garnishing you will find canned whole chestnuts or chestnut pieces in vanilla syrup. Do not confuse them with chestnuts packed in water.

Coffee

Coffee is a classic dessert flavor, with or without chocolate. Normally, to use it properly as a flavoring, we require maximum taste with minimum liquid. Rather than use coffee extract or flavoring from a bottle, I use one of the premium brands of instant coffee or espresso powder (but not freeze-dried crystals), dissolved in a few drops of water, or liquid, where necessary. Two brands that I like are Medaglio d'Oro and Café Salvador.

If (like me) you are too much of a coffee snob to ever dream of actually drinking instant coffee, you are probably thinking of using strong, brewed coffee or real espresso to flavor your desserts. I recommend against this. A strong cup of coffee or even a cup of very concentrated espresso usually will deliver too much liquid and not enough coffee flavor for most dessert recipes. So, relax this time and open the jar.

Chocolate

See Working with Chocolate, pages 24–29, for types and uses of chocolate.

Citrus Fruit

Whether or not you are concerned about ingesting pesticides used to grow produce, orange and lemon slices poached with their skins left on (see Lemon Bombe, page 70, and Citrus Tart, page 142) taste and smell measurably better if the fruit was grown organically. If you are a stickler, you will consider this also when using the grated zests of citrus fruit.

Cream

Unless otherwise stated, use the richest, purest cream you can find. This means pasteurized heavy cream, or whipping cream with at least 38 percent butterfat. It should have the fewest possible ingredients on the label! The very best-tasting cream usually has only one ingredient printed on the carton: "cream." Other creams may have a stabilizer, such as carrageenan, which makes the texture seem thicker. If you buy large cartons of cream from a dairy or producer, you may be able to find something called "manufacturing cream" with as much as 40 percent butterfat. This is a good choice, if you can get it.

Creams vary in taste and texture. Choose by tasting. The best will taste fresh and natural, not cooked or processed. The cream that you buy should be pasteurized, but avoid creams labeled "ultrapasteurized" or "sterilized." Both of these terms indicate that the cream has been treated with additional heat—cooked at high temperatures—to make it last for weeks without spoiling. The flavor is similar to canned milk. I am willing to go out of my way to avoid buying this type of cream because the flavor is very disappointing. Regular pasteurized cream is available in most areas of the country, but you may have to read labels carefully or phone several local stores to find one that carries it. If you have the luxury of having more than one brand of cream available (other than ultrapasteurized or sterilized) in your market, buy a small carton of each one on a day when you plan to make a dessert with lots of cream. Conduct your own blind tasting to decide which you like the best. For techniques and details on working with cream, see Frosting with Whipped Cream, page 179.

Cream of Tartar

This white acidic powder is a natural by-product of wine making. It is one of the ingredients in baking powder. It also stabilizes beaten egg whites (meringue), helping to keep them from becoming dry and grainy. Add ⅛ teaspoon for every three to four egg whites before beating. If you beat your egg whites in an unlined copper bowl (page 23), do not use cream of tartar.

Crème Fraîche

This is the thick, rich, slightly fermented cream so beloved in France. It tastes like exotic, rich sour cream. It is rich enough to cook with or to whip. It can be purchased here in the U.S. at a very high price. When I use crème fraîche, I like to use lots, so I make a close approximation of the real thing myself by allowing a small amount of buttermilk to ferment a larger amount of cream. See the recipe, page 169, and remember to prepare it several days in advance. It must not only have time to ferment slightly, but it will need additional time to chill before it is used for whipping.

Eggs

Recipes in this book are based on large grade AA eggs. Buy the freshest available in your area and store them in the refrigerator. Bring eggs to room temperature before baking. See Shortcuts, page 23, for quick ways to bring eggs to room temperature.

Extracts

Use pure extracts. Artificial flavorings are not worthy of the time and other good ingredients you put into your favorite recipes!

Flour

All-purpose flour is used throughout this book except where otherwise specified. Cake or pastry flour, which is made from softer wheat and milled finer, makes superior sponge and génoise cakes. Cake flour does not refer to self-rising flour, which contains some baking powder and salt. Cake flour comes in a 2-pound box made by General Mills and labeled Softasilk. Pastry flour, available in some areas, may be used in place of cake flour, but try not to substitute all-purpose flour for cake flour unless otherwise stated. If you must do so anyway, use 2 tablespoons less flour per cup, or measure by weight without adjusting.

Gelatin (Unflavored)

I use gelatin infrequently—only in light fruit mousses and in Bavarian creams that ordinarily would not set without it. The recipes in this book call for ordinary Knox brand granulated unflavored gelatin, and the method is spelled out in each recipe. Do not take shortcuts. Gelatin must be softened before melting or it will not dissolve, even in a hot mixture. To soften gelatin, sprinkle it onto the surface of cold water and, without stirring, allow it to swell up and absorb the water. The newer gelatins soften in only about a minute, instead of the 5 or more minutes that it used to take. Check the package and, if in doubt, soften for 5 minutes. (If you rush or skip the softening step, the gelatin will remain gritty and it will not set the dessert.) Softened gelatin is then melted gently in a water bath or microwave (at LOW or 30% power) just until it liquefies and there are no visible granules, or it can be stirred directly into a hot mixture. Do not overheat or cook gelatin, or it will lose its power to gel.

Liqueurs and Spirits

Use drinking-quality liqueurs and spirits, never liquor "flavorings" or anything that you would not care to sit and sip. There is no need, however, to pour a highly prized, rare, or extravagantly expensive, aged bottle into a dessert recipe.

I use Myers's dark rum because it has lots of flavor. For Cognac, brandy, and whiskey a good medium-price California or imported bottle, or your own favorite, is fine. I am very fussy about the high-proof, clear fruit spirits called *eaux-de-vie*—Kirschwasser, Framboise, etc. Domestic brands of Kirsch and Framboise (raspberry) are exceedingly poor, and I refuse to use them. A notable exception is made by St. George Spirits in California. St. George makes five different *eaux-de-vie*—Raspberry (Framboise), Cherry (Kirsch), Pear (Poire), Quince, and Kiwi. These are very good and reasonably priced, compared to European brands. French (Alsatian) and German brands are expensive but superb. Do not confuse these very special spirits with the sweet, colored, fruit-flavored brandies available.

Nuts

Shelled nuts may be purchased natural (raw with skins left on) or blanched (raw, with skins removed). Freshness is important. Buy nuts whole or in large pieces for the greatest freshness and grate or chop your own. If you bake a lot, buy nuts from a bulk source in the fall and store them in the freezer. They will keep, well wrapped, for several months. Do not buy nuts that are already toasted—they may be stale or even rancid, and nothing compares to your own freshly toasted nuts. Toasting brings out the richest flavors in many nuts and virtually transforms the flavor of nuts such as almonds and hazelnuts. Recipes will specify if nuts should be toasted; otherwise, use them raw.

To toast nuts, spread them in a single layer on an ungreased cookie sheet. Bake in a preheated oven for 10–20 minutes, depending on whether the nuts are whole, sliced, or slivered. For even toasting, sliced and slivered nuts should be stirred once or twice while in the oven. When chopped toasted nuts are called for, toast the nuts whole and chop them afterwards. Toast almonds and hazelnuts at 350°. Taste-test them for doneness, first biting them in half to inspect the centers. Look for a golden brown color and a rich nutty flavor with no bitterness. Toast more delicate walnuts and pecans very lightly at 325° for 10–15 minutes. Test by tasting after 10 minutes; it is hard to tell by color. Macadamias are extremely delicate; toast at 300° until they barely color, about 10 minutes. Toasted nuts can be stored in the freezer, well wrapped, for several months.

Toasted hazelnut skins are somewhat bitter. We usually remove as much of the skin as possible by rubbing the nuts together, after toasting, in a dishtowel or coarse wire mesh colander or strainer. The latter helps to rub the skins off faster and allows the dust and pieces of skin to fall through the mesh. The traditional method is to do this while the nuts are still hot. In my experience just as much skin comes off of the nuts after they have cooled. In either case there is no need to remove 100 percent of the skins unless the nuts are to be used for decoration.

Nuts can also be toasted in the microwave using HIGH (100%) power. Spread the nuts in a single layer as above. One cup of nuts takes 3–5 minutes, stirring once, depending on the type and size of the nut. Observe carefully and use the taste test.

To blanch almonds or hazelnuts drop them, untoasted, into a pan of simmering water for about 1 minute. Use a skimmer or a strainer to remove them from the hot water and transfer them to a bowl of cold water. The skins will slip off between your fingers as you "pinch" each nut. If the skins do not slip off easily, put the nuts back into the simmering water for another few seconds and try again. Put the nuts aside to dry completely or dry them in a warm oven. Let them cool completely before grating or grinding.

Raspberries (Frozen) for Purées and Sauces

Fresh raspberries, even in season, are a thing of beauty and some expense in most parts of the country. For this reason I have no hesitation about the judicious use of frozen raspberries for purées and sauces. Choose a brand with little or no sugar if you have the choice. To retain the sweet/tart fresh flavor and brilliant color of the berries, thaw them gently. To heat or cook them, even gently, is to assassinate them—transforming a breathtakingly fresh fruit sauce into a mundanely flavored, dull-colored cooked syrup.

Sugar

Ordinary granulated sugar is used in most of my recipes, unless otherwise specified. Superfine granulated sugar is best, but not essential, for making meringues because it dissolves quickly. Superfine sugar is available in 1-pound boxes in many supermarkets. If you don't have it or cannot get it, process ordinary granulated sugar, after measuring, in a food processor (using the steel blade) for several seconds to reduce the particle size.

Confectioners' or powdered sugar is granulated sugar that has been milled to a powder with cornstarch added. I use it almost exclusively for dusting and stenciling the tops of desserts.

Brown sugar, light or dark, is granulated sugar with molasses added. It has a lovely rich caramel-like flavor that enhances many American-style desserts and cookies. I use light and dark interchangeably. Brown sugar is always measured in "packed" cups. (A packed cup weighs approximately 7 ounces, if you prefer to use your scale.)

Shortcuts and Production Tips

Finding a simpler way is part of the fun and challenge of perfecting any craft. Many cooking and baking methods have been done in one certain way for so long that we assume it is the only way. I don't mind working on a complex recipe, but I don't like unnecessary steps or messy procedures. I frequently break some of the old "rules" in order to simplify—always making sure that my shortcuts are not compromises. On the contrary, they often improve the final dessert!

Well-meaning magazine food editors often assume that I am either ignorant or have simply forgotten to write in the "right" technique, and they helpfully re-edit my simplified method back to the old accepted, but more complicated, procedure.

At last here is my chance to explain that when I don't say butter and flour a pan, you really don't have to do it—so long as you use parchment paper. This and several other streamlining techniques are outlined here.

Preparing Pans for Baking

Unless otherwise indicated, I do not butter and flour my cake pans.

Buttering and flouring pans is not foolproof—there are always times when a portion of the cake sticks to the pan anyway. Lining the bottoms of cake pans with parchment paper eliminates this uncertainty, as well as the messy nuisance of smearing pans with butter and shaking flour around the kitchen.

Line only the bottom of the pan and don't worry about the sides. The sides of a cake release easily with a small metal spatula. There is no need to butter the bottom of the pan before putting in the parchment circle, nor is it necessary to butter the parchment paper itself! Keep lots of parchment circles on hand so you don't have to cut one out each time you bake. Parchment circles may be purchased at specialty cake decorating shops, or you may make your own. To do this, stack several parchment sheets on a cutting board, hold a cake pan firmly on the top sheet, and cut around the pan with an X-acto knife.

To line a jelly-roll pan, cut the parchment to the exact width of the bottom of the pan (don't worry about the sides) but long enough so that it hangs over the ends of the pan. When the cake is cool, release the sides with a small spatula; use the extra parchment at the ends as handles to lift the delicate cake sheet up and out of the pan, and to help you flip the cake over before peeling off the paper.

Cooling Cakes and Tortes—in the Pan

Most of the time I cool cakes *in the pans*, on a rack. I have not found this to damage the taste or texture of cakes or tortes. The benefits are several:
— no need to handle hot pans when you unmold your cake.
— no need to stop and unmold the cake at a precise time after it is taken from the oven.
— a torte cooled in the pan will have a nice flat bottom that later can become a nice flat top (see the technique for unmolding and preparing a torte to be glazed, page 175).

The traditional method for making roulades and jelly rolls is to remove the hot sheet of sponge cake from the pan immediately after it comes out of the oven. You must then roll it up in a moist towel, to "train" it to roll later without cracking. Once cooled, it is unrolled, filled, and re-rolled. I find this procedure unnecessarily delicate and inconvenient. And who needs extra damp, sticky dishtowels to launder?

Instead, I cool jelly-roll and roulade sheet cakes in the pan. My Hot Milk Sponge Cake (page 160) remains perfectly flexible after cooling flat in the pan, with no extra fuss. Génoise sheets, inherently less flexible, do have a tendency to crack when rolled.

My remedy is to leave the cake in the pan and cover it with foil as soon as it is taken from the oven. The cake steams slightly as it cools and so remains flexible for later rolling.

Working with Parchment Paper

Parchment paper is one of a baker's best friends. In addition to lining cake pans (see above), parchment paper provides an easy release for meringues and macaroons. Hot caramel and praline can be poured onto a sheet of parchment placed on a cookie sheet or on a marble slab. It is not necessary to oil or butter the paper. When the praline or caramel is cool and brittle the parchment will peel away from it cleanly and quickly. If you use parchment on a marble slab you get the best of both worlds — the cold surface under the parchment cools the candy quickly but the parchment saves you from having to clean and oil the marble afterward. Cookies bake beautifully on parchment-lined baking sheets. I cannot think of anything baked that does not release from parchment paper! Use parchment paper triangles — purchased or cut yourself — to make disposable paper decorating cones for fine writing and lacy chocolate filigree.

Sifting Dry Ingredients

Strainers are easier than sifters. They shake out and wash easier, they are easier to store, and they can be held and used in one hand.

Sifting flour and dry ingredients has two unrelated functions. The first function is measuring accuracy. Flour that has been sitting in a sack or cannister for any length of time may be quite compacted or relatively loose — we never know for sure. We sift before measuring to undo any compacting and increase the accuracy of measuring by the cup. Sifting before measuring is unnecessary if you measure your flour by weight, since one pound of compacted flour is the same as one pound of loose flour.

The second function of sifting is to aerate and lighten the flour to make it easy to fold into delicate batters. It takes fewer strokes to fold sifted flour into any batter; the fewer the strokes, the less the batter will deflate. For some recipes I sift two or three times for this purpose. In these cases sifting is important especially if you have first measured the flour unsifted, by weight. Follow the sifting instructions in each recipe. Where no mention of sifting is made, you don't have to do it.

Using a Scale

Life would be simpler if we all weighed ingredients instead of measuring them. Scales save time and steps, and they decrease the number of bowls and measuring cups that need washing when you have completed a recipe. A scale is a special blessing for dry and chunky ingredients and gooey or greasy ingredients that we use frequently.

For Flour: Normally you must sift flour, spoon it gently into a measuring cup, and then sweep off the excess into the cannister. With a scale you weigh out the exact amount needed, and then sift only that amount. You use fewer steps and fewer containers and probably make less of a mess on the counter. All recipes in this book give weights as well as cup measures for flour.

For Chocolate: In my pantry, away from light, I keep closely covered mason jars of chocolate, cut up in small pieces and ready to melt. I simply scoop out and weigh the quantity needed. This is especially convenient if you buy chocolate in bulk or in random weights instead of premeasured bars or squares.

For Nuts: Nuts are sold by weight, not by cup. When a recipe calls for 1 cup of ground almonds, you must guess how much to buy. Since 1 cup of whole almonds does not equal 1 cup after grinding, you often have to grind and measure a couple of times before you get it right. You often end up with small quantities of leftover pulverized nuts.

If you know the weight of one cup of pulverized nuts, you can weigh out the exact quantity of nuts needed (no matter what size the pieces are) and then pulverize them. All recipes in this book give weights as well as cup measures for nuts.

For Butter: Most of us already use butter by weight since the butter we buy is marked off in ounces on the wrapper. A scale is helpful if you buy butter in larger quantities without marked measures.

Propane Torch

This is the neatest way to unmold molded desserts, from Jell-O to the Strawberry Carrousel. It is also convenient for caramelizing the tops of desserts. Unfortunately, a hand-held hair dryer is not powerful enough to substitute for a torch.

Water Bath or Bain Marie

I do not like double boilers. For melting chocolate or warming other delicate ingredients I prefer a water bath that allows the ingredient container to sit directly in warm or barely simmering water.

Double boilers are often the wrong size for the quantity of ingredients involved, and so they are cumbersome and inflexible. What if a recipe has two or more ingredients that must be warmed, melted, or reheated in succession and you have only one double boiler insert?

Unless the double boiler is glass, it is not easy to see if the water is boiling too rapidly or just barely simmering as desired. The steam from a rapidly boiling double boiler is hot enough to burn chocolate anyway, so there is no advantage over the water bath. (See Working with Chocolate, page 25–26.)

A water bath is very flexible. I use a wide skillet filled with an inch of two of water into which I can place any small bowl, saucepan, or jar as needed. I can always see how hot the water is and I can put a succession of vessels (sometimes two at a time if they are small) in and out of the bath as needed (to melt chocolate, keep melted butter warm, soften buttercream, etc.). Sometimes when I'm testing lots of recipes at once, I have two baths on the stove. If the water bath becomes too hot I can always turn the heat off and use the heat that remains in the water.

Microwave

Only the microwave oven is more convenient and less messy than the water bath for melting chocolate, softening buttercream, melting butter, and reheating anything.

Bringing Eggs to Room Temperature Quickly

I often forget to take eggs out of the refrigerator in advance of baking. To remove the chill from cold eggs, submerge them, in their shells, in a bowl of warm water for a few minutes before using.

If you have stored egg whites in the refrigerator, you will want to warm them to room temperature before beating them. Place them in a stainless-steel or unlined copper bowl (I like my stainless mixer bowl) and swirl the bowl an inch or two above a gas burner flame until they no longer feel cold to the touch, or set the bowl in a pan of barely simmering water for just a few seconds, stirring until the whites are no longer cold. Watch them carefully lest they begin to cook.

Beating Egg Whites

Many cakes and desserts are leavened or lightened only by the air beaten into egg whites. Most recipes ask that you beat egg whites until "stiff but not dry." Unless you are very experienced, you may not know what this means or when to stop beating. Here are a few tips about handling egg whites, including what to do when you have accidentally overbeaten them:

—Beat egg whites in a clean, dry bowl, free of grease. For maximum volume, egg whites should be at room temperature (or even slightly warmer) before they are beaten.

—⅛ teaspoon of cream of tartar beaten with every three or four egg whites helps keep them stable. Salt does not, as formerly believed, serve the same purpose.

—Alternatively, beat egg whites in an unlined copper bowl. The chemical reaction caused when the whisk strikes the copper stabilizes the egg whites. Do not use cream of tartar in a copper bowl. Wash the copper bowl with salt and vinegar, rinse, and dry well before each use.

—Egg whites beaten without any sugar become dry the quickest, so you must beat them only until barely stiff. If in doubt, stop. Underbeating is preferable to overbeating because the air bubbles that are formed remain elastic enough to withstand folding and to expand during baking without collapsing. Overbeaten egg whites are hard to fold. The air bubbles are brittle and burst easily. Instead of blending easily with another mixture and lightening it, dry, overbeaten whites form boulder-shaped chunks that are hard to disperse without stirring. Stirring breaks the air bubbles, deflates the mixture, and defeats the purpose of the egg whites in the first place.

—The more sugar is added to the egg whites, the longer and stiffer they can be beaten before they become dry. Sugar should be sprinkled in gradually, and only after soft peaks (nearly stiff) are formed. Adding sugar too early prevents the whites from achieving maximum volume.

—Dry, overbeaten egg whites can be remoistened and rescued by adding an additional unbeaten egg white to the overbeaten batch and then beating briefly to combine. The recipe can then be completed as written. This technique works perfectly as long as it is executed before any other mixture or ingredient (including a spatula that has chocolate or batter on it) has contaminated the bowl of egg whites. Sometimes it is hard to tell whether the whites are too dry until after you have tried to fold the first portion of them into the batter. Because of this, I always scoop the first portion of whites out with a clean, dry spatula. If, while folding them into my batter, I discover that they are too dry, I can still rescue the remaining egg whites as described above.

Planning Quantities, Larger Crowds, and Smaller Parties

Serving sizes are confusing these days because our eating habits are changing. Many of my desserts are very rich. For the diet and exercise crowd, or for anyone after a very elaborate meal, an 8-inch torte will serve up to 16 people. Other people will find the same cake serves only 10. The number of servings that I have indicated in each recipe assumes a generous but not huge slice, considering the richness of the dessert. Where the range of servings seems large, such as 16 to 20, this simply means that the dessert is very, very rich and a very small serving may be appropriate on some occasions or for certain kinds of groups.

When you plan dessert, consider your guests and the occasion. Are they hale and hearty eaters? Is it a dainty ladies' tea party? Older people and small children will eat smaller servings and rarely come back for seconds. A group of women will, in general, eat less than a group of men. My husband's graduate students and their spouses are big dessert eaters. Be generous in your planning for a dessert party that has no dinner immediately preceding it. If you are serving a variety of different desserts at such a party, your guests will want to taste a small piece of several different choices, and this will add up to more than just one average serving per person. Plan accordingly, and abundantly for this kind of party.

What about small dinner parties? My recipes generally serve 10 or more people. Many are large enough to serve 16 or 20, making them ideal party cakes. Don't disregard them if you want dessert for only six or eight. Many recipes can be made into two smaller desserts — one to serve now and one to freeze for your next small party. This saves you time and energy, and it is easier than getting out your calculator and figuring out how to divide the recipe in half. The bonus is that you will have an extra dessert ready and waiting in the freezer. In general, recipes such as chocolate tortes, génoise, and sponge for layer cakes normally baked in 8- or 9-inch round pans can be made and baked in two 6-inch round pans instead. Baking time may be as much as 10 to 15 minutes less. Complicated cakes like Pavé d'Amour or Marjolaine can be made and assembled as directed, and then cut in half to make two rectangles — and one can be frozen. A very rich dessert like Tricolor Mousse serves 16 or more. It is molded in an 8-inch round pan, 3 inches tall, but the recipe divides perfectly into two 6-inch round pans, 3 inches tall.

If you are ever confused about the relative size of one pan compared to another, just fill them both with water and measure the number of cups in each. This will tell you, for example, if one pan is half the size of another.

What about doubling recipes and saving time? If you plan to bake a lot, create a larder. All of the batters, doughs, fillings, mousses, glazes, and buttercreams in this book can be increased. When you bake a génoise, double the recipe and put the extra cake in the freezer. Do the same with buttercream. Store extra simple syrup in the fridge; keep caramelized nuts in the freezer. If you make an especially complicated cake, make it in an 8-inch square, cut it in half, and finish only half. Or, make and assemble two cakes at the same time. Wrap and freeze the other half, or the second cake, along with the buttercream needed to finish it. It may take parts of several days to make, assemble, and finish a cake like the Pavé d'Amour, but it is worth it if you plan two parties and make both cakes at the same time. Alternatively, stretch out the parts of a complex cake over several days or a week, using the freezing and timing tips in the recipes.

Do be careful if you plan to double or increase a recipe in order to make one larger dessert. Pan size must be proportionately larger, baking time may change, and the time it takes to chill a dessert before unmolding will change. Proceed with caution unless you are experienced at this sort of thing.

Working with Chocolate
A Guide for Dessert Makers

The extraordinary interest in chocolate desserts in the last decade means that we cook, bake, and decorate with chocolate at home as never before. Whereas our mothers and grandmothers used unsweetened baking chocolate, cocoa, and chocolate chips to make brownies, chocolate chip cookies, and devil's food cake, we frequently use premium-quality bittersweet, semisweet, and even white and milk chocolate to make sophisticated European-style desserts, tortes, and mousses.

The amount of chocolate in a given recipe and the cocoa butter content of that chocolate make the critical difference between Mom's desserts and some of our contemporary favorites. Cocoa butter, the natural fat of the cocoa bean, contributes an exquisite aroma and incomparable melt-in-your-mouth quality to chocolate desserts.

Cocoa butter makes chocolate especially demanding and unpredictable to work with. The neophyte finds that chocolate burns without warning; sometimes it melts smoothly, sometimes it tightens into an unmanageable lump; it dulls and streaks or remains shiny for no discernible reason; silky smooth molten chocolate may suddenly become gritty when added to another mixture. To make matters worse, milk and white chocolates, because of their milk content, are even more delicate to work with than dark chocolate.

Chocolate is like a "difficult" personality. A successful working relationship depends on knowing why it behaves as it does and how to make it work for, instead of against, you.

The vast body of knowledge, and the rules, about working with chocolate presume that all users are confectioners — candy makers. In fact, dessert chefs and candy makers use chocolate differently. The "rules" about chocolate are either ignored completely by dessert makers, or followed slavishly for no good reason. In fact, we need to know enough about chocolate to know when the rules apply and when they do not.

To Temper or Not to Temper

To begin with, there is not a dessert, cake, glaze, or special decoration in this book that requires you to know how to temper chocolate.

The number one mystique that surrounds chocolate has to do with tempering. In the last decade, I have noticed that everyone who loves and wants to work with chocolate is eager to become an expert. Everyone wants to temper! Many do not quite understand what tempering is, or why they want to do it, but do it they must. From the dessert maker and pastry chef's point of view, I take a radical position: I do not think it is necessary or practical to temper. But what are we talking about anyway?

Briefly, tempering is a process of slowly raising and lowering the temperature of melted chocolate, stirring constantly, until the complex fat crystals in the cocoa butter stabilize and "behave" in concert with each other. At a cool room temperature, chocolate which has been tempered will dry rapidly to a hard and shiny piece that breaks with a snap. It shrinks slightly as it dries, enabling it to release easily from a mold. A tempered chocolate piece keeps at room temperature for months without losing its luster or snap. Any bar of chocolate that you purchase to eat or to melt has been tempered. Once melted or exposed to heat, however, it loses its temper, though it can be retempered.

Chocolate that is melted but not tempered will dry slowly, at room temperature, to a soft, almost cakey texture. It will stick inside of a mold. Untempered chocolate "blooms"—that is, it becomes dull and streaky, or it takes on a mottled appearance—unless it is refrigerated immediately.

Candy makers almost always temper the chocolate they use. A piece of candy that must sit on the shelf or in a package for days or weeks *without refrigeration* must remain shiny and hard. A molded chocolate rabbit must first release from its mold, then remain lustrous and stable in an Easter basket.

But dessert chefs have little need to temper. There is no reason to temper the chocolate used in cake and torte batters, buttercreams, and most ganaches. The same is true for mousses, custards, and creams. Chocolate that will be stored in the refrigerator or consumed quickly need not be tempered. Chocolate glazes, properly handled, do not require tempering to remain shiny for the short life of the dessert.

This is good news because *tempering is not easy to master unless you do it almost every day*—despite the detailed, and sometimes even simple-sounding directions that you may find. Each brand of chocolate behaves differently and even may require slightly different temperatures during each stage of tempering. The temperature and humidity of the kitchen can also affect tempering. It takes a lot of experience to adjust for this. Unless you temper often, there are too many variables to guarantee success even most of the time. It may come easily one

time and take hours the next. This is impractical for the home dessert chef. Instead of tempering, the dessert maker should become familiar with more practical issues:
— how to melt chocolate properly—alone and with other ingredients.
— how chocolate responds to moisture.
— why chocolate seizes, and how to avoid or correct this.
— when and why chocolate is refrigerated.

Melting Chocolate

Read six cookbooks and learn six different "foolproof" ways of melting chocolate without burning it. Some say microwave, others advise a double boiler. Some say covered, still others say uncovered. Many warn you never, *ever*, let the water come to a boil or even permit the container of chocolate to touch the water.

The fact is, *unless you exercise care*, chocolate burns easily, in the microwave or the double boiler, covered or uncovered, and whether or not the container touches the water. There is no such thing as foolproof. Melting chocolate must be done carefully. (I always keep extra chocolate on hand in case of an "accident," as well as for spur-of-the-moment dessert making.)

Knowing this, you at least can discard *unnecessary* precautions and pay attention to what is important:

Remember that you are trying to melt chocolate, not cook it. Whether you use a microwave, water bath, or double boiler, do not heat dark chocolate above 120°. White and milk chocolates should not be heated above 110°. These temperatures are warm, not hot. (Remember, normal body temperature is 98.6°.) Chocolate is too frequently overheated. Even if it doesn't burn, seize up, turn gritty, or taste bad, overheated chocolate can cause handling problems. Take it easy.

Chocolate melts smoothest and fastest if it is done slowly. This is not a contradiction. Use low heat and cut or break dark chocolate up into small bits to expose lots of surface area°. Use a large, dry chef's knife and cutting board. Cut white and milk chocolate into dice—no larger than ¼ inch—or thin matchsticks. Dark chocolate can be left in larger pieces if they are less than or about ⅜ inch thick. Melt dark chocolate in a barely simmering water bath or double boiler. Melt white and milk chocolate in a water bath or double boiler that has first been brought to a simmer and then turned off for 60 seconds. (Reheat the water only if necessary.) Stir frequently to hasten the melting process. You

°Think of the chocolate as though it were frozen butter: if a large chunk of frozen butter is placed in a hot skillet, the butter will burn as it melts, even while part of it is still frozen! If it is cut up into small pieces and put it in a warm skillet instead, it will melt very quickly, without burning.

will be surprised at how quickly and smoothly the chocolate melts. Take the chocolate off the heat before it is completely melted and it will continue to melt, safely, on its own. You can always rewarm the chocolate for a few seconds if it hasn't completely melted or if it cools too much before you need it. Chocolate can also be melted in a microwave oven (see instructions below).

A double boiler is OK but unnecessary. Suspending the bowl of chocolate over hot water is no safer than placing the bowl directly in hot water. In both cases the chocolate will burn if the water is simmering or boiling too rapidly, or if the chocolate is left there too long. Unless the double boiler is glass, it is impossible to see whether the water is simmering gently or boiling hard.

Do not create a top-heavy double boiler or water bath by placing a large bowl on top of a much smaller pot. Invariably, without your noticing, the flames from the burner will lick up and around the small pot and scorch the sides of the larger bowl and burn the chocolate.

Do not cover the bowl of chocolate while it is melting. This is an unnecessary step and it may cause condensation to form under the cover and damage the chocolate.

Melting Chocolate in the Microwave Oven

The microwave has become my favorite method for melting chocolate because it is quick, simple, and clean.
—Cut or break the chocolate into small pieces.
—Use a microwave-safe bowl, jar, or measuring cup.
—Remember that chocolate holds its original shape, even when melted. You cannot tell if it is melted by looking—you must stir it.

Melt chocolate uncovered. Use MEDIUM (50%) for dark chocolate and LOW (30%) for milk and white chocolates. Despite the microwave manuals, HIGH (100%) for chocolate is risky. The chocolate gets too hot too fast and there is great risk of burning. Earlier I said that chocolate melts fastest if it is done gently. This is also true in the microwave. At MEDIUM and LOW, it doesn't seem to take longer to melt the chocolate than it does at HIGH (100%). The difference is that the melted chocolate will be warm, instead of hot, which is good.

The following are some average times for melting different quantities of chocolate in the microwave. These times are for melting chocolate alone, without water, butter, or any other ingredient. I tested this in a 600-watt microwave, and I cut my chocolate into small bits. After microwaving, expect to stir the chocolate for several seconds until smooth and until the last few lumps are melted. Add 5- to 10-second increments, always at the appropriate power level, if the chocolate still is not melted (after stirring) or warm enough for your purpose.

Semisweet or bittersweet chocolate, at MEDIUM (50%):
1 ounce: 1 minute and 30 seconds
2 ounces: 2 minutes
4 ounces: 2 minutes and 20–30 seconds
6 ounces: 3 minutes

Milk chocolate, at LOW (30%):
1 ounce: 1 minute and 45 seconds
2 ounces: 2 minutes and 25–35 seconds
4 ounces: 2 minutes and 40–50 seconds
6 ounces: 3 minutes and 45 seconds

White chocolate, at LOW (30%):
1 ounce: 1 minute and 20 seconds
2 ounces: 2 minutes and 10 seconds
4 ounces: 2 minutes and 30–40 seconds
6 ounces: 3 minutes and 30 seconds

Note: The above times are not appropriate if the chocolate being melted is accompanied by a liquid or butter. The addition of these ingredients shortens the melting times because the moisture warms more quickly, surrounding the chocolate pieces and helping them to melt.

Moisture

A chocolate technologist will tell you that chocolate is incompatible with moisture. More precisely, chocolate *alone* is incompatible with *small* amounts of moisture, which cause it to thicken and seize. Chocolate is quite compatible with larger amounts of moisture, or with small amounts of moisture in the presence of a larger quantity of fat, like butter.

Chocolate melts smoothly with a liquid if there is enough liquid. As a rule of thumb, 1 tablespoon of liquid for each 2 ounces of chocolate is usually a safe ratio. The liquid can be water, milk, cream, liquor, coffee, etc. Each brand of chocolate has a slightly different tolerance for liquid (depending on how much cocoa butter it contains)—so this rule of thumb is safe by a good margin for some chocolates and more borderline for others.

Chocolate melted with butter, cream, or other liquids burns less readily, and of course it is not necessary to observe the strict precautions about dry bowls and implements. Nonetheless, I still recommend low temperatures, I still use the water bath or microwave, and I still cut or break the chocolate—as well as the butter, if any—into small pieces to obtain more surface exposure.

Why Chocolate Seizes

Almost everyone who has worked with chocolate has seen it transformed from a shiny, smooth, fluid mass to a dull, thick paste. There are three possible explanations:

The chocolate is burned. Chocolate melted alone, with no other ingredients, is the most delicate. Too much heat will burn it. White and milk chocolates are most vulnerable. Even at temperatures that are not too hot for your finger, these chocolates start to become thicker, less fluid, and ultimately burned. Stick your finger into the seized chocolate. If it is very hot or too hot to touch it may be burned. Taste it. If it tastes burned, throw it away and start over.

A small amount of moisture has contaminated the chocolate. Small quantities of moisture or liquid increase the viscosity of the chocolate to such a degree that it ceases to be fluid—it actually seizes up, looks dull, will not flow, and cannot be remelted.

To melt chocolate alone, without any other ingredient, it is essential that no moisture or liquid whatever come in contact with the chocolate. It is important to use a perfectly dry bowl. The knife and cutting board used to cut the chocolate must also be dry. Even a wet spoon used to stir melted chocolate may cause the chocolate to thicken or seize. This is why it is impossible to flavor a few ounces of melted chocolate with "just a splash" of your favorite liqueur. Dipping even slightly moist strawberries in chocolate will eventually cause the chocolate to thicken and dull.

Bars of chocolate to be used for melting must be stored well wrapped, because chocolate actually attracts moisture and may absorb it from the air. This is especially true of white and milk chocolates, which are even more susceptible to moisture damage. Chocolate may be stored, well wrapped, in the freezer. If so, it should not be unwrapped until after it has thawed to prevent condensation from forming on the surface of the chocolate.

If chocolate has seized because of moisture and your recipe does not call for any liquid to be added to it, you will have to throw it out or use it for another purpose. Scrape it onto a piece of waxed paper and let it harden. Save it for a recipe that does call for melting the chocolate together with butter or cream or a safe quantity of liquid (see below). Remelt a fresh measure of chocolate for your current project.

Cold liquid has been added to warm chocolate. Despite the compatibility of chocolate with large quantities of liquid, seizing will occur if the liquid is cool or cold and is added to already melted, warm chocolate. What happens? The cool or cold moisture immediately starts to harden the chocolate, either causing it to thicken uniformly or to form gritty particles—usually the latter. This is precisely what happens when you attempt to pour warm melted chocolate into whipped cream or cold buttercream. Nine times out of 10, the result is a bowlful of whipped cream or buttercream streaked with hard, gritty, chocolate flecks.

The problem of seizing caused by temperature difference can be reduced or eliminated if you combine the cut-up chocolate with the required liquid, and then warm them *together* in the water bath or microwave. If the ratio of liquid to chocolate is safe, there should be no seizure.

When combining chocolate with whipped cream, melt the chocolate first with a safe amount of water or cream (1 tablespoon of liquid per 2 ounces of chocolate). Stir it until smooth, and allow it to cool to room temperature. (This pre-loosens the chocolate so that it won't seize or turn gritty on contact with a colder mixture.) Beat the cream much less stiffly than usual, and fold it quickly into the chocolate mixture. Use immediately, as it stiffens quickly and becomes hard to spread. (The recipe for Chocolate Buttercream on page 182 incorporates this technique of pre-loosening the chocolate, as do the instructions for the chocolate crème fraîche in the recipe for Cranberry Christmas Cake (page 145).

Note: It is not impossible to combine a cool liquid with warm melted chocolate. Someone who works with chocolate all of the time, knows his/her brand well, has good timing, and has a fast whisking wrist can often do it. But the home dessert maker shouldn't count on it. I once saw it done successfully by accident by someone quite innocent of the hazards. Thereafter, she was unable to repeat the success and couldn't understand why. It is much better to use techniques that reduce the risk in the first place.

What if you've carefully melted chocolate with a safe amount of liquid and you know it's not burned, but it seizes anyway? Chances are the chocolate you are using requires a little more liquid than usual. You must increase the liquid by an additional tablespoon or two—just enough to loosen the chocolate. Be careful not to compound the problem by adding cold liquid, which will stiffen the chocolate even more. The liquid should be approximately the same temperature as the seized chocolate. Touch the chocolate with your finger. Turn on the tap until the water feels about as warm, to your finger, as the chocolate. Add 1 tablespoon of the warm water all at once to the troubled chocolate and whisk vigorously. Add an additional tablespoon if necessary.

Many chefs recommend adding shortening to save seized chocolate. This does not work as well. Besides, why add shortening to a recipe that had none in it in the first place?

Refrigerating Chocolate

Refrigerating chocolate is tricky; it can work for or against you. For example, tortes and cakes that are glazed, stored, and served at room temperature are ruined by refrigeration. Chilling makes the torte dense and hard, and it dulls the chocolate glaze and spoils its appearance. Refrigeration can also dull an otherwise shiny piece of tempered chocolate or cause it to collect droplets of moisture. On the other hand, a *cold* cake or dessert should be glazed cold (page 174) and must be chilled again immediately to *maintain* the shiny appearance of the glaze. For the best results, follow temperature and refrigeration instructions in each recipe carefully. They will vary depending on the temperature at which the dessert will be stored and served.

Refrigeration can also be used to avoid tempering. Untempered chocolate coating is the secret to the softest-centered chocolate truffles imaginable (page 155). The more sophisticated decorations and special effects that I have included in these chapters—curls, ruffles, cigarettes, and chocolate cups—are often made with tempered chocolate. When they are, they remain crisp and shiny, at room temperature for days, even weeks until needed. But these very special decorations are also made beautifully, and easily, *without* tempering. To keep them from blooming or becoming soft, they must be refrigerated immediately, and stored in the refrigerator until needed. Refrigeration is normally considered against the rules for handling chocolate, but here, it is used as a trick to "freeze" the fat crystals in the chocolate and prevent blooming. Decorations and chocolate cups made from untempered chocolate keep several weeks in the refrigerator, between layers of waxed paper, in a covered container.

Types of Chocolate

Unsweetened Chocolate/Chocolate Liquor: To the American home cook, the most familiar baking and cooking chocolate is unsweetened chocolate or "baking chocolate," technically called chocolate liquor. It often comes in packages of 8 individually wrapped 1-ounce portions. It is the usual chocolate for making brownies, fudges, frostings, and sauces and many popular American-style cakes as well. Unsweetened chocolate is the cleaned and roasted cocoa bean which has been milled to a molten state and then molded into cakes. It is about 53 percent cocoa butter, and 47 percent cocoa solids. With absolutely no sugar it is too strong and bitter for nibbling. Unsweetened chocolate should not be confused with bittersweet chocolate.

Very few of the recipes in this book call for unsweetened chocolate. Unsweetened chocolate has remarkable keeping qualities. Store it, well wrapped, in a cool, dry place.

Semisweet and Bittersweet Chocolate: These are the types of chocolate most frequently used in this book. These two chocolates are deliciously suitable for nibbling as well as for making candy and desserts. They may be used interchangeably, although I generally prefer bittersweet, for its stronger flavor. In fact, there is no standard technical definition of what makes one chocolate "bittersweet" and one "semisweet." Both contain chocolate liquor, additional cocoa butter, sugar, vanilla or vanillin, and sometimes lecithin. These terms are applied differently from brand to brand. However, *in general,* bittersweet will be stronger

and more pronounced in chocolate flavor and less sweet, owing to the higher chocolate liquor and lower sugar content.

Whether you use semisweet or bittersweet, there is no need to compensate by altering any part of the recipe. Choose chocolate based upon the flavor characteristics you prefer.

The tips and instructions outlined here are geared specifically to working with good-quality semisweet and bittersweet chocolates.

Some of the brands I like are Callebaut, Ghirardelli Bittersweet, Lindt, and Valrhona. Both semisweet and bittersweet chocolates have remarkable keeping qualities. Store them, well wrapped, in a cool, dry place and they will keep for a year or longer.

Chocolate Chips or Chocolate Bits: Whether these are the familiar semisweet, milk chocolate, or white chocolate chips, this type of chocolate is formulated especially for use in chocolate chip cookies and other desserts and sweets in which the chocolate is meant to remain in chip or bit form. The fat content and viscosity are such that the bits can take high heat, even direct contact with a hot cookie sheet, without scorching. They retain their pleasing eating qualities after the cookie has cooled.

On the other hand, chocolate chips are not well suited for other uses. Do not substitute semisweet chocolate bits or chips when a torte, mousse, or other dessert recipe calls for semisweet or bittersweet chocolate. Do not substitute white or milk chocolate chips in recipes that specify white chocolate or milk chocolate. The chips will not melt and behave in the same way as their non-chip counterparts; flavor, texture, and quality are not as good. By the same token, resist the urge to use chopped up, good bittersweet, semisweet, milk, or white chocolate instead of chocolate chips in cookies and other applications where packaged chocolate chips are called for. Regular, good-quality chocolates are likely to scorch during baking and have a poor eating texture in the finished product.

Cocoa: Cocoa is chocolate liquor with a portion of the cocoa butter pressed out. The remaining mass is then pulverized to make cocoa powder. Cocoas contain from 10 to 24 percent cocoa butter and no sugar whatever. Cocoa powder delivers a strong and direct chocolate flavor, marvelously suited for some desserts. Cocoa is less tricky to work with than chocolate, and there are no special concerns about melting, since cocoa generally is sifted into dry ingredients or dissolved into liquid before heating or baking.

There are two types of cocoa: natural or nonalkalized, and Dutch-processed. Cocoa that has been "Dutched," or alkalized, is less acidic and often a richer, more appealing color. I use a good-quality Dutch-processed cocoa made by De Zaan, unfortunately unavailable to the retail shopper (except by mail order, see Resources, page 197). Dröste is the most widely available of the better-quality Dutch-processed cocoas, but do try Lindt, Bensdorp, or Pernigotti cocoa, available in some specialty and gourmet shops. Do not use sweetened cocoas or hot chocolate mixes in place of cocoa powder.

Milk Chocolate: Milk chocolate actually contains milk, in a dry or concentrated form, in addition to chocolate liquor, cocoa butter, and sugar. Milk makes this type of chocolate milder and sweeter than dark chocolate. Milk chocolate is mostly used for eating—in candy bars, chocolates, and other confections. It is the preferred eating chocolate in the United States, although dark chocolate is gaining in popularity with the spread of more gourmet trends in this country. The milk ingredient makes this chocolate largely unsuitable for cooking and baking, per se, as it cannot take even moderate heat without burning. I use milk chocolate to great advantage, however, in mousses and glazes that require only minimal heat. In these recipes the delicate flavor and marvelously smooth eating qualities so appreciated in a good piece of milk chocolate can be enjoyed in dessert form as well. Do not try to substitute milk chocolate for dark chocolate in a cake or torte that will be baked. Also be aware that milk chocolate melts, handles, and combines with ingredients differently from semisweet or bittersweet chocolate. If you take your favorite bittersweet chocolate mousse recipe and try substituting milk chocolate, you are likely to be disappointed in the taste and/or texture.

I, personally, prefer the flavor of European milk chocolate best, including brands like Callebaut, Lindt, Tobler, and Valrhona, as well as the special Cocolat blend called "Albert's Milk," available by mail order (see Resources, page 197). But do select your own favorite milk chocolate for any recipes that call for this ingredient.

Milk chocolate does not keep as well as dark chocolate. Do not buy too far ahead unless you plan to freeze it. Keep milk chocolate—and all chocolates—well wrapped to avoid absorbing moisture and odors from the air. Frozen chocolate should be thawed completely, without unwrapping, in order to prevent moisture from forming directly on the chocolate.

White Chocolate: I had a difficult time finding high-quality white chocolate when I began using it in the 1970s. This product has grown tremendously in popularity since then, and is much more available today. But white chocolate is confusing to the consumer. Legally, there is no such thing as white chocolate, because, in this country, nothing can be called "chocolate" unless it contains chocolate liquor—the pulverized roasted cocoa bean consisting of cocoa butter and cocoa solids. What we call "white chocolate" contains no cocoa solids. Technically it must be called "white confectionery coating." The problem is that there are two types of white confectionery coating, both informally called white chocolate. Only one of them, however, contains cocoa butter, preferably as its *only* fat. I strongly believe that this latter type

should be allowed the legal distinction of being called "white chocolate." The other type of confectionery coating is made with vegetable fats instead of cocoa butter, so it bears no relation, whatsoever, to the cocoa bean. To lessen the confusion to the consumer, I believe one should be called "white confectionery coating" and the other "white chocolate." If you are going to make wonderful desserts you must read the ingredient label carefully to be sure that you are buying white chocolate that is made with cocoa butter. Good brands are Callebaut, Lindt, Nestlé, Tobler, and Valrhona. Some of these are available only from specialty stores or by mail order (see Resources, page 197). Beware of so-called white chocolate that is too inexpensive; chances are it is *not* made with cocoa butter.

Note that the best white chocolates are ivory or cream colored, never absolutely white. This is because of the cocoa butter. The best white chocolates share many characteristics with fine milk chocolates—both contain milk and cocoa butter, although milk chocolate contains cocoa solids in addition. Like milk chocolate, white chocolate does not tolerate high heat and is usually not cooked or actually baked. Also like milk chocolate, white chocolate usually cannot be substituted in recipes originally created for dark chocolate. For the pastry chef and dessert maker, white chocolate is best in mousses, glazes, and sauces in which its taste and texture can be enjoyed to advantage. Milk and white chocolates are similar enough to each other to substitute, in some recipes, one for the other.

White chocolate does not keep well. Buy it from sources that sell a lot. Be sure that it is well wrapped—white chocolate attracts moisture and odors from the air. Buy only enough for immediate use or plan to store the excess in the freezer. Frozen chocolate should be thawed completely without unwrapping, in order to prevent moisture from forming directly on the chocolate.

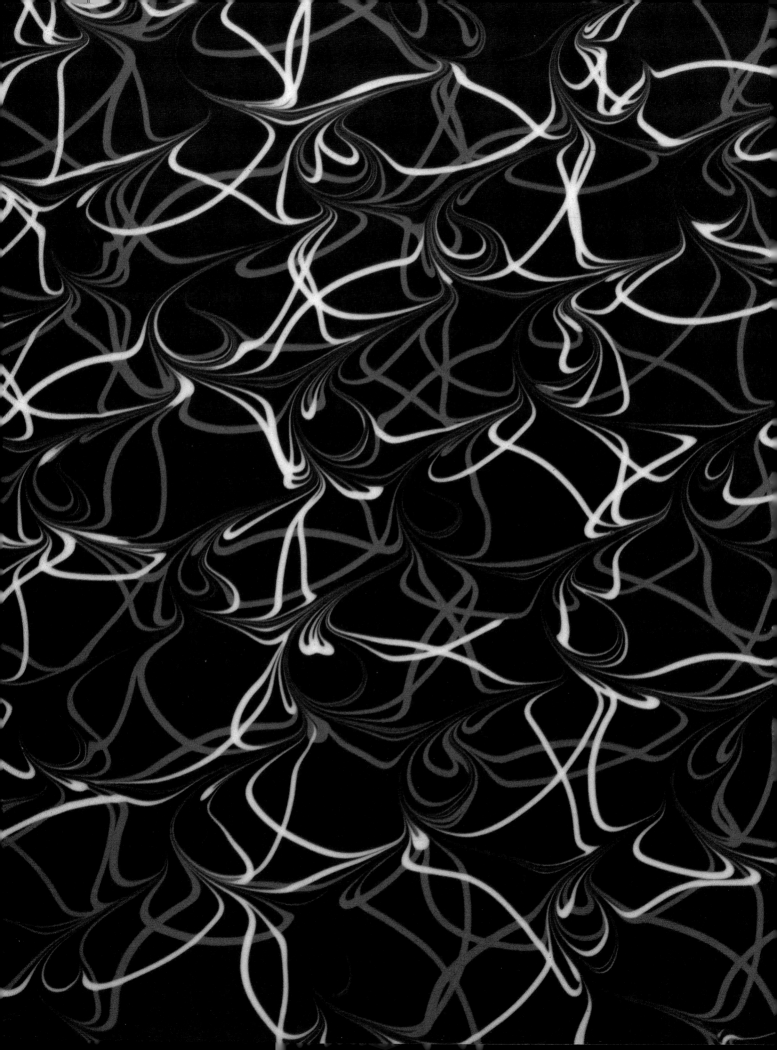

Chocolate Tortes

A dessert for lovers of dark, bittersweet chocolate . . .

a dessert for the purist . . .

a cake so chocolatey that icing or glaze is unnecessary,

except to add a sleek finishing touch . . .

a cake so rich in texture and flavor that the smallest piece

is pure satisfaction . . .

- - - - - -

My love affair with chocolate desserts started with the first bite of a simple, intensely chocolate, one-layer torte homemade in a tiny Paris apartment. The oven didn't even have a thermostat. ▪ ▪ ▪

It was a dessert for lovers of dark, bittersweet chocolate—a dessert for the purist, a "cake" so chocolatey that icing or glaze were unnecessary, except to add a sleek finishing touch. The smallest piece was pure satisfaction. I couldn't believe that something so simple could be so divine. ▪ ▪ ▪

I started my business inspired by this one sublime recipe. At Cocolat we literally celebrate the chocolate torte in all its variations. ▪ ▪ ▪

I smile to think that these exquisite recipes originally came from the home kitchens, cookbooks, and notebooks of generations of European grandmothers, aunts, mothers, and daughters. They were not the recipes of professional pastry chefs. They are as down-to-earth and soul-satisfying as home cooking and, indeed, may be presented with the utmost simplicity—a dusting of confectioners' sugar or a dollop of cream. It is my special delight to present them, sleek and glamorous, to grand company. ▪ ▪ ▪

The words "torte" or "torta" simply mean cake, in several European languages. Americans use the term "torte" for the specific type of European cake that is made with ground nuts or crumbs and with little or no flour. These are rich desserts, usually denser, more flavorful and somehow more exotic than the Anglo-American layer cake, pound cake or butter cake. This is especially true when chocolate plays the starring role! This first chapter deals exclusively with the rich, single-layer chocolate beauties that have become a Cocolat signature. ▪ ▪ ▪

When Cocolat opened in 1976, customers were accustomed to tall, sweet airy cakes bedecked with swirls of sticky frosting made primarily of shortening and confectioners' sugar. When they saw our low, svelte chocolate tortes, some said, "How beautiful, how elegant, but what are they?" But people were soon hooked on these rich, understated-looking desserts—all chocolate with a lovely nuance of brandy and almonds, fragrant toasted hazelnuts, or walnuts. To a large handful of relatively well-traveled locals in 1976, here was Vienna remembered, or that neighborhood restaurant in Paris. - - -

The recipes that follow are treasures. They are quick and easy to make, keep well, and freeze beautifully. Subtle variations result in different tortes—from light, creamy textures, to coarser, nuttier versions, to tortes so chocolate rich that they are more confection than cake! One great secret of these desserts is that most are slightly "underbaked," resulting in an indescribably rich, moist texture. - - -

If possible, I serve a chocolate torte at room temperature rather than cold. The texture is softer and smoother, the flavors are more luscious and forthcoming, and the fragrance of the chocolate is more intense. Tortes frosted with whipped cream may be removed from the refrigerator 45 minutes to an hour before serving, to restore the flavor and texture. - - -

When I started making desserts over 14 years ago, a chocolate torte was an exotic foreign pleasure. Today, there is hardly an excellent restaurant in the country that doesn't have one on the menu—plain or fancy. These chocolate tortes revolutionized our concept of dessert; they taught us that small can be beautiful, and that less definitely can be more!

Chocolate Hazelnut Torte

Serves 10–12

Torte tastes best if baked at least one day ahead.

Ingredients:
6 ounces semisweet or bittersweet
  chocolate, cut into small pieces
6 ounces sweet butter, cut into
  pieces
4 large eggs, separated
¾ cup sugar
½ cup (2 ounces) ground toasted
  hazelnuts
¼ cup (1 ounce) flour
⅛ teaspoon cream of tartar
Bittersweet Chocolate Glaze (page
  174) or Chocolate Honey Glaze
  (page 174)
12 plain or caramelized hazelnuts
  (page 172; optional), for
  decoration, or
1 ounce each, milk and white
  chocolate, for piped decoration
  (page 185; optional)

Special Equipment:
8-inch corrugated cake circle
Parchment paper cone(s) for
  piping decoration (optional)

1. Preheat oven to 375°. Line bottom of an 8 × 3-inch round cake pan or springform pan with a circle of parchment or waxed paper.

2. Melt chocolate and butter in a small bowl placed in a barely simmering water bath on low heat, stirring occasionally until completely melted. Remove from heat. Or, microwave on MEDIUM (50%) for about 2 minutes. Stir until smooth and completely melted.

3. Beat egg yolks with ½ cup of sugar until pale and thick. Stir in warm chocolate mixture, nuts, and flour. Set aside.

4. Beat the egg whites and cream of tartar at medium speed until soft peaks form. Gradually sprinkle in remaining ¼ cup sugar, beating at high speed until stiff but not dry. Fold one-fourth of whites into chocolate batter to lighten it. Quickly fold in remaining whites. Turn mixture into prepared pan and smooth top if necessary. Bake for 40–45 minutes, or until a toothpick or wooden skewer plunged into center of torte shows moist crumbs.

5. Cool torte completely in pan on a rack. It will have risen and then fallen in the center, leaving a higher rim of cake around sides and possibly some cracking. Level and unmold torte onto an 8-inch corrugated cake circle according to instructions, page 175. Torte may be completed to this point, wrapped and kept at room temperature up to 3 days in advance. Or freeze for up to 3 months. Let come to room temperature before glazing.

6. Glaze with Bittersweet Chocolate or Chocolate Honey Glaze. To decorate place plain or caramelized hazelnuts around the top edge of the cake or pipe overlapping zigzags of melted white and milk chocolate (see photograph). Do not refrigerate.

The rich flavor of toasted hazelnuts (filberts) bowled me over for the first time in a creamy gelato ice cream cone just yards from the Leaning Tower of Pisa! In this torte that memory mingles with my favorite— bittersweet chocolate.

In Italy Amareno cherries in syrup are served right out of the jar, spooned over ice cream or gelato. Try them in this moist, fruity, bittersweet torte glazed with sweet white chocolate.

Italian Cherry Torte

1. Preheat oven to 375°. Line bottom of 8 × 2-inch round cake pan with a circle of parchment or waxed paper.

2. In small bowl, combine cherries with liqueur and almond extract; set aside.

3. Melt chocolate and butter in a small bowl placed in a barely simmering water bath, stirring occasionally until melted and smooth. Remove from heat. Or, microwave on MEDIUM (50%) for about 2 minutes. Stir until smooth and completely melted.

4. Beat egg yolks with ½ cup sugar until pale and thick. Stir in chocolate mixture, flour, and almonds. Add the cherries and liqueur. Set aside.

5. Beat egg whites and cream of tartar at medium speed until soft peaks form. Gradually sprinkle in remaining 3 tablespoons sugar, beating at high speed until stiff but not dry. Fold one-fourth of whites into chocolate mixture to lighten it. Fold in remaining whites. Turn batter into prepared pan and smooth top if necessary. Bake for 30–40 minutes, or until a toothpick inserted about 1 inch from edge of torte shows moist crumbs. The center of cake will test very moist.

6. Cool torte completely in pan on a rack. The cake will have risen and then fallen in the center, leaving a higher rim of cake around sides and possibly some cracking. Level and unmold torte onto 8-inch corrugated cake circle according to instructions, page 175. Torte may be completed to this point, wrapped well, and kept at room temperature up to 3 days in advance. Or freeze for up to 3 months. Let come to room temperature before glazing or serving.

7. Serve simply, with a dusting of confectioners' sugar, or accompany with whipped cream or vanilla ice cream. Or glaze with White Chocolate Glaze. Decorate, if desired, with fresh rose petals, cherry blossoms, or chocolate piping. Once the torte is glazed, do not refrigerate.

Serves 10–12

Torte tastes best if baked at least one day ahead.

Ingredients:
¼ cup Amareno cherries,* drained and quartered
¼ cup Kirsch or Maraschino liqueur
⅛ teaspoon almond extract
6 ounces semisweet or bittersweet chocolate, cut into small pieces
4 ounces sweet butter, cut into pieces
3 large eggs, separated
½ cup plus 3 tablespoons granulated sugar
¼ cup (1 ounce) flour
⅔ cup (2½ ounces) ground blanched almonds
⅛ teaspoon cream of tartar
White Chocolate Glaze (page 175), confectioners' sugar, whipped cream, or vanilla ice cream, for decoration or serving
1 ounce white or dark chocolate (optional) for piped decoration (page 185)

*Amareno cherries in syrup are available in gourmet sections of many department stores, and in some supermarkets. Amareno cherries are firm and have a unique flavor. Canned or frozen cherries are too soft and do not have enough flavor to substitute.

Special Equipment:
8-inch corrugated cake circle
Parchment paper cone for piping decoration (optional)

Chestnut Chocolate Torte

Serves 10–12

Torte tastes best if baked at least one day ahead.

Ingredients:
4 ounces semisweet or bittersweet chocolate, cut into pieces
4 ounces sweet butter, cut into pieces
4 large eggs, separated
1 cup canned sweetened chestnut purée
1 teaspoon vanilla extract
¼ cup (1 ounce) flour
⅛ teaspoon cream of tartar
¼ cup granulated sugar
2–3 tablespoons confectioners' sugar (optional, for stencil)
Chilled Crème Fraîche (page 169), made at least 3 days in advance

Special Equipment:
8-inch corrugated cake circle
Homemade stencil (page 187) or doily (optional)

1. Preheat oven to 350°. Line bottom of 8 × 2-inch round cake pan with parchment or waxed paper.

2. Melt chocolate and butter in a small bowl placed in a barely simmering water bath over low heat, stirring occasionally until smooth. Remove from heat. Or, microwave on MEDIUM (50%) for about 1 minute and 30 seconds. Stir until completely melted and smooth. Set aside.

3. In bowl, whisk egg yolks, chestnut purée, vanilla, and flour. Stir in chocolate mixture; set aside.

4. Beat egg whites and cream of tartar in a clean, dry mixing bowl at medium speed until soft peaks form. Gradually sprinkle in granulated sugar, beating at high speed, until stiff but not dry. Fold about one-quarter of egg whites into chocolate batter to lighten it. Quickly fold in remaining whites. Turn mixture into prepared pan and smooth top. Bake for 40–45 minutes, until a toothpick or wooden skewer plunged into the center comes out moist, but not gooey.

5. Cool torte completely in pan on a rack. It will have risen and then fallen in the center, leaving a higher rim of cake around sides and possibly some cracking. Level and unmold torte onto an 8-inch corrugated cake circle according to instructions, page 175. Torte may be made to this point up to 3 days in advance. Wrap well and refrigerate until needed, or freeze for up to 3 months. Let come to room temperature before serving or decorating.

Simply dust or stencil with confectioners' sugar. Serve with Crème Fraîche.

I admit to a
weakness for
sweetened chestnut
purée—yes, the
kind that comes in
a can. It used to be
served for dessert
in French cafés
with lots of crème
fraîche. Here is a
chocolate torte
inspired by that
memory. It could
be finished with
Bittersweet
Chocolate Glaze,
but I love it best
with a great dollop
of crème fraîche!

Chocolate Orange Torte for Passover

Serves 10-12

Torte tastes best if baked at least one day ahead.

Ingredients:
4 ounces semisweet or bittersweet chocolate, cut into pieces
4 ounces sweet butter, at room temperature
⅔ cup sugar
⅛ teaspoon almond extract
Finely grated zest of 1 orange
3 large eggs
¾ cup (3 ounces) ground blanched almonds
¼ cup matzoh meal
Chocolate Honey Glaze (page 174)
½ cup (about 2 ounces) sliced toasted almonds (optional)

Special Equipment:
8-inch corrugated cake circle

Here is a chic bittersweet chocolate torte with lots of freshly grated orange zest—devised especially for Passover, but lovely all year round. No flour, a generous quantity of ground almonds, and a handful of matzoh meal give this dessert a characteristic nubbly texture. You don't have to be Jewish to enjoy it!

1. Preheat oven to 375°. Line bottom of 8 × 2-inch round cake pan with a circle of parchment or waxed paper.

2. Melt chocolate very gently in a clean, dry bowl set into a barely simmering water bath, stirring frequently until melted and smooth. Or, microwave on MEDIUM (50%) for about 2 minutes and 20–30 seconds. Stir until completely melted and smooth. Be sure the stirring implement is dry. When chocolate is melted and smooth, remove from heat and set aside.

3. Beat butter, sugar, almond extract, and orange zest with an electric mixer until very light and creamy. Add eggs, one by one, beating very well after each addition. Turn mixer to low speed and add chocolate, beating only until incorporated. Stir in almonds and matzoh meal just until combined. Turn batter into prepared pan and smooth top. Bake for 25–30 minutes, until a toothpick or a wooden skewer plunged into center of cake shows moist crumbs (the torte should be neither completely dry nor runny in the center).

4. Allow torte to cool completely in pan on a rack. Level and unmold torte onto 8-inch corrugated cake circle according to instructions, page 175. Torte can be made to this point up to 3 days in advance. Wrap well and keep at room temperature until needed, or freeze for up to 3 months. Let come to room temperature before serving or glazing and decorating.

5. Glaze with Chocolate Honey Glaze and press toasted sliced almonds around the sides. Once glazed, do not refrigerate.

Gâteau Royale

Our Cocolat customers think this chocolate cake, with red raspberry preserves and a fine layer of almond paste, is even moister and more delicious than the much-touted Sacher Torte! What can I say?

1. Preheat oven to 350°. Line bottom of 9 × 2-inch round cake pan with a circle of parchment or waxed paper.

2. Melt together chocolate, butter, and 3 tablespoons water in a barely simmering water bath over low heat, stirring occasionally until smooth. Remove from heat. Or, microwave on MEDIUM (50%) power for about 1 minute. Stir until completely smooth. Set aside.

3. Beat egg yolks and ½ cup sugar together until pale and thick. Stir in warm chocolate mixture; stir in flour. Set aside.

4. Beat eggs whites with cream of tartar in a clean, dry mixing bowl at medium speed until soft peaks form. Gradually sprinkle in remaining ¼ cup sugar, beating at high speed until stiff but not dry. Fold one-fourth of whites gently into chocolate batter to lighten it. Fold in remaining whites. Turn batter into prepared pan. Bake for 20–25 minutes, until a toothpick or wooden skewer plunged into the center comes out just dry. Do not overbake.

5. Cool cake for 10 minutes in pan on a rack. Run a small knife or spatula around the edge and invert onto cake circle. Peel off parchment. Invert once more onto a rack so that the cake is right side up. Save the cake circle. Cool cake completely on the rack before using. Cake may be prepared to this point, wrapped well, and kept at room temperature up to 2 days in advance, or frozen for up to 3 months. Let come to room temperature before glazing or serving.

6. **To Assemble the Cake:** Place cooled cake right side up on cake circle. With a serrated bread knife, split cake horizontally into 2 thin layers. Set upper layer aside. Spread bottom layer evenly with half of preserves. Place top layer on preserves and spread with remaining preserves.

7. Roll almond paste between 2 sheets of plastic wrap until about ⅛ inch thick and at least 8 inches in diameter. Cut almond paste into a neat 8-inch round; save the scraps for another use. Center almond paste round on top of cake.

8. Glaze cake with Bittersweet Chocolate Glaze. Once glazed, do not refrigerate the cake.

Serves 10–12

Ingredients:
5 ounces semisweet or bittersweet chocolate, cut into pieces
2 ounces sweet butter, cut into pieces
3 large eggs, separated
¾ cup sugar
¾ cup (3 ounces) sifted cake flour
⅛ teaspoon cream of tartar
½ cup raspberry or apricot preserves
4–5 ounces almond paste
Bittersweet Chocolate Glaze (page 174)

Special Equipment:
9-inch corrugated cake circle

Diabolo

Serves 10–12

Torte tastes best if baked at least one day ahead.

Ingredients:
6 ounces semisweet or bittersweet
  chocolate
6 ounces sweet butter
4 large eggs, separated
¾ cup plus 2–3 tablespoons sugar
⅛ teaspoon almond extract
½ cup (2 ounces) ground almonds
¼ cup (1 ounce) flour
⅛ teaspoon cream of tartar
3 cups heavy cream
25–30 chocolate fans (pages
  189–91)

Special Equipment:
9-inch corrugated cake circle

1. Preheat oven to 375°. Line bottom of 8 × 3-inch springform pan with parchment or waxed paper.

2. Melt chocolate and butter in small bowl placed in barely simmering water bath over low heat, stirring occasionally until smooth. Or, microwave on MEDIUM (50%) for about 2 minutes. Stir until completely melted and smooth. Remove from heat and set aside.

3. In bowl, whisk egg yolks with ½ cup of sugar and almond extract until pale and thick. Stir in warm chocolate mixture, almonds, and flour. Set aside.

4. In clean, dry mixing bowl, beat egg whites and cream of tartar at medium speed until soft peaks form. Gradually sprinkle in ¼ cup sugar, beating at high speed until stiff but not dry. Fold about one-quarter of the egg whites completely into the chocolate batter to lighten it. Quickly fold in remaining whites. Turn mixture into prepared pan and smooth top if necessary. Bake for 40–45 minutes, until a toothpick or wooden skewer plunged into the center of the cake shows moist crumbs (center of torte should be neither completely dry nor runny).

5. Cool torte completely in pan on a rack. It will have risen and then fallen in the center, leaving a higher rim of cake around sides and possibly some cracking. Level and unmold torte onto a 9-inch (1-inch bigger than the cake) corrugated cake circle according to instructions, page 175. Torte may be prepared to this point up to 3 days in advance. Wrap well and store in the refrigerator until needed, or freeze for up to 3 months.

6. Whip cream with remaining 2–3 tablespoons of sugar until fairly stiff and mask the cake with all of it, making sure to cover the edges of the cake circle (see Frosting with Whipped Cream, page 179). Decorate with a ruffle of plain or striped chocolate fans. Refrigerate in a covered container.

7. Cake may be finished to this point up to 12 hours in advance of serving. Remove from refrigerator about 1 hour before serving.

This is the lightest and most subtle of chocolate tortes. With so little flour and such a small quantity of nuts, it resembles a chocolate soufflé served at room temperature. This one even tastes good cold — so I give it an exotic finish of whipped cream and fancy chocolate ruffles.

This dessert is in a class by itself. Closer to a baked bittersweet chocolate truffle than a cake or torte, it is practically all chocolate, butter, and eggs. Versions have circulated around this country for years. This sublime dessert pairs whipped cream with a tangy, tart fresh fruit sauce to offset the richness. Raspberry Puree is the traditional accompaniment, but do try Sauce Bijou or Orange Sauce.

Chocolate
Decadence

1. Preheat oven to 425°. Line 8 × 2-inch round cake pan with parchment or waxed paper.

2. Melt the chocolate and butter in a small bowl placed in a barely simmering water bath over low heat, stirring occasionally until smooth. Or, microwave on MEDIUM (50%) for about 3 minutes and 30 seconds. Stir until completely melted and smooth. Whisk in egg yolks and flour. Set aside.

3. Beat egg whites with cream of tartar in a clean, dry mixing bowl at medium speed until soft peaks form. Gradually sprinkle in 1 tablespoon sugar, beating at high speed, until stiff but not dry. Fold about one-quarter of eggs whites into the chocolate mixture to lighten it. Quickly fold in remaining whites. Turn mixture into prepared pan. Bake for exactly 15 minutes.

4. Remove from oven and cool in pan. Cake will rise somewhat, especially around edges, but will still seem undercooked. As it cools, it will sink in the center. This is correct! Let the dessert cool completely in the pan on a rack. Cover and chill for several hours in refrigerator.

5. Run a knife or small spatula around the edge to release it from pan. Warm the bottom of the pan on a stove burner on low heat for just a few seconds; invert it onto a plate to unmold. Peel the parchment liner from bottom and invert again onto serving plate or corrugated cake circle (if you plan to frost it with whipped cream). The cake circle will be ½ inch bigger than the dessert all around. The dessert will be right-side-up and higher around the edges than in the middle. It may be made to this point up to 4 days in advance. Wrap well and refrigerate until needed, or freeze for up to 3 months.

To Serve Simply: Remove from refrigerator at least 1 hour in advance. Cut in wedges and pass lightly sweetened whipped cream and sauces separately.

To Serve More Formally: Whip cream with remaining 3 tablespoons of sugar and mask cake thickly with about three-quarters of it (see Frosting with Whipped Cream, page 179, for details and tips). Scrape the remaining whipped cream into pastry bag and pipe large rosettes or swirls around the top edge of the cake.

Serves 10–12

Ingredients:
16 ounces semisweet or bittersweet chocolate, cut into small pieces
5 ounces sweet butter
5 large eggs, separated
1 tablespoon flour
¼ teaspoon cream of tartar
3–4 tablespoons sugar
4 cups heavy cream
One or a pair of the following sauces: Raspberry Sauce (page 171), Sauce Bijou (cranberry/ raspberry) (page 171), Orange Sauce (page 171)

Special Equipment:
9-inch corrugated cake circle, if you plan to frost the dessert with whipped cream
Pastry bag fitted with Ateco #7 closed star tip, if you plan to frost with whipped cream

There are countless variations on this French housewife's classic. As a rule, pastry shops in France do not make this cake. To me, it is one of the ultimate chocolate desserts.

Queen
of Sheba

1. Preheat oven to 375°. Line bottom of 8 × 3-inch springform pan with parchment or waxed paper.

2. Combine chocolate and butter in a small bowl placed in a barely simmering water bath over low heat, stirring occasionally until melted and smooth. Remove from heat. Or, microwave on MEDIUM (50%) for about 2 minutes. Stir until completely melted and smooth. Stir in brandy and almond extract. Set aside.

3. In bowl, whisk egg yolks with ½ cup sugar until pale and thick. Stir in the warm chocolate mixture, almonds, and flour. Set aside.

4. Beat the egg whites and cream of tartar at medium speed until soft peaks form. Gradually sprinkle in remaining ¼ cup sugar, beating at high speed until stiff but not dry. Fold about one-quarter of the egg whites completely into the chocolate batter to lighten it. Quickly fold in remaining whites. Turn mixture into the prepared pan and smooth top if necessary. Bake for 40–45 minutes, until a toothpick or wooden skewer plunged into the center of the cake shows moist crumbs (the center of the cake should be neither completely dry nor runny).

5. Cool torte completely in pan on a rack. It will have risen and then fallen in the center, leaving a higher rim of cake around sides and possibly some cracking. Level and unmold torte onto an 8-inch corrugated cake circle according to instructions, page 175. Torte may be prepared to this point up to 3 days in advance. Wrap well and store at room temperature until needed, or freeze for up to 3 months. Bring to room temperature before serving, glazing, or decorating.

6. Glaze torte with Bittersweet Chocolate Glaze, plain or marbled, and press sliced toasted almonds around the sides.

Serves 10–12

Torte tastes best if baked at least one day ahead.

Ingredients:
6 ounces semisweet or bittersweet chocolate, cut into pieces
6 ounces sweet butter, cut into pieces
3 tablespoons brandy
⅛ teaspoon almond extract
4 large eggs, separated
¾ cup sugar
½ cup (2 ounces) ground blanched almonds
¼ cup (1 ounce) flour
⅛ teaspoon cream of tartar
Bittersweet Chocolate Glaze (page 174)
1 ounce each white and/or dark chocolate (optimal) if you plan to marble the glaze (page 177)
½ cup (about 2 ounces) sliced toasted almonds

Special Equipment:
8-inch round corrugated cake circle

Mocha Pecan Torte

Serves 10–12

Torte tastes best if baked at least one day ahead.

Ingredients:
6 ounces semisweet or bittersweet
  chocolate, cut into pieces
6 ounces sweet butter, cut into
  pieces
4 large eggs, separated
¾ cup sugar
1 cup (4 ounces) ground pecans
2 tablespoons (½ ounce) flour
⅛ teaspoon cream of tartar
Mocha Glaze (page 175)
1 ounce each white and/or dark
  chocolate (optional) if you plan
  to marble the glaze (page 177)
½ cup (2½ ounces) chopped
  lightly toasted pecans

Special Equipment:
9-inch round corrugated cake circle
1 or 2 paper cones to marble glaze
  (optional)

1. Preheat oven to 350°. Line bottom of 9 × 2-inch round cake pan with parchment or waxed paper.

2. Combine chocolate and butter in a small bowl placed in a barely simmering water bath over low heat, stirring occasionally until melted and smooth. Remove from heat. Or, microwave on MEDIUM (50%) for about 2 minutes. Stir until completely melted and smooth. Set aside.

3. In bowl, whisk the egg yolks with ½ cup sugar until pale and thick. Stir in warm chocolate mixture, pecans, and flour. Set aside.

4. Beat egg whites and cream of tartar at medium speed until soft peaks form. Gradually sprinkle in remaining ¼ cup sugar, beating at high speed until stiff but not dry. Fold about one-quarter of egg whites completely into the chocolate batter to lighten it. Quickly fold in remaining egg whites. Turn mixture into the prepared pan and smooth top if necessary. Bake for 40–45 minutes, until a toothpick or wooden skewer plunged into the center of the cake shows moist crumbs (the center of the torte should be neither completely dry nor runny).

5. Cool the cake completely in pan on a rack. It will have risen and then fallen in the center, leaving a higher rim of cake around sides and possibly some cracking. Level and unmold torte onto an 9-inch corrugated cake circle according to instructions, page 175. Torte may be prepared to this point up to 3 days in advance. Wrap well and store at room temperature until needed, or freeze for up to 3 months. Let come to room temperature before serving, glazing, or decorating.

6. Glaze torte with Mocha Glaze (p. 175), marbled or plain, and press chopped toasted pecans around the sides.

A European-style torte with distinctive American flavors. Loads of nutty, sweet-flavored, Georgia pecans with luscious Mocha Glaze.

Designer
Desserts

Like exquisite jewels or haute couture,

designer desserts are the work of culinary artists

with keen eyes and very clever hands,

as well as great palates ...

Each is executed to make a strong visual statement,

and each tastes even more delicious than it looks.

- - - - - -

I have always loved desserts—from the homiest apple pie to the most elegant Viennese creation. But I never really looked at desserts until my husband and I went to live in Paris in 1973. Like so many before us, we made a virtual career of visiting pastry shops. Most French desserts tasted better to us than anything we were accustomed to at home. But something else was different, too. Desserts were less frilly, overdressed, and overdecorated than Americans were used to. Some of the most magnificent and delicious were downright understated! I saw simple lines and dramatic use of form and color. In short, I saw a sense of design used to create incredibly glamorous and appetizing desserts. ▪ ▪ ▪

Like exquisite jewels or haute couture, desserts displayed in Parisian store windows were not just the work of dedicated pastry cooks with great palates and good recipes. They were the work of culinary artists with keen eyes and very clever hands, as well as great palates. The elegant simplicity, clean lines, and dramatic sculptural shapes brought out the problem solver and puzzle doer in me. How was that deceptive simplicity achieved—that flawless chocolate glaze, that high-fashioned topknot of ruffled chocolate that crowned the chocolate dessert of my dreams? A lifetime interest in crafts, architecture, and graphics was suddenly connected to my passion for everything culinary. I began to view dessert making as a contemporary art form—one that posed a significant design challenge, in addition to the traditional culinary hurdles. ▪ ▪ ▪

Since opening Cocolat, my aim has been to create desserts that please the eye and tantalize the mind as well as the palate. I think of my desserts as a collection—

just the way a designer might. "Designer" desserts may sound pompous, but to me the label describes the very special qualities of my favorite recipes. **- - -**

Designer desserts may be simple or quite elaborate, classic or contemporary. But each makes a strong visual statement. Even the simplest dessert exudes a certain sophistication. None of these desserts could be described as homey or amateurish in presentation. None is fussy, overly frilly, or rococo. Finally, no matter how dramatic or stylish they look, taste and quality are never sacrificed for glamour or special effect. One of the things I love best is that mixture of astonishment and reverence when, after the very first bite, the taster realizes the dessert tastes even more delicious than it looks. A designer dessert must never disappoint—the proof of the pudding is still in the eating. **- - -**

I especially love to make desserts that are architectural: the dessert is assembled in such a way that its elements and ingredients also become its decoration. This is so much more fun than making the cake first, then covering it completely with frosting, and *then* decorating it—usually with rosettes squeezed from a pastry bag! Architectural desserts like Strawberry Carrousel and Tricolor Mousse make people stare and wonder, "How on earth was that done?" Happily, these fabulous-looking desserts are much simpler to make than they look. **- - -**

My concept of designer desserts is a statement about style *and* quality. It profoundly influences all of my dessert making. The desserts in this chapter are the quintessence of the concept—the most dramatic and contemporary looking, and the most fun to make.

Tricolor
Mousse

*Serves 16–18
(or makes two small desserts,
each to serve 8–9)*

Ingredients:
*1 ounce semisweet or bittersweet
    chocolate*
Chocolate Marquise (page 165)
Mocha Mousse (page 166)
*White Chocolate Mousse (page
    166)*
*2–3 chocolate fans or 16–20
    chocolate cigarettes (pages 189–
    91), plain or striped (optional,
    for decoration)*

Special Equipment:
*Piece of parchment or waxed paper
    with an 8-inch circle traced on it
    8 × 3-inch round springform pan
    or cheesecake pan with removable
    bottom, or an 8-inch dessert ring
    plus an 8-inch corrugated cake
    circle (if you plan to make two
    small desserts, use two 6 × 3-
    inch round pans or dessert rings,
    two 6-inch corrugated cake
    circles, and two 6-inch circles
    traced on parchment or
    waxed paper)*
Propane torch (optional)

1. If you are using dessert ring(s), place on a flat plate or tray. If not, have ready the springform or cheesecake pan. Turn parchment(s) with the traced circle(s) upside down on a baking sheet (you should still see the tracing through the paper) and tape the edges to the baking sheet to keep them from curling later.

2. Melt chocolate gently in water bath or microwave at MEDIUM (50%) about 1 minute and 30 seconds. Spread chocolate evenly in traced circle(s). Refrigerate for at least 10 minutes, until hardened. When hard, remove tape. Turn paper upside down and peel gently away from chocolate. Place chocolate disk(s) in bottom of each pan or ring; return to refrigerator until needed. (It is OK if disk breaks or cracks; just put pieces in place. This thin chocolate disk will facilitate serving by keeping mousse from sticking to bottom of pan.)

3. Make the Chocolate Marquise. Turn immediately into pan on top of chocolate disk. If you are making two smaller desserts put half of the Marquise in each pan and do the same in steps 4 and 5. Level Marquise with a spatula; wipe inside sides of pan clean above top of Marquise. The pan will be less than half-full. Refrigerate.

4. Make the Mocha Mousse. Turn immediately into pan and spread on top of Marquise, leaving about ¾ inch of space at the top of the pan. (If there is excess mousse, nibble.) Wipe inside sides of pan clean above top of mousse. Refrigerate.

5. Make the White Chocolate Mousse. Turn immediately into pan on top of mocha. Use a metal spatula to level top of mousse perfectly even with rim of pan. Refrigerate dessert for 4–6 hours, or until set, before unmolding. Dessert may be completed to this point and refrigerated in the pan, covered, up to 2 days in advance. Or, freeze for up to 2 months.

6. **To Unmold:** Before unmolding dessert ring(s), tilt and slide cake circles under each dessert. Warm the sides of ring briefly with a hot, wet, wrung-out towel, or a propane torch and slip it off of dessert by pulling up with both hands. The sides of a cheesecake pan must be pulled down, so you must place the pan on top of a can or other sturdy support before warming and sliding the sides down. If you have used a springform pan, warm as described, then release sides of pan. The springform will not release as cleanly as the dessert ring or cheesecake pan, so you may need to smooth sides of dessert with a metal spatula.

7. Decorate dessert with a cluster of chocolate fans or chocolate cigarettes.

*Three stunning
chocolate
mousses in one
dessert earned
San Francisco
Focus magazine's
"Dessert of
the Year" award
in 1987.*

A merry-go-round of strawberries makes a high-tech strawberry shortcake. This is the most festive strawberry dessert I know. The white chocolate mousse splashed with Kirsch is sensational, but I sometimes replace it with something simpler—lightly sweetened, whipped crème fraîche or just plain whipped cream!

Strawberry Carrousel

1. Cut one even layer, ¾ inch thick, from cake. (Wrap and freeze remainder of cake for another use.) Place cake layer in bottom of pan or dessert ring. (If you are using dessert ring, slide corrugated cake circle underneath cake layer and dessert ring.)

2. Choose about 10 large berries of equal height. Cut them in half vertically. Arrange them, pointed ends up, fitting cut sides snugly against inside circumference of pan. Cut additional berries, if necessary, to completely line the sides of the pan. Leave remaining berries whole and arrange them, pointed ends up, close together all over top of cake in pan. Berries must be at least ⅛ inch shorter than sides of pan. (If necessary, trim bottoms of any berries that are too tall.)

3. Make White Chocolate Mousse. Pour immediately over berries. Spread mousse, pushing it into all the spaces between berries and making sure that it is in contact with sides of pan between cut berries. (If mousse is too stiff to pour, scrape into a pastry bag fitted with a large, plain, open tip. Fill mold by piping the mousse first around edges of pan between and among the berries. Then fill in the center. Use a broad spatula to smooth top even with pan. Ripple top surface of mousse with a serrated bread knife, if desired. Refrigerate in a covered container for at least 4 hours, until set. Dessert may be completed to this point up to 24 hours before serving. Refrigerate in a covered container. Do not freeze.

4. **To Unmold and Serve:** Warm pan or dessert circle briefly with a hot, well wrung-out wet towel or a propane torch. Remove sides of springform carefully; smooth sides of dessert with a warm, dry metal spatula if necessary. If you have used a dessert ring, lift ring upwards off dessert.

5. Simmer strained apricot preserves in a very small saucepan for 1–2 minutes to create a glaze. Using a pastry brush, carefully glaze only the sides of sponge cake and cut surfaces of strawberries. Avoid brushing glaze on mousse. Press minced pistachios against very lowest edge of cake layer. Refrigerate in a covered container until serving time.

Serves 12–16

Ingredients:
8-inch-round Hot Milk Sponge Cake (page 160) or Génoise (page 159)
2 pints whole ripe strawberries, rinsed, drained, and hulled
White Chocolate Mousse with Kirsch (page 166)
¼ cup strained apricot preserves
2 tablespoons finely minced pistachios

Special Equipment:
8 × 3-inch springform pan, or dessert ring with an 8-inch-round corrugated cake circle
Propane torch (optional)

- - -

When strawberries are at their ripest and best, this cake is perfect as it stands. If your berries need a "lift," crush enough of them to make 3 tablespoon of purée. Add 1 tablespoon of good Kirsch and sugar to taste. Spread this mixture over cake before arranging berries.

Bittersweet
Chocolate Truffle
Tart

Serves 12–16

Ingredients:
10 ounces bittersweet or semisweet
chocolate, cut into small pieces
1¼ cups heavy cream
9½-inch Chocolate Tart Shell
(page 164), baked and cooled
1–2 tablespoons unsweetened cocoa
powder (optional, for stenciling)

Special Equipment:
Homemade stencil (page 186) or
doily, for decoration (optional)

- - -

For the shiniest tart:
—If possible, avoid using a knife
or spatula to spread or smooth the
surface of the filling once it is
poured into the tart.
For the smoothest, creamiest
filling:
—Do not whisk or stir the truffle
filling too briskly or you will
create air bubbles and foam, which
cause a dry, grainy texture.

1. Place chocolate in a medium-size heatproof bowl; set aside.

2. In a small saucepan, bring cream to a simmer over medium heat. Immediately pour hot cream over chocolate; let stand for 30 seconds. Stir very gently just until chocolate melts completely and mixture is smooth.

3. Pour chocolate mixture through a fine strainer directly into cooled Chocolate Tarte Shell. Tilt or shake pan gently, if necessary, to spread chocolate evenly over shell. Refrigerate for 3–4 hours, until set. Tart may be made to this point up to 2 days in advance. Cover and refrigerate until ready to decorate.

4. Center a stencil or doily over well-chilled tart. Use a fine strainer to sift cocoa over the stencil. Remove the stencil carefully. Refrigerate tart in a covered container.

5. Remove finished tart from refrigerator 45 minutes or more before serving to soften filling slightly and bring back its shine. (Be sure that you applied the stenciled cocoa to the cold tart *before* allowing it to soften.)

*Ultra chocolate.
This is like
eating the
richest, smoothest,
bittersweet
chocolate truffles—
with a fork!*

*To me, a
chocolate dessert
with a ruffle
is the ultimate
chocolate
romance—the most
flirtatious
look of all.*

Chocolate Ruffle Torte

1. Before beginning, check to see that you will be able to fit the 26-inch cardboard into your refrigerator. I fit it into my home refrigerator at a slant and kitty-corner, often balanced on top of the milk cartons. This is precarious but adequate.

2. Reverse cooled sponge sheet onto a sheet of foil or waxed paper and remove pan liner. Reverse sponge again so that top side faces up. Cut out two 8-inch cake circles, plus 2 strips of sponge, each 1½ inches wide and 13 inches long (fig. 1).

3. Brush tops of cut cake pieces liberally with Curacao. Line pan with sponge as follows: place 1 sponge circle, moist side up, in bottom of 8 × 3-inch springform or cheesecake pan with a removeable bottom. Lay strips, standing on their sides, around insides of the pan, moist sides facing in, trimming to fit if necessary. Reserve second cake circle.

4. Make Chocolate Velvet Mousse. Pour immediately into lined mold. Top mousse with remaining cake circle, moist side down. Cover and refrigerate for 2–3 hours, at least, to set before finishing. Dessert may be prepared to this point, wrapped well and refrigerated, up to 2 days ahead, or frozen for up to 2 months.

5. **To Finish the Torte:** In a small saucepan, simmer strained jam for 1–2 minutes until reduced and thickened. Remove sides of cake pan to unmold. Transfer dessert to cardboard circle or directly onto serving platter. (If you leave it on the bottom of springform pan, the edges will show.) Spread sides and top with hot jam. Refrigerate.

6. Meanwhile, place paper strip flat on counter. Fold *under* 1 inch of paper at each end, to be used later as handles. Melt chocolate in a water bath on low heat or microwave on MEDIUM (50%) for about 2 minutes and 10 seconds. Use an offset spatula to spread carefully over paper strip, reserving ½ teaspoon of melted chocolate. Keep reserved chocolate warm. Transfer chocolate-coated paper on cardboard support and refrigerate until chocolate is set but still flexible, about 10 minutes.

7. Remove mousse and chocolate strip from refrigerator. If the chocolate strip is too cold and brittle, wait a few minutes until it is flexible again, but not melting or gooey. If it becomes too soft or gooey, refrigerate for a few minutes. Leave chocolate attached to paper while you work. Pick up strip, using the folded paper ends as handles. Wrap strip snugly around sides of **mousse**, placing chocolate side against apricot-coated dessert (fig. 2). The bottom edge of strip should cover bottom edge of dessert and edge of corrugated cardboard, if you have used it. When the 2 ends of chocolate strip meet, peel away enough paper to overlap the strip and

Serves 12–14

Ingredients:
11 × 17- or 12 × 16-inch Hot Milk Sponge Cake sheet (page 160), baked and cooled
About ¼ cup Curaçao or rum
Chocolate Velvet Mousse (page 165)
½ cup strained apricot jam
2½ ounces semisweet or bittersweet chocolate, cut into bits
1½ cups heavy cream
2 tablespoons sugar
1 teaspoon vanilla extract
Chocolate fans (pages 189–91)

Special Equipment:
Piece of stiff cardboard, 26 inches long and 4 inches wide
8-inch corrugated cardboard cake circle (optional)
Strip of parchment or waxed paper 28 inches long by 2½ inches wide

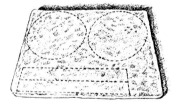

figure 1

figure 2

attach with a dab or two of reserved melted chocolate. Trim excess length from strip with a razor blade or scissors, if necessary. The chocolate strip will be about ½ inch taller than the dessert it encircles. Leave paper attached. Refrigerate to harden the chocolate.

8. Whip cream with sugar and vanilla until stiff. Spread cream over top of mousse, reaching nearly to rim of chocolate strip. Arrange chocolate fans all over the whipped cream, starting from perimeter and working toward center. Dessert may be prepared to this point, covered with a cake dome or plastic cake container, and refrigerated up to 1 day ahead. Peel paper from sides of dessert before serving.

Apricot Soufflé

1. **To Make Apricot Purée:** Place dried apricots in a small heatproof bowl. Pour boiling water over them. Cover bowl tightly with plastic wrap; set aside to steep for at least 1 hour or longer. In blender or food processor, purée apricots, their soaking liquid, and 1 cup sugar until as smooth as possible. Set aside.

2. **To Assemble Cake and Purée:** Run a knife around edges of sponge sheet to release from pan. Reverse cooled sponge onto a piece of waxed paper; peel off parchment from bottom. Carefully turn sponge over again so that top side faces up. Cut sponge into 2 pieces: One piece should measure 7 × 11 inches; remaining piece will be about 10 × 11 inches. Spread smaller piece with about 6 tablespoons apricot purée. Cut apricot-coated sponge into 4 strips, each 1¾ inches wide and 11 inches long. Use a metal spatula with a long blade to lift and stack the coated strips one on top of the other, lining up all edges. You will have a long, narrow 4-layer apricot and sponge "sandwich" about 11 inches long and about 1¾ inches wide, with apricot purée on top. Wrap tightly in plastic wrap. Freeze until needed, or for at least 2 hours.

3. Cut one paper circle in half. Cut one whole circle and two half-circles out of the remaining piece of sponge, using the paper patterns (fig. 1). Spread 5 tablespoons of apricot purée on sponge circle. Place half-sponge circles together on top to form a whole circle. Spread with 5 tablespoons of purée. You will have a 2-layer 7¼-inch round sandwich with purée on the top. Wrap and freeze until needed. Recipe may be completed to this point and frozen several weeks in advance. If so, freeze the remaining apricot purée as well.

4. **To Line Mold:** Remove frozen sandwich strip from freezer. Use a sharp knife to cut it, still frozen, into 25 or more slices, each ⅜ inch wide. Stand slices on end like dominoes with cut surface of each slice against the inside circumference of cake pan or dessert ring (fig. 2). Fit slices tightly together to form vertical stripes around the sides of pan about 1⅝ inches tall. (If you are using a dessert ring lift the lined ring and place it on the corrugated cake circle—the cake strips should be tight enough not to fall out!) Place the round sandwich in the bottom of the lined pan, apricot side facing up. Set aside.

5. **To Make Apricot Mousse and Fill Mold:** Sprinkle 2 teaspoons gelatin over ¼ cup water in a small cup. Allow gelatin to soften, without stirring, for about 5 minutes. Place cup in a barely simmering water bath until gelatin is completely melted, or melt gently in a microwave on LOW (30%) for 40 seconds.

Serves 10–14

Ingredients:
8 ounces dried apricots, coarsely chopped
1¼ cups boiling water
1 cup plus 7 tablespoons sugar
11 × 17- or 12 × 16-inch Hot Milk Sponge Sheet (page 160), baked and cooled
2¾ teaspoons unflavored gelatin
¼ cup fresh lemon juice
¾ cup fresh orange juice
1 cup heavy cream
½ cup (3–4) egg whites
¼ teaspoon cream of tartar
½ cup strained apricot jam

Special Equipment:
8 × 3-inch round springform pan, or cheesecake pan with removable bottom, or dessert ring
8-inch corrugated cake circle, if using dessert ring
2 paper circles, 7¼ inches in diameter, to use as patterns
Propane torch, if using a dessert ring

figure 1

A cloud of apricot mousse embraced by a deliciously "optical" cordon of sponge cake with more apricots, topped with a fine halo of shiny apricot gelée.

6. In a bowl, combine 1 cup apricot purée, the lemon juice, ⅓ cup orange juice, and the melted gelatin.

7. In another bowl, beat cream until it holds a soft shape—not too stiff. Refrigerate until needed.

8. In a clean, dry mixing bowl, beat egg whites and cream of tartar at medium speed until soft peaks form. Gradually sprinkle 6 tablespoons sugar over the whites, beating at high speed, until stiff but not dry.

9. Check the apricot mixture; if it has begun to set, place the bowl in a pan of warm water and stir to soften before proceeding. Fold one-third of whites into apricot mixture to lighten it. Scrape remaining whites and whipped cream over the apricot mixture and fold together. Turn the mousse immediately into the cake-lined mold and use a metal spatula to smooth mousse almost level—slightly concave works best—with top of pan. Refrigerate at least 3 hours, until set.

figure 2

10. **To Finish the Top with Gelée:** Sprinkle remaining ¾ teaspoon gelatin over 2 tablespoons orange juice in a small cup. Set aside, without stirring, until gelatin softens, about 5 minutes. Place cup in a barely simmering water bath until gelatin melts completely, or melt gently in microwave on LOW (30%) for 25 seconds.

11. Combine 2 tablespoons apricot purée with remaining 5 tablespoons orange juice. Strain through a very fine sieve and combine with melted gelatin. Chill just until syrupy, 10–15 minutes. Spoon mixture over top of mousse. Use the back of a spoon and/or tilt the pan to spread a thin layer of gelée evenly over mousse. Transfer to a level shelf in refrigerator. If dessert is not level, gelée layer will settle to one side of dessert. Chill until set, 20–30 minutes.

12. **To Unmold and Serve:** If dessert was made in a springform pan, carefully run a thin, sharp knife around upper half of dessert to separate mousse from pan. Release and remove sides of pan. If necessary, dip a metal spatula in hot water and use to smooth sides of mousse. If dessert was made in a ring, warm sides with a hot, wrung-out, wet towel or propane torch—just enough for ring to slip off when pulled straight up. Smooth sides with a spatula, if necessary.

13. Simmer apricot jam and remaining 1 tablespoon sugar in a small saucepan. Using a pastry brush, glaze sponge and apricot layers. Do not glaze the mousse. May be completed to this point and refrigerated in a covered container up to 1 day before serving. Do not freeze.

I love the intense and slightly nutty flavor of bittersweet chocolate cheesecake. For me, the best marbled cheesecake has great pockets of plain and chocolate cheesecake juxtaposed so that you can appreciate the contrast.

Black and White Cheesecake

1. Preheat oven to 350°.

2. Mix the Chocolate Tart Pastry according to instructions, until dough is still crumbly and has not yet formed a ball. Firmly pat three-fourths of mixture into bottom (only) of an 8-inch springform pan or cheesecake pan with a removable bottom. Use a fork to toss and spread the remaining crumbly dough loosely in a shallow baking pan. Place bottom crust and pan of extra dough in oven together. Bake for 10 minutes. Remove baked crumbs. Bake bottom crust for an additional 5 minutes. Let crust and crumbs cool completely on a rack. Reduce oven temperature to 325°.

3. Butter the bare sides of cake pan above bottom crust, or spray with a quick-release baking spray such as Pam. Pulverize the cooled crumbs. Store in airtight container until needed.

4. Melt chocolate with ¼ cup water in a small bowl placed in a barely simmering water bath on low heat, stirring occasionally until chocolate is melted and smooth. Or, microwave on MEDIUM (50%) for 1 minute. Stir until smooth and keep warm.

5. Place cream cheese in the bowl of an electric mixer and beat on medium speed, until it begins to smooth out. Stop mixer and scrape bowl and beaters well. Continue to beat, gradually adding the sugar. Beat just until completely smooth (scraping beaters and bowl as often as necessary). Add vanilla and eggs, one by one, beating only until well mixed.

6. Measure and set aside 1 cup of cheesecake batter. Pour remaining batter over chocolate crust; set aside.

7. Stir warm chocolate into reserved cheesecake batter. Pour chocolate batter in a thick ring, about ½ inch in from sides of pan, on top of plain batter, leaving a bull's-eye of plain batter in center. Use a soup spoon to marble the chocolate, scooping just enough to create a lovely, dramatic marbled pattern. Try not to blend the batters together too much. If necessary, use your finger to wipe the sides of the pan clean above the batter after marbling.

8. Bake for 20–25 minutes, or until cheesecake shows signs of puffing around the edges but is still very soft in center. Remove cake from oven, and run a thin knife blade carefully around the edges to release cake from sides of pan.

9. Cool in the pan, on a rack, covered with an inverted large mixing bowl. Refrigerate, covered with plastic wrap, after completely cool. Cake may be made to this point and refrigerated up to 4 days in advance. Unmold cheesecake. Press reserved cookie crumbs around the sides of cake, being careful not to get crumbs on top.

Serves 12–14

Ingredients:
Chocolate Tart Pastry (page 164),
prepared only till crumbly
5 ounces semisweet or bittersweet
chocolate, cut into bits
3 large packages (8 ounces each)
cream cheese, slightly softened
1¼ cups sugar
½ teaspoon vanilla extract
2 large eggs

- - -

Tips for great cheesecakes:
—If the cheese and sugar mixture
is overbeaten, it will thin out and
lose body and the resulting
cheesecake with not have a creamy
texture. Do not mix in the food
processor.
—Add eggs only when the cheese
and sugar mixture is completely
smooth. Once eggs are added, it is
impossible to smooth out lumps.
—Cover the cheesecake with a
large inverted mixing bowl to slow
the cooling and prevent cracking

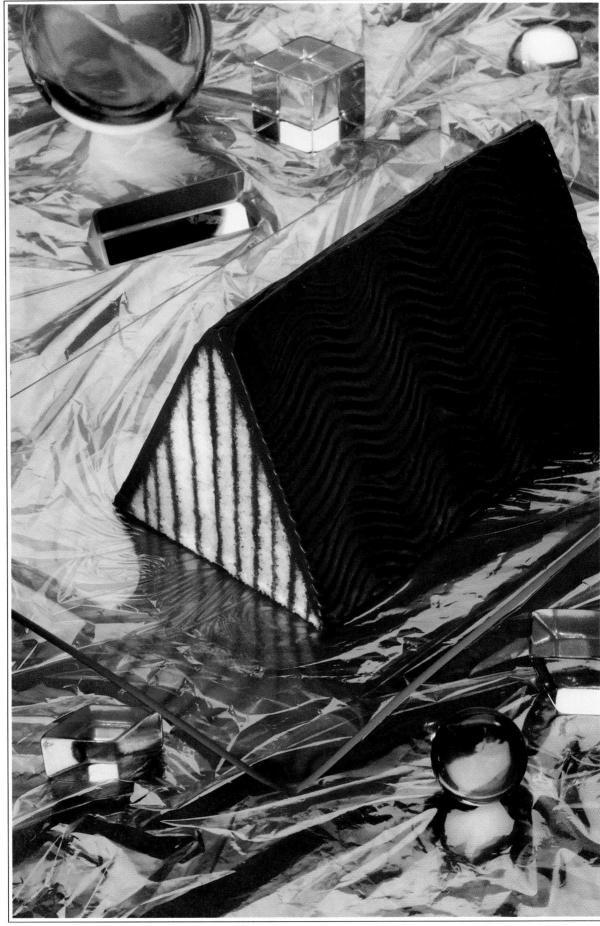

The mystery of this intriguing triangle is "how"? A clever sleight of hand turns six luscious layers into delicious dessert geometry.

Triangle

1. Run a knife around edges of sponge cake to release it from pan. Reverse cake onto a piece of waxed paper and peel off the parchment paper liner. Brush sponge all over with liqueur. Spread evenly with about 1½ cups of Chocolate Buttercream. Cover and refrigerate remaining buttercream until needed.

2. Cut chocolate-covered sponge into 6 equal pieces, each about 4 inches by 8 inches, as follows: First cut the sponge lengthwise into 3 equal strips, each 4 inches wide and 16–17 inches long (depending on which pan you used). Cut all 3 strips crosswise in half.

3. Pile sponge pieces on top of each other. Line up edges as neatly as possible. If some pieces are thicker on one edge than the other, alternate pieces so that thick edges offset thin ones and resulting cake is relatively level. You will end up with a 6-layer sandwich of cake and buttercream, with buttercream on the top. Wrap the whole thing tightly in plastic wrap. Level it, if necessary, by pushing on the top with a flat cardboard or the bottom of a cake pan. Freeze until firm, several hours or overnight. Dessert may be completed to this point and frozen several weeks in advance. If so, remember to freeze remaining buttercream as well.

4. When ready to finish cake, thaw and/or re-soften cold buttercream in a water bath or microwave (see page 181 for details), and beat or stir until smooth.

5. Remove assembled cake from freezer. Unwrap and even long sides, using a serrated knife. Turn the cake upside down on a piece of waxed paper and place it at the edge of the counter. While still frozen, cut cake diagonally, as shown in fig. 1. Turn the 2 pieces on their sides. Warm the layer of buttercream that was formerly on the top with a hot spatula or hair dryer. The former top and the former bottom are now standing perpendicular to the counter, as shown in fig. 2. Push the pieces firmly together, using a little extra buttercream between them if necessary. The cake will now be triangular. Trim the piece of cardboard so that it is exactly the same width, but ¼ inch shorter in length than the cake. Transfer cake carefully onto cardboard—it will hang over about ⅛ inch at each end.

6. Spread reserved buttercream evenly over sides, but not the ends. Texture it with a serrated knife or cake comb that has been dipped in hot water and wiped dry. Defrost the cake before serving. Cake may be completed, covered, and refrigerated up to 2 days before serving. Before serving, trim about ⅛ inch off each end of the chilled cake, pressing straight down with a sharp knife dipped in hot water and wiped dry. Remove cake from the refrigerator about 1 hour before serving to soften the texture and bring out the aroma and flavors.

Serves 10–12

Ingredients:
11 × 17- or 12 × 16-inch Hot Milk Sponge Sheet (page 160), baked and cooled
⅓–½ cup Grand Marnier or other liqueur
Small batch Chocolate Buttercream (page 182)

Special Equipment:
5 × 8-inch piece of cardboard
Cake comb (optional) or a straight-bladed serrated knife, for texturing surface of cake

figure 1

figure 2

Lemon
Bombe

Serves 10–12

Ingredients:
1½ cups sugar
3 bright-skinned, unblemished
  organic lemons
8-inch Génoise (page 159)
Lemon Mousse (page 167), with
  the larger amount of gelatin
2–3 tablespoons minced unsalted
  pistachios (optional)

Special Equipment:
3-quart mixing bowl or colander
  shaped like a hemisphere, 8½ or
  9 inches in diameter and about 4
  inches deep
Plastic wrap
8- or 9-inch cardboard cake circle

- - -

Poached organic lemons not only
taste superior, but their skins
become especially tender during
poaching so that the dessert can be
sliced without damaging the
delicate mousse inside. Use a gentle
back-and-forth sawing stroke with
a very sharp, non-serrated knife.
Occasionally the lemon skins resist
the knife a little. I then whisk the
dessert into the kitchen and snip
the skins with sharp kitchen shears
or slice just through the lemons
with a clean razor blade. Desperate
measures, but worth it!

1. **To Prepare Lemon Slices and Line Mold:** Stir sugar and 1½ cups water together in a small saucepan. Bring to a simmer. Meanwhile, wash and slice lemons ⅛ inch thick; you will need about 18 good slices. Poach lemon slices gently in simmering syrup, covered, until tender, 15–20 minutes. Cool poached fruit in syrup. Cover and chill until needed, up to 2 weeks in advance. Drain cooled slices in one layer on a rack; pat dry with paper towels before use.

2. Oil the bowl or colander lightly before lining it neatly with plastic wrap, leaving long ends overhanging sides. (The oil will help the lining to stick and stay smooth.) Arrange drained and blotted lemon slices in the bottom and up sides of bowl. Be sure that the prettiest side of each slice faces the sides of the bowl. Set aside.

3. **To Assemble the Dessert:** Cut the Génoise, horizontally, into 2 layers; set one aside. Wrap and freeze the other for another use. Make the Lemon Mousse and turn it immediately into the bowl lined with lemon slices. Trim the cake layer (if necessary) enough to nestle into the mousse with about ¼ inch of mousse showing all the way around it. Place a cardboard cake circle on top of cake and press to level. (If there are lemon slices sticking up higher than the level of the cardboard, they can be trimmed later when the dessert is chilled and firm.) Cover mold. Refrigerate for at least 4 hours, or up to 1 day in advance of serving. Do not freeze.

4. **To Unmold and Serve:** Uncover the mold. Use a sharp knife to trim any lemon slices that stick up higher than the corrugated cardboard. Pull a little on overhanging ends of plastic lining to help release lining from mold. Hold cardboard cake circle in place while you invert mold on a platter. Remove mold; peel plastic liner gently away from dessert. Press minced pistachios around the very bottom edge of the bombe to finish it, if desired. Refrigerate until time to serve.

Lemony and light and pretty as can be, this cool, creamy citrus sensation demands the spotlight. I serve it with bite-size, classic bittersweet chocolate truffles and coffee.

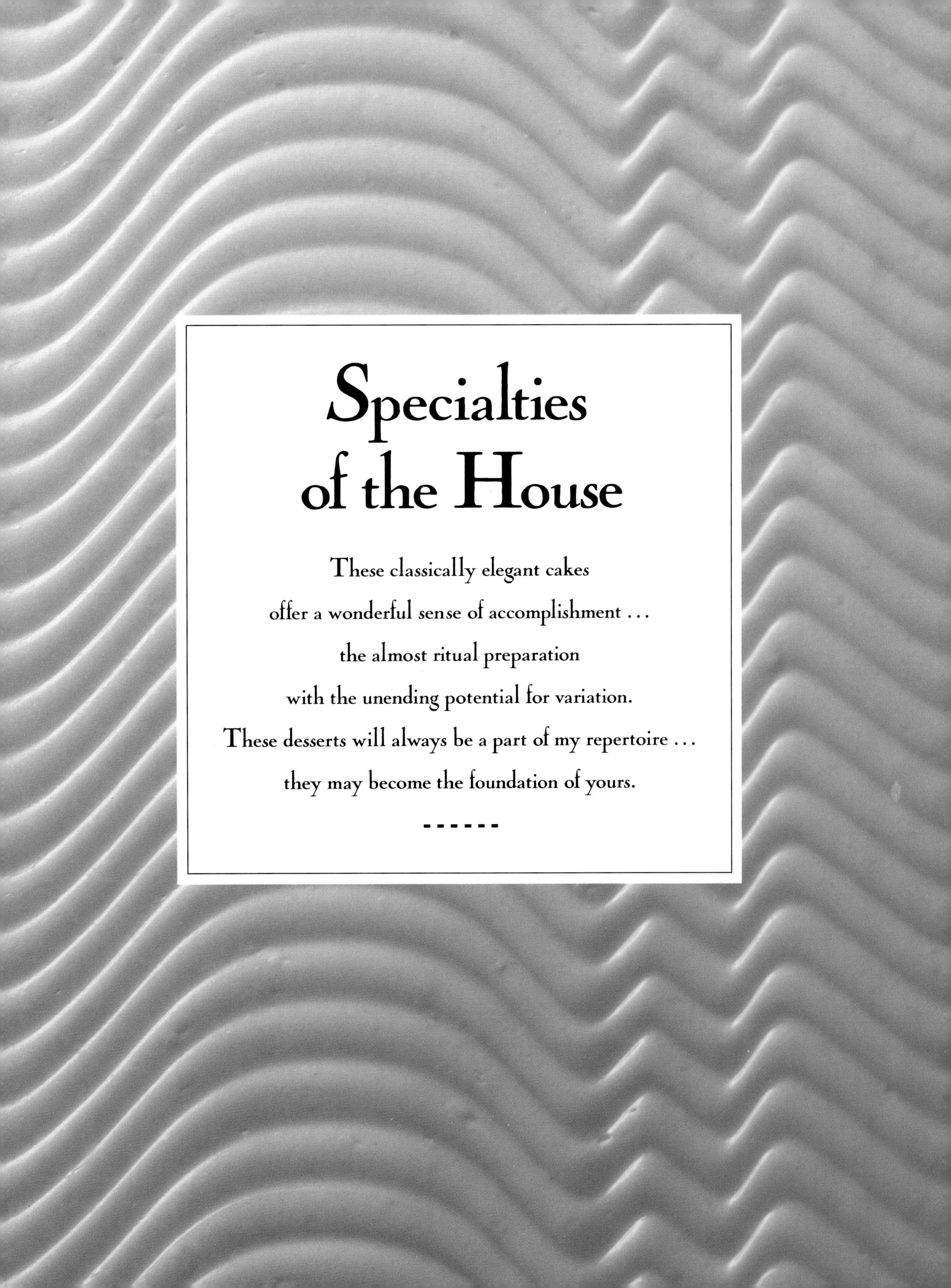

Specialties of the House

These classically elegant cakes

offer a wonderful sense of accomplishment . . .

the almost ritual preparation

with the unending potential for variation.

These desserts will always be a part of my repertoire . . .

they may become the foundation of yours.

- - - - - -

When I began Cocolat, the Big Idea (besides chocolate) was to offer desserts that were otherwise unavailable in this country. In 1976 this meant purity and integrity of ingredients—real chocolate, freshly ground nuts, fresh citrus juices and peels, sipping-quality liqueurs as fine or finer than any in your own home liquor cabinet, sweet butter, and fresh ranch eggs. If this litany of freshness and purity sounds cliché-ridden today, it was groundbreaking and unprecedented in 1976. It meant separately beaten egg whites folded into batters by hand. It meant no shortening, no artificial extracts or flavors, no commercial mixes, no stabilizers, no shortcuts, no compromise. It meant European desserts that you might purchase in the finest *patisserie*, or make yourself at home if you had the knowledge, the skill, the time, and the access to superb ingredients. ▪ ▪ ▪

If one part of the Cocolat menu was dominated by the simpler, homemade-style chocolate tortes of Chapter One, the other side of the menu was replete with these traditional European classics—the gâteaux and torten of Paris, Vienna, and beyond—Marjolaine, Linzer torte, charlottes, and layer cakes of delectable richness and finesse—the complex and challenging desserts of the great pastry chefs of Europe that inevitably became "Cocolat Versions" and finally "Cocolat Originals." ▪ ▪ ▪

To make these desserts is to draw upon the pastry chef's repertoire of basic recipes and skills. Some of the cakes are assembled in classic fashion—layer by layer. Thin génoise or sponge cake layers, or crisp or soft nutted meringues are filled and neatly reassembled to be masked and decorated with buttercream and/or glazed with chocolate. Here a little practice goes a very long way as you gain facility with knife and spatula, experience making and working with buttercream, practice with pastry bag and paper cone. ▪ ▪ ▪

I love to make these desserts. They offer a wonderful sense of accomplishment—the almost ritual preparation and completion of each part necessary to assemble the whole and, of course, the unending potential for variation and personal versions. ▪ ▪ ▪

In the last few years the vogue for mousse desserts—with very little cake at all—has partially eclipsed the grand old tradition of European layer cakes. Yet these classically elegant cakes celebrate the pastry chef's true craftsmanship and mastery of basic technique. They are not necessarily the showiest desserts, or the most contemporary-looking, but in their quiet complexity and sublime taste you will appreciate the art of the pastry chef at its highest point of achievement. These desserts will always be a part of my repertoire—they may become the foundation of yours.

Gâteau Grand Marnier

Serves 10–12

For best flavor and texture, assemble cake at least one day ahead.

Ingredients:
⅓ cup Grand Marnier
⅓ cup Simple Syrup (page 171)
8-inch Chocolate Génoise (page 159)
½ cup strained apricot jam
Small batch Chocolate Buttercream (page 182)

Special Equipment:
8-inch corrugated cake circle
Pastry bag fitted with a plain tip with a ⅛-inch opening (optional, for decorating)
Cake comb (optional, for decorating)

1. Combine Grand Marnier with Simple Syrup; set aside.

2. Use a serrated knife to cut the Génoise, horizontally, into 3 layers. Place the top layer upside down on the cake circle. With a pastry brush, moisten it with some of Grand Marnier syrup. Spread half the apricot jam over moistened cake layer. Spread ⅓ cup Chocolate Buttercream evenly over jam. Brush the second cake layer with syrup. Place it, moist side down, on top of chocolate buttercream. Brush dry side of layer, facing up, with syrup. Spread with remaining jam. Spread with ⅓ cup buttercream. Brush third layer with syrup. Place it, moist side down, over buttercream. Moisten again with remaining syrup. Level the cake by pressing the top firmly with the bottom of a cake pan. If the cake is leaning to one side, press where necessary to make it symmetrical.

3. Crumb coat and mask entire cake with remaining chocolate buttercream (see Finishing a Cake with Buttercream, page 182). Texture top with a long serrated knife, if desired. Comb sides with a cake comb. Pipe a decorative border around edge of cake. The cake may be made to this point up to 3 days in advance. Store in a covered container in the refrigerator, or freeze for up to 3 months. Remove cake from refrigerator about 1 hour before serving to soften buttercream and develop flavors.

Chocolate layers drenched in luscious orange liqueur and filled with apricot and rich chocolate buttercream. This Cocolat classic makes a sophisticated party dessert, or an unconventional wedding cake. · Vary it by substituting white chocolate buttercream for dark.

Forget the sweet, sticky coconut creations of your childhood. Here is a dreamy, moist cake flavored with freshly squeezed lemon juice, dark rum, cool whipped cream, and coconut. People who "don't like coconut" find this cake absolutely delicious.

Coco Cabaña

1. In a small bowl or jar, combine lemon juice, rum, 1½ teaspoons sugar, and 3 tablespoons water. Set aside.

2. Whip 1 cup cream with 2 teaspoons sugar just until it holds soft peaks. Fold in shredded fresh coconut; set aside.

3. Use a serrated knife to cut the génoise dome, horizontally, into 3 layers. Place the bottom (widest) layer of the dome, cut side up, on the cake circle or a platter. Use a pastry brush to moisten it liberally with the rum mixture. Spread almost two-thirds of the preserves over moistened layer. Top with almost two-thirds of cream and coconut filling, spreading evenly. Moisten bottom side of second layer. Place it, moist side down, over filling. Moisten the dry top side of layer, spread with remaining preserves. Spread on remaining coconut filling. Finally, moisten bottom of third layer. Place on filling. (You will have reassembled the original dome with filling between each layer. Push and pat the cake with your hands if necessary to reshape the dome so that it is neat and symmetrical.) Brush any leftover rum mixture over top and sides of dome. Cake may be made to this point up to 2 days in advance. Wrap well and refrigerate, or freeze up to 1 month.

4. Whip remaining 1½ cups cream with the remaining 1 tablespoon sugar until nearly stiff. Spread cream over dome to mask it as evenly as possible. Cover with dried large-flake coconut and a few candied lemon zests for color.

Serves 10–12

Ingredients:
2 tablespoons fresh lemon juice
¼ cup dark rum
6½ teaspoons sugar
2½ cups heavy cream
¾ cup shredded dried unsweetened
  coconut°
7-inch Génoise dome (page 159)
¼ cup puréed apricot preserves
1 cup dried unsweetened large-flake
  coconut°
Candied lemon zests (page 173,
  optional)
°Available from natural and bulk
  food stores. If you must use
  sweetened coconut, choose the
  longer "fancy" shred. Eliminate
  the sugar in the whipped cream.

Special Equipment:
7-inch corrugated cake circle

- - -

One San Francisco food maven is so enamored of this cake that she is convinced it is made with fresh coconut. The secret? Assemble the cake at least a day in advance so that the dried coconut has time to absorb plenty of moisture from the slightly under-whipped cream.

Lutèce

Serves 10–12

*For best flavor and texture,
assemble cake at least one day
ahead.*

Ingredients:
½ cup dark rum
*Small batch plain
  Buttercream (page 181)*
*⅔ cup (3½ ounces) finely chopped
  toasted walnuts*
⅓ cup Simple Syrup (page 171)
8-inch Génoise (page 159)
*Sarah Bernhardt Chocolate Glaze
  (page 175)*
*12 plain or caramelized walnut
  halves (page 172)*

Special Equipment:
8-inch corrugated cake circle

1. Briskly stir 3 tablespoons of the rum into the Buttercream with a rubber spatula. In a separate bowl, combine the walnuts with ⅔ cup of the rum buttercream. Combine the remaining rum with the Simple Syrup.

2. Using a serrated knife, cut Génoise, horizontally, into 3 layers. Invert top layer onto the cake circle. Brush layer with rum syrup. Spread half of the walnut buttercream evenly over moistened layer. Brush second layer with syrup and place it, moist side down, over the walnut buttercream. Moisten dry side of layer, facing up, and spread with remaining walnut buttercream. Top with third génoise layer, moist side down. Moisten top of assembled cake. Level the cake by pressing the top firmly with the bottom of a cake pan. If the cake is leaning to one side, press where necessry to make it symmetrical.

3. Mask entire cake with a thin layer of rum buttercream. Cover and chill cake for at least 1 hour before glazing it. Cake may be made to this point and refrigerated up to 3 days in advance. Or, freeze for up to 3 months.

4. Glaze cake with Sarah Bernhardt Chocolate Glaze. Decorate by pressing plain or caramelized walnut halves around top edge of cake. Refrigerate immediately to set glaze. Remove cake from refrigerator about 1 hour before serving to soften buttercream and develop flavors.

Rum-soaked génoise layers filled with toasted-walnut and rum buttercream. This sophisticated Paris lady is cloaked in bittersweet chocolate and adorned with sparkling caramelized walnuts.

Exotic,
baunting flavors.
Coffee, cinnamon,
and ground pecans
mingle with crisp
meringue, two
buttercreams, and
tender chocolate
génoise.

Aztec
Layer Cake

1. Combine chocolate with 2 tablespoons water in a small bowl. Melt gently in a barely simmering water bath or microwave at MEDIUM (50%) for about 45 seconds. Stir until smooth; remove from heat. When chocolate mixture has cooled to lukewarm, stir in ½ cup of the buttercream; set aside.

2. Dissolve coffee powder in ½ teaspoon water. Stir mixture into remaining plain buttercream.

3. Split Chocolate Génoise, horizontally, into 2 layers with a serrated knife. Turn top layer upside down on the cake circle. Brush with one-third of the Kahlúa. Spread with about ⅓ cup chocolate buttercream; top with 1 Aztec Meringue. Spread meringue with another ⅓ cup chocolate buttercream. Brush second génoise layer with half of remaining Kahlúa. Place it, moist side down, on buttercream. Moisten génoise again with remaining Kahlúa. Spread with remaining buttercream. Top with remaining meringue. Be sure assembled cake is level and even on top. If not, press gently with the bottom of a cake pan. The sides of the cake should be symmetrical—all sides straight up and down or equally slanted all the way around. If not, correct by pushing on it where necessary to slide the layers into place. Ragged edges can be corrected later. Cover and chill until firm, 15–20 minutes.

4. Trim, crumb coat, and mask entire cake, top and sides, with coffee buttercream, texturing the sides, if desired. (See Finishing a Cake with Buttercream, page 182.) Double-stencil the top, if desired, first with cocoa, then with cinnamon. (See Stencils, page 186.) Cake may be made to this point up to 3 days in advance. Store, refrigerated, in a closed container, or freeze for up to 3 months. Remove from the refrigerator about 1 hour in advance of serving to soften textures and enhance flavors.

Serves 10–12

For best flavor and texture, assemble cake at least one day ahead.

Ingredients:
4 ounces semisweet or bittersweet chocolate, cut into bits
Small batch Buttercream (page 181)
1 teaspoon powdered instant coffee
9-inch Chocolate Génoise (page 159), baked and cooled
About ⅔ cup Kahlúa
Two 9-inch Aztec Meringue layers (page 163), baked and cooled
Cocoa and cinnamon, for decoration (optional)

Special Equipment:
9-inch corrugated cake circle
Stencil (optional)
Cake comb or serrated bread knife (optional), for texturing buttercream

Café Express

Serves 10-12

For best flavor and texture, assemble cake at least one day ahead.

Ingredients:
¼ cup Simple Syrup (page 171)
½ cup Kahlúa
9-inch Coffee Génoise (page 159)
Large batch Coffee Buttercream (page 182)
Two 9-inch Coffee-Almond Meringues (page 164)
Several candy coffee beans, or real ones, for decoration

Special Equipment:
9-inch corrugated cake circle
Pastry bag with tip (optional), for decoration

I like the idea of using coffee, a favorite flavor, over and over again in a dessert with several different textures. Layers of crisp coffee almond meringue and tender coffee génoise are suffused with Kahlúa and filled with creamy coffee buttercream. Serve it with—what else?—a great cup of strong coffee.

1. In a small bowl, combine Simple Syrup with Kahlúa.

2. Split Coffee Génoise into 2 horizontal layers with a serrated knife. Place top layer upside down on the cake circle. Brush with Kahlúa syrup. Spread with about ⅓ cup Coffee Buttercream. Top with 1 Coffee-Almond Meringue. Spread the meringue with another ⅓ cup coffee buttercream. Brush the second génoise layer with Kahlúa syrup. Place it, moist side down, on coffee buttercream. Moisten dry side of layer, facing up. Spread with buttercream; top with second meringue. Level the cake by pressing the top firmly with the bottom of a cake pan. If the cake is leaning to one side, press where necessary to make it symmetrical.

3. Crumb coat and mask the entire cake, top and sides, with coffee buttercream. Pipe a decorative border with a pastry bag if desired, and decorate with real or candy coffee beans. (See Finishing a Cake with Buttercream, page 182.) Cake may be made to this point up to 3 days in advance. Store, refrigerated, in a closed container, or freeze up to 3 months. Remove from refrigerator about 1 hour in advance of serving to soften textures and enhance flavors.

Raspberry Banana
Charlotte

My favorite fruit charlotte of all is colorful, light, and richly flavored all at the same time—and it is made without a trace of gelatin.

1. Combine ⅓ cup sugar with ¼ cup water in a small saucepan. Cover and bring to a simmer. Simmer, covered, for 1 minute. Uncover and let cool. Add ½ teaspoon vanilla.

2. Slice bananas about ⅜ inch thick. Toss with vanilla syrup; set aside.

3. Crush enough raspberries to equal 2 tablespoons. Sweeten with ¼ teaspoon sugar; set aside.

4. Drain bananas and reserve syrup. Using a pastry brush, lightly moisten all inside surfaces of ladyfingers in the mold with reserved vanilla syrup. Spread crushed, sweetened berries in bottom of mold. Spread half of the Pastry Cream over crushed raspberries. Place a layer of whole raspberries all over pastry cream, using ¾ cup of raspberries.

5. Whip cream with remaining 1 tablespoon sugar and ½ teaspoon vanilla until stiff but still spreadable. Spread half the whipped cream over berries. Top with ladyfinger round; press gently to compact layers. Brush the ladyfinger round with vanilla syrup. Spread remaining pastry cream over it. Place banana slices all over pastry cream. Top with remaining whipped cream. Heap the remaining 1¼ cartons of berries on top of whipped cream. Cover and chill dessert for 4–5 hours before unmolding.

6. Dessert may be completed and refrigerated 1 day ahead. Do not freeze. Remove sides of pan. Transfer charlotte to a serving platter. Tie a ribbon around the finished dessert, if desired.

Serves 10–12

Ingredients:
½ cup sugar
1 teaspoon vanilla extract
2 ripe bananas
*2 half-pint cartons fresh
   raspberries*
*8-inch springform or cheesecake
   pan with removable bottom,
   bottom and sides lined with
   Ladyfingers (page 160), plus an
   additional 7-inch-round
   Ladyfinger layer*
Pastry Cream (page 169)
1 cup heavy cream

Chocolate
Banana
Charlotte

Serves 10–12

Ingredients:
⅓ cup plus 2–3 tablespoons sugar
2½ tablespoons dark rum
1½–2 ripe bananas
8-inch springform or cheesecake
pan with removable bottom,
lined, bottom and sides, with
Ladyfingers (page 160)
Chocolate Velvet Mousse, made
with rum (page 165)
2 cups heavy cream
2 teaspoons vanilla extract
Chocolate shavings (optional)
(page 188)
Bright colored ribbon (optional)

Special Equipment:
Pastry bag fitted with closed star
tip (Ateco #9)

- - -

Don't pass up this recipe because
you dread the usually fussy and
time-consuming task of lining a
mold with ladyfingers. The
professional trick of making them
in one continuous strip reduces the
task to child's play. See page 160.

1. Combine ⅓ cup sugar and 3 tablespoons cold water in a very small saucepan. Simmer, covered, for 1–2 minutes, to dissolve sugar. Allow to cool. Stir in rum; set aside.

2. Slice bananas about ½ inch thick. Pour the rum syrup over them; set aside for at least 15 minutes, or until needed.

3. Drain the bananas, reserving the syrup. Using a pastry brush, moisten all of the inside surfaces of the ladyfingers in the mold with the reserved rum syrup. Place drained pieces of banana all over the bottom of the lined mold, overlapping if necessary.

4. Make Chocolate Velvet Mousse. Turn immediately into lined pan. Chill for at least 3–4 hours, until set. Dessert may be completed to this point, wrapped, and refrigerated in the mold, up to 2 days in advance.

5. Whip cream with vanilla and remaining 2–3 tablespoons sugar until fairly stiff. Scrape whipped cream into pastry bag. Pipe decorative swirls all over mousse so that it peaks up and above the ladyfingers. Decorate with chocolate shavings, if desired. Dessert may be completed up to 12 hours in advance of serving. Refrigerate in a covered container until needed. Do not freeze.

Remove the sides of the mold and transfer the charlotte to a serving platter. If desired, tie a pretty ribbon around the dessert to present.

Bananas are simply not given their due. They make a seriously delicious and sophisticated dessert buried in Chocolate Rum Mousse and surrounded by old-fashioned ladyfingers.

Fernand Point's French classic with three buttercreams, Cocolat style. A symphony of almonds and hazelnuts for the truly sophisticated palate. This cake is best if made at least one day ahead.

Marjolaine

1. **To Make Nut Meringue Pastry:** Preheat oven to 325°. In a blender or food processor fitted with steel blade, pulverize 5 ounces of the toasted hazelnuts, 5 ounces of the toasted almonds, and the flour until a fine meal forms. Add ⅔ cup sugar and pulse just to mix. Set aside.

2. In a large clean, dry mixing bowl, combine egg whites and cream of tartar. Beat at medium speed until soft peaks form. Turn to high speed and gradually beat in remaining ⅓ cup sugar; beat until stiff but not dry. Fold pulverized nut mixture into the beaten egg whites. Spread meringue evenly in lined pan.

3. Bake for 30–35 minutes, or until golden brown and springy to the touch. Cool the nut meringue in pan on a rack. Nut meringue may be prepared, left in the pan and covered well, and stored at room temperature up to 2 days ahead.

4. **To Prepare Nuts for Decoration and Flavor Buttercreams:** Chop remaining 2 ounces toasted hazelnuts medium fine; reserve for decoration. Chop remaining 3 ounces toasted almonds medium fine; reserve for buttercream and decoration.

5. In a food processor or blender, process ¼ cup of chopped toasted almonds until reduced to a paste or as fine as possible. Add ¼ cup plus 2 tablespoons plain Buttercream. Process again to combine. Set toasted almond buttercream aside until needed.

6. Stir hazelnut Praline powder into ¼ cup plus 2 tablespoons plain buttercream. Set praline buttercream aside until needed.

7. Melt the chocolate with ¼ cup water in a small bowl placed in a barely simmering water bath. Stir occasionally until melted and smooth. Or, melt in microwave on MEDIUM (50%) for about 1 minute and 30 seconds. Stir until completely melted and smooth. Stir melted chocolate into remaining plain buttercream. Set chocolate buttercream aside.

8. **To Assemble the Cake:** Run a small knife or spatula around the edges of the pan to release the cooled meringue. Invert onto a sheet of waxed paper; remove pan and peel off parchment paper liner. Cut the pastry into 4 equal strips, each about 4 inches wide and 12 inches long. Cut a piece of corrugated cardboard to the exact size of 1 pastry strip; set aside.

9. Place 1 pastry strip on a cookie sheet or level platter. Spread with ½ cup chocolate buttercream. Place the second pastry strip on top; spread with all the praline buttercream. Center third pastry strip on top; spread with all the toasted almond buttercream. Top with fourth strip of pastry. Align all the strips so that they are as even as possible on all sides and the

*Makes 1 large cake
to serve 12–16
or 2 small cakes
to serve 6–8 each*

*For best flavor and texture,
assemble cake at least one day
ahead.*

Ingredients:
*7 ounces toasted hazelnuts, skins
 rubbed off*
8 ounces toasted almonds
2 tablespoons (½ ounce) flour
1 cup sugar
*1 cup plus 2 tablespoons egg whites
 (about 7), at room temperature*
½ teaspoon cream of tartar
*Large batch Buttercream (page
 181)*
*¼ cup hazelnut Praline powder
 (page 171)*
*8 ounces semisweet or bittersweet
 chocolate, cut into bits*
*1 ounce milk or dark chocolate
 (optional), for decoration*
*30–36 whole caramelized hazelnuts
 (page 172, optional)*

Special Equipment:
*12 × 16- or 11 × 17-inch half-sheet
 or jelly-roll pan, lined with
 parchment paper*
*Corrugated cardboard cut to fit the
 assembled cake (see below)*
*Parchment paper cone (optional),
 for piped decoration*
*Pastry bag fitted with Ateco tip
 #27 (very small star), for
 border decoration*

assembly is symmetrical. Level top by pressing down firmly with a cookie sheet or the bottom of a pan. If there is time, cover and chill until firm, 15–20 minutes.

10. Remove chilled cake; trim any ragged edges with a serrated knife. If you are making 1 large cake, slide the cardboard under cake now; otherwise, wait. Spread top and sides with chocolate buttercream. If you plan to make 2 small cakes, cut cake in half now. Cut the corrugated cardboard in half to match. Slide a spatula under the cake halves and place each on its own cardboard. Spread chocolate buttercream on the 2 cut ends and re-smooth tops, if necessary.

11. **To Decorate the Cake(s):** Melt 1 ounce of milk or dark chocolate. Scrape into a parchment-paper cone. Pipe a loose diagonal crosshatching on top of cake (see Piping with Chocolate, page 185). Combine reserved chopped toasted hazelnuts and almonds. Press them into the soft buttercream on the cake sides. Scrape remaining chocolate buttercream into pastry bag and pipe a dainty border of rosettes or scallops along the top edges of cake. Place whole caramelized hazelnuts next to the border.

12. **To Make a Simpler Decoration:** Omit the piped melted chocolate crosshatching and the caramelized hazelnuts. Press the reserved chopped toasted hazelnuts and/or almonds into the soft buttercream sides of the cake, as above. *If desired,* use pastry bag and tip to pipe a shell border along the top edge of the cake.

13. Cake may be completed, put in a closed container, and refrigerated up to 3 days ahead, or frozen for up to 3 months. Thaw in the container in the refrigerator for several hours or overnight. Remove cake from refrigerator at least 1 hour before serving to soften textures and develop aroma and flavors.

Pavé D'Amour

1. Run a knife around the Chocolate Soufflé Pastry sheet to release it from pan. Use ends of paper liner to lift pastry from pan onto work counter. Do not remove pastry from parchment paper. Use scissors or a sharp knife to cut through pastry and paper to make two 8-inch squares. Set aside.

2. Run a knife around Hot Milk Sponge Cake to release it from pan. Invert onto a cookie sheet and peel off paper liner. Use a serrated knife to cut the cake, horizontally, into 3 even layers. Remove the top 2 layers and set aside. Using a pastry brush, lightly moisten bottom layer of sponge with liqueur.

3. Remove cold Chocolate Ganache from refrigerator. Beat until it stiffens and holds its shape like very thick whipped cream. (Overbeating causes granular appearance and texture and makes ganache too stiff to spread—so, easy does it.) Spread half the beaten ganache evenly over moistened sponge. If ganache is too stiff to spread, warm the spatula by dipping it in hot water and wiping it dry.

4. Pick up one chocolate soufflé pastry square by holding onto attached paper. Invert it onto ganache-covered sponge layer. Adjust the position, if necessary; peel off parchment from pastry. Spread chocolate pastry with ½ cup of Coffee Buttercream.

5. Moisten a second layer of sponge with liqueur. Place it, moist side down, on top of coffee buttercream layer. (If sponge layer is too delicate to moisten and flip, omit moistening and carefully move the layer into place using a cookie sheet or spatula.) Moisten top of the sponge layer with liqueur. Spread it with remaining ganache. Top with remaining chocolate soufflé pastry. Spread with ½ cup coffee buttercream.

6. Moisten the third layer of sponge with liqueur. Place it, moist side down, on coffee buttercream. Moisten top side of sponge. Level cake by pressing firmly with the back of the square cake pan. Examine cake to be sure that it is symmetrical; press where necessary to correct the shape if it is leaning. Cover and chill the cake for 20 minutes or more to firm up for easier handling.

7. Remove cake from refrigerator. Trim off any ragged edges with a serrated knife. Transfer whole cake to cardboard square. Or, cut it in half. Place each half on cardboard. Spread a small amount of coffee buttercream all over the top and sides of the cake(s) to seal in crumbs; reserve remaining buttercream. Chill cake(s) again for a few minutes to set the crumb coat.

Makes 1 cake to serve 20–25, or 2 cakes to serve 10–12 each

For best flavor and texture, assemble cake at least one day ahead.

Ingredients:
11 × 17- or 12 × 16-inch Chocolate Soufflé Pastry (page 163)
8-inch-square Hot Milk Sponge Cake (page 160)
½ cup or more Orange Curaçao or Grand Marnier
Chocolate Ganache (page 169), made and chilled at least 5–6 hours in advance
2 small batches Coffee Buttercream (page 182)
2 fresh roses, for decoration (optional)
1 ounce white chocolate, for decoration (optional)

Special Equipment:
8-inch-square piece of corrugated cardboard (cut in half if you plan to make 2 smaller cakes)
Cake comb (optional)
Paper cone (optional) for decoration
Pastry bag fitted with small closed star top (Ateco #26)

A Cocolat signature. Two different cakes and two different fillings form a multi-layered stack of complementary flavors, textures, and colors when sliced. The effort is justified by making one large cake into two smaller ones.

8. Remove chilled cake(s) from refrigerator. Mask cake(s) smoothly with coffee buttercream. Comb sides with a cake comb or serrated knife, if desired. Pipe a decorative border with a pastry bag fitted with a small closed star tip. (See Finishing a Cake with Buttercream, page 182.) Cake may be completed, covered, and refrigerated up to 3 days in advance, or frozen for up to 3 months in an airtight plastic container.

9. Decorate cake with fresh roses. Use a paper cone filled with melted white chocolate to pipe dainty curlicue (see Piping with Chocolate, page 185). Remove cake from refrigerator about 1 hour or more before serving to soften textures and enhance flavor.

Note

You may want to make this dessert over a few days. Make the ganache and buttercream any time within 5–6 days of serving. Cover and store in the refrigerator. (See page 181 for reconstituting cold buttercream.) The Chocolate Soufflé Pastry can be made a couple of days in advance. Bake the Sponge Cake, assemble the layers, and finish the cakes up to 2 days before serving.

Petite Rewards

There is something exquisitely tempting about

a complete dessert for one person.

Any large dessert can be redesigned as a small one.

And any small dessert can be

made even smaller and offered in glorious miniature.

Enticing, mouthwatering seductions ...

- - - - - -

There is something exquisitely tempting about a complete dessert for one person. A small pastry evokes the childlike response "It's so beautiful and it's all for me!" During my year in Paris, our great friends were an English family with two small boys, 7 and 8 years old. The younger memorialized his Paris year by creating a series of woodblock prints depicting éclairs and tartelettes. Today, with an advanced degree in art history and philosophy from a prestigious London university, he has not lost his early passion for pastry. ▪ ▪ ▪

The "fancy" pastries that made my eyes grow wide as a child were often too-sweet disappointments, so I was unprepared for my first taste of France in the late 60s. Of all the mouth-watering, diet-defeating seductions in Europe, the most enticing were the rows and rows of small, jewel-like pastries beckoning from every window. How delicious they were—impossible not to dart in for a small éclair filled with real custard, a tartelette of wild strawberries, a little round cylinder of tender mousse surrounded by cake, just big enough for one. We often stood outside the shop to devour the morsel on the sidewalk, letting the crumbs fall to our feet. This is such a common tourist sight in France that I'm sure small pastries are the universal cure for tired feet and museum malaise. ▪ ▪ ▪

Almost any large dessert can be redesigned as a small one. And any small dessert can be made even smaller and offered in glorious miniature. At teatime or on the dessert table an assortment of bite-size desserts invites everyone to try several. I have never seen a more effective icebreaker than a mosaic of miniature desserts and the invitation "Please help yourself!" ▪ ▪ ▪

I like the variety of shapes and sizes possible with small desserts. Some, like Petite Charlottes, are literally small replicas of large desserts. Something in their very smallness makes them especially elegant. Others, shaped like kisses, small roulades, or free-form chocolate shells, seem uniquely suited to their size. ▪ ▪ ▪

The collection that follows is pure Cocolat, my favorites—from the innocent Lemon Roulades to the seductive chocolate Sarah Bernhardts. Some are miniature masterpieces that you will serve with a great sense of accomplishment. Others are no more than what used to be humbly called "cake squares" (actually torte squares in this case), cleverly presented. Dressy or informal, each is a work of art designed to tease the eye and dazzle the taste buds. ▪ ▪ ▪

Happily, the individual dessert is just as appropriate on the grandest table as it is gobbled gleefully on foreign sidewalks!

Kiss-shaped mounds of chocolate cream on top of almond macaroons, entirely glazed with bittersweet chocolate. Petite pastries as divine as the legendary Sarah.

Sarah Bernhardts

1. **To Make Macaroons:** Line a baking sheet with parchment paper. In a food processor fitted with the steel blade, grind almonds and sugar until fine. Add egg whites and almond extract and process to a paste.

2. Transfer mixture to the pastry bag. Pipe 1½-inch rounds about ½ inch high, leaving about 1 inch between macaroons on the parchment-lined baking sheet. Let stand for 30 minutes.

3. Meanwhile, preheat oven to 300°.

4. Bake macaroons until they begin to color, about 20 minutes. Cool on baking sheet on a wire rack. When cool, carefully peel each cookie from the parchment paper. Macaroons may be completed up to 3 days ahead. Wrap well and refrigerate.

5. **To Assemble and Finish Pastries:** Wash and dry pastry bag and tip, then re-assemble. Beat chilled Chocolate Ganache until the color lightens and mixture becomes stiff enough to hold its shape. Do not overbeat or ganache will have a granular texture. Transfer ganache to pastry bag. Pipe a 2-inch-high kiss-shaped mound on top of each macaroon. Refrigerate until well chilled, at least 1 hour.

6. Meanwhile, prepare Sarah Bernhardt Chocolate Glaze. Strain glaze through a fine strainer. Allow to cool until a small dab on your upper lip feels barely cool, about 88°. Transfer glaze to a narrow container tall enough to dip the pastries. Hold the cookie part of each pastry carefully and dip each one, upside down, into the glaze, reaching deep enough just to cover ganache. Set pastry upright and top with a pinch of pistachio, if desired. Refrigerate pastries immediately; keep chilled until ready to serve. If you are decorating with gold leaf, omit pistachios. Before applying gold leaf, chill pastries until glaze is set.

7. Apply gold leaf by touching the thin gold sheets with a tiny artist's brush; the gold will come off in tiny pieces and stick to the brush. Touch the brush to the pastry to transfer the gold to the pastry. Pastries may be completed up to 2 days in advance of serving. Refrigerate in a covered container.

Makes about 24 pastries

Ingredients:
⅔ cup (3½ ounces) whole blanched almonds
¾ cup sugar
3 tablespoons (1–2) egg whites
½ teaspoon almond extract
2 recipes Chocolate Ganache (page 169), made and chilled at least 5–6 hours in advance
Sarah Bernhardt Chocolate Glaze (page 175)
Gold leaf° (optional), or 2 tablespoons minced, unsalted, shelled pistachios
°Edible, real gold and silver leaf is available from art supply stores and from Indian grocery stores, where it is called vark.

Special Equipment:
Pastry bag fitted with a plain #9 tip (⅝ inch)

Walnut Squares

Makes sixteen 2-inch squares

These taste best if baked at least one day ahead.

Ingredients:
6 ounces semisweet or bittersweet
   chocolate, cut into pieces
6 ounces sweet butter, cut into
   pieces
3 tablespoons dark rum
4 large eggs, separated
¾ cup sugar
¾ cup (3 ounces) ground walnuts
¼ cup (1 ounce) sifted flour
¼ teaspoon cream of tartar
Confectioners' sugar and/or
   unsweetened cocoa powder, to dust
   the top

Special Equipment:
Decorative stencil, if desired (page
186)

1. Preheat oven to 375°. Line bottom of an 8-inch square cake pan with a square of parchment or waxed paper.

2. Melt chocolate and butter in a small bowl placed in a barely simmering water bath, stirring occasionally until melted and smooth. Remove from heat. Or, microwave on MEDIUM (50%) for about 2 minutes. Stir until completely melted and smooth. Stir in rum and set aside.

3. Beat egg yolks with ½ cup sugar until pale and thick. Stir in warm chocolate mixture, nuts, and flour. Set aside.

4. In a clean, dry mixing bowl, beat egg whites and cream of tartar at medium speed until soft peaks form. Gradually sprinkle in remaining ¼ cup sugar and continue to beat at high speed until stiff but not dry. Fold one-quarter of whites into chocolate batter to lighten it. Fold in remaining whites.

5. Turn batter into prepared pan. Bake for 30–40 minutes, or until a toothpick or wooden skewer plunged into the center of the cake shows moist crumbs. Allow cake to cool completely in the pan on a rack.

6. When cool, cake will settle in the center, leaving a higher rim around edges. Press edges gently with your fingers to flatten and level cake. Run a small knife around the edge of pan to release cake. Unmold it upside down onto a cutting board. Cake may be prepared to this point, wrapped well, and refrigerated for up to 3 days, or frozen for up to 3 months.

7. Cut cake into 2-inch squares. Use a fine strainer to dust with confectioners' sugar or cocoa. Stencil a simple pattern on each square, if desired. Serve at room temperature.

A San Francisco food critic once called these chocolate-walnut torte squares "brownies with a college education."

Chocolate almond meringue cookies seem to merge with a light, buttery, chocolate mousse so it's hard to know where one starts and the other leaves off. But who cares?

Autumn Leaves

1. **To Make the Chocolate Almond Meringues:** Preheat oven to 200°. Stir together ¼ cup sugar with the almonds, cocoa, and cornstarch. Set aside.

2. Combine ½ cup egg whites, cream of tartar, and vanilla in a clean, dry mixing bowl. Beat at medium speed until soft peaks form. Gradually sprinkle in remaining ½ cup sugar, beating on high speed until stiff but not dry.

3. Fold dry ingredients into the stiff meringue. Scrape mixture into the pastry bag. Pipe about 24 disks, each 2½ inches in diameter and about ⅝ inch thick, spacing them ½ inch apart on the parchment-lined cookie sheet.

4. Bake for 30 minutes. Turn oven off, but leave meringues in still-warm oven until completely dry and crisp, about 30 minutes more. Let cool completely. Store airtight, at room temperature, until needed. Meringues may be completed 3–4 weeks in advance.

5. **To Make the Mousse:** Melt chocolate gently in a clean, dry container set in a barely simmering water bath or microwave on MEDIUM (50%) for about 3 minutes. Keep chocolate warm until needed.

6. Meanwhile, cream butter in the bowl of an electric mixer. Beat in eggs yolks and continue to cream until very soft and fluffy. Set aside.

7. Combine the 3 egg whites plus the additional ½ cup egg whites and the cream of tartar in a clean, dry mixing bowl. Beat at medium speed until soft peaks form. Gradually sprinkle in sugar, beating at high speed until stiff but not dry.

8. Stir the warm melted chocolate into the soft egg yolk and butter mixture with a rubber spatula. Fold one-fourth of the egg whites into chocolate mixture to lighten it. Fold in remaining whites.

9. **To Assemble and Finish the Pastries:** Scoop or pipe a mound of mousse (about 3 tablespoons) on top of 12 of the meringues. (If mousse is very soft, refrigerate meringues for 10–15 minutes to firm up the mounds of mousse and the bowl of mousse, as well.) Embed a second meringue, upside down, into the mousse on the first meringue to make a tall "sandwich" cookie about 1½ inches high. Gently pick up each sandwich with thumb and forefinger. Use a small spatula to fill in and smooth sides with more mousse, forming a cylinder. Smooth mousse on the tops as well. (If at any time the pastries are too soft or difficult to work with, refrigerate or freeze them for a few minutes to stiffen them.) You will have small cylindrical pastries, about 1½ inches tall, covered in chocolate mousse. Leftover mousse may be divvied up and spread on

Makes 12 individual pastries

For best flavor and texture, assemble pastries at least one day ahead.

Ingredients:
For Chocolate-Almond Meringues:
¾ cup sugar
¾ cup (3 ounces) ground blanched almonds
2 tablespoons plus 2 teaspoons unsweetened cocoa powder
1 tablespoon plus 1 teaspoon cornstarch
½ cup (3–4) egg whites, at room temperature
¼ teaspoon cream of tartar
1 teaspoon vanilla extract
For Mousse:
9 ounces semisweet or bittersweet chocolate, cut into bits
4 ounces sweet butter (1 stick), slightly softened
3 large eggs, separated
½ cup (3–4) additional egg whites, at room temperature
½ teaspoon cream of tartar
¼ cup sugar
Chocolate shavings made by scraping a chunk or block of chocolate (page 188)

Special Equipment:
Heavy-duty baking sheet, lined with parchment paper
Pastry bag fitted with Ateco #9 plain round tip (⅜-inch opening)

the tops of each pastry. Pastries may be completed to this point, covered and refrigerated for up to 2 days, or frozen for up to 2 months.

10. The surface of the mousse will have to be softened slightly in order for the chocolate shavings to adhere. If necessary, wave a warm hair dryer near the pastries to warm up just the surface of the mousse for this purpose. Use a metal spatula to gently apply chocolate shavings to tops and sides of each pastry. Scoop the biggest and prettiest shavings on the tops of the pastries first, then press the remaining shavings against the sides. Remember to use the spatula—the shavings will melt in your hands. Pastries may be completed and refrigerated in a closed container for 1 day before serving.

Chocolate Dessert Cups

1. Place chocolate in a 1-quart heatproof container about 5 inches deep and at least 6 inches in diameter. Melt chocolate gently in a barely simmering water bath, stirring frequently until melted and smooth, about 120° for dark chocolate and 110° for white or milk chocolate. Or, melt in the microwave on MEDIUM (50%), stirring once or twice, for about 5 minutes for dark chocolate, or on LOW (30%) for about 7 minutes for milk and white chocolate.

2. **To Make the Molds:** The chocolate cups are be formed by dipping handmade cellophane molds into melted chocolate. The molds are made by wrapping lightweight paper or Styrofoam cups in cellophane. The cellophane is gently peeled away from the chocolate after it has hardened. While chocolate is melting, place a disposable cup in the center of a cellophane square. Pull one side of the cellophane up loosely around the side of the cup and tuck the edges into the cup to secure them. Continue to "wrap" the cup so that the cellophane forms loose pleats all around it (fig. 1). Adjust the cellophane so that the folds and pleats are not too tight, sharp, or close together. If the folds are too tight, the chocolate cups will break when you peel the cellophane from them. Make more molds than you need, in case of breakage.

3. **To Form the Chocolate Cups:** Hold the rim of a cellophane-wrapped cup with your fingers. Dip the bottom of it into the melted chocolate (fig. 2) as deep as the desired height of the finished dessert cup, usually 2–3 inches. Remove and shake excess chocolate from bottom. Immediately place the bottom of dipped mold, right side up, directly on the lined cookie sheet. Proceed to dip remaining molds. Refrigerate dipped molds, on the cookie sheet(s), as soon as possible. Allow cups to harden in refrigerator; they will be ready to peel in 1 hour or so, but they will be much less fragile and easier to work with if you allow them to harden for several hours or overnight. If you allow them the longer period of time, cover them as soon as they are set, to protect from odors and moisture in the refrigerator.

4. **To Unmold the Cups:** Remove cups, one at a time, from refrigerator. Use sharp scissors to snip cellophane all around the top of the mold just below the rim of the disposable cup. Try to avoid touching the chocolate with your fingers. Remove the disposable cups and the excess snipped cellophane, but leave the cellophane that adheres to the chocolate (for now). Replace each cup in the refrigerator after you have done this.

5. When all of the cups have been completed to this point, remove them, again one by one, and carefully peel the cellophane away from the chocolate cup. Do this by holding the cup, at the base, with the fingertips of your left hand (if you are right-handed). If your hands are

Ingredients:
2 pounds premium white, milk,
semisweet, or bittersweet
chocolate, finely chopped to
hasten melting

Special Equipment:
12 or more 6- or 8-ounce
Styrofoam or paper cups
12 or more pieces of cellophane
measuring 12 × 12 inches for 6-
ounce size or 15 × 15 inches for
8-ounce size
1–2 cookie sheets or trays lined
with parchment or waxed paper
Space cleared in your refrigerator
for the cookie sheets, while the
cups are hardening

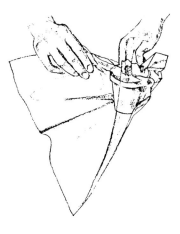

figure 1

Each sculptural, handmade chocolate cup is a delicious, dramatic one-of-a-kind container for homemade mousses, sorbets, or fresh seasonal fruits. And, homemade chocolate cups mean that you control the quality of the chocolate.

very warm, hold the cup with a square of waxed paper between your fingers and the chocolate. Use your other hand to peel the cellophane carefully away from the sides of the cup, pulling the cellophane down and towards the center of the cup until all of the sides are free (fig. 3). Finally, pull cellophane from the bottom inside of the cup; return the cup to the refrigerator. Cups may be completed and refrigerated in a covered container 2–3 weeks ahead. Cups may be frozen, in an airtight container, indefinitely.

Note

Because the cups are made with untempered chocolate, they are very fragile, must be handled very, very carefully, and must be kept refrigerated until serving time. The untempered chocolate also makes them literally melt in your mouth!

figure 2

figure 3

These light, lemon pastries are always on our menu. Year-round, they are a perfect finish to a rich or spicy repast, and a grand alternate for those who don't prefer chocolate.

Lemon
Roulades

1. Run a small knife or spatula around the edges of the pan to release the cooled sponge. Invert onto a sheet of waxed paper; peel off paper liner. Turn sponge right side up. Reserving ⅓ cup of the Lemon Curd, spread evenly with remainder of lemon curd.

2. Divide coated sponge sheet into 5 equal strips (each about 3¼ inches wide and 11–12 inches long, depending on size of pan sponge was baked in). Cut strips in half to make 10 short strips, each about 5½–6 inches long.

3. Roll each strip into an individual jelly roll. (If you have time, refrigerate the lemon roulades until firm, for easier handling. Otherwise, proceed.) Roulades may be made to this point, covered, and refrigerated up to 36 hours in advance, or frozen for up to 1 month.

4. Spread the ends of each roulade with any lemon curd that may have oozed out, plus some of the reserved lemon curd, as needed. Press toasted almonds against each end (or dip each end into the nuts). Cover and refrigerate until serving. Just before serving, sieve confectioners' sugar over each roulade.

Makes 10 roulades

Ingredients:
11 × 17- or 12 × 16-inch Hot Milk
  Sponge Cake (page 160), baked
  and cooled
Lemon Curd (page 169),
½ cup (2 ounces) shaved, toasted
  almonds
2–3 tablespoons confectioners'
  sugar, to finish

- - -

Instead of toasted shaved almonds,
try pistachios, chopped toasted
hazelnuts, or lightly toasted
shredded coconut.

Make miniature roulades, only 2
inches wide, to serve as cookies or
petits fours.

Petite Charlottes

Makes 8 individual desserts

Ingredients:
Eight 3-inch molds, lined with
  plain or Chocolate Ladyfingers
  (page 160 or 163)
¼ cup liqueur of your choice
  (optional)
Filling Recipe such as:
—Coffee, Vanilla, Caramel, or
Banana Bavarian Cream (pages
  167–68)
—Chocolate Velvet Mousse or
Chocolate Marquise (page 165)
—Lemon Mousse (page 167)
—White Chocolate or Mocha
Mousse (page 166)
Topping and/or Garnish such as:
—1 cup heavy cream, whipped
—Fresh raspberries
—Candied citrus zests (page 173)
—Chocolate shavings (page 188)
—Praline (page 171), powdered or
coarsely crushed
Sauce such as:
—Caramel, Raspberry, Chocolate,
Crème Anglaise, or Blueberry
(pages 170–71)

Special Equipment:
Pastry bag fitted with Ateco #6 or
  #7 closed star tip for piping
  whipped cream, if necessary

1. Select the combination of Ladyfingers (chocolate or plain), liqueur, filling, topping, garnish, and sauce that pleases you most.

2. Make the ladyfingers. Line molds according to instructions on page 162. Brush inside surface of the ladyfingers very lightly with liqueur, if desired.

3. Make filling. Spoon immediately into lined molds, leaving room at the top for whipped cream, if desired. Chill for at least 2 hours. Charlottes may be prepared to this point, covered, and refrigerated 1 day in advance. To unmold, lift cardboard rings off of each charlotte.

4. Meanwhile, prepare garnish and sauce. To serve, place each charlotte on a large dessert plate. Pipe whipped cream on top, if desired. Pour sauce around charlotte and garnish.

Note

As fussy as these charlottes sound, the sauces and garnishes can be made a few days in advance and the molds can be lined and filled a day ahead. On serving day simply add toppings and garnish. Pour the sauces around the charlottes just before serving.

Several of my favorite charlotte combinations follow:

Mocha Raspberry: Chocolate Ladyfingers brushed with Kahlúa, filled with Coffee Bavarian Cream, garnished with fresh raspberries, and served with Chocolate Sauce.

Classic Bittersweet: Chocolate Ladyfingers brushed with Grand Marnier, filled with Chocolate Velvet or Chocolate Marquise, topped with chocolate curls, and served with Coffee or plain Crème Anglaise.

Lemon Blueberry: Plain Ladyfingers, filled with Lemon Mousse, topped with whipped cream and lemon zests, served with Blueberry Sauce.

Southern Belles: Plain Ladyfingers, filled with Coffee or Banana Bavarian Cream, topped with whipped cream and crushed pecan praline, served with Caramel Sauce.

Adorably pretty miniature masterpieces. You'll enjoy creating your own flavor combinations.

Special Occasions

We always commemorate really grand events with

Very Special Desserts.

I love pretty or elegant or whimsical cakes

that capture the spirit of the celebration subtly...

Must a cake for Dad or husband

always come in the shape of a necktie?

- - - - - -

Although dessert makes any day an occasion, we commemorate the really grand events in our lives—birthdays, anniversaries, and marriages—with Very Special Desserts. We say "Congratulations," "Bon Voyage," "Good Luck," and "Thanks"—with cakes of all descriptions made especially for the occasion. ▪ ▪ ▪

I love pretty, or elegant, or whimsical cakes that capture the spirit of the celebration with subtlety. Cute "theme" cakes just really aren't my forte. To me, the ideal baby shower cake is a delicious light luncheon dessert with pure, white, whipped cream and pretty, pastel chocolate ribbons. If you must, nest a plastic baby rattle or tiny toy amongst the ribbons. ▪ ▪ ▪

Lucy's Birthday Cake? Liv Blumer, my editor, asked me to include a child's birthday cake. I loved the idea, as I was expecting my first baby, Lucy; but I didn't want to do a Teddy bear or a clown. It finally came to me. A whimsical tower of miniature brownie cupcakes with sparklers would delight children (and adults too, it turns out) every bit as much as a red and blue clown cake. The brownie pyramid is a natural invitation to "help yourselves." As a bonus to parents, cutting and serving is eliminated, and so are messy plates. Children can easily take extra portions home to siblings, and Moms and Dads who arrive to collect children at the end will surely want "just one." I've included a recipe for miniature banana cakes, and lovely peanut cakes, that can be substituted for, or interspersed with the brownies, which are very bittersweet. ▪ ▪ ▪

Why does a cake for Dad or husband always come in the shape of a necktie? Don't your special men deserve a grown-up delicious chocolate cake? So, why not "package" it as a sophisticated, but still masculine wrapped gift. - - -

A meringue vacherin "basket" of fruit is a perfect expression of spring or summer. I love it for Mother's Day and even Easter if good early berries are available. The method for producing the meringue basket is significantly updated from the old-fashioned three-day ordeal in egg whites. My procedure is astonishingly simple and quick. The finished dessert will knock the socks off your guests, not to mention Mom herself. - - -

The *Pâte Trompé?* Just a delicious joke and a little dig at some of the sophisticated foods that we like to eat. Still, I bet more people love this chocolate than love even the best liver pâté—*en gelée* or not! - - -

I hope you will enjoy these celebration desserts. Perhaps the approach will inspire you to dream up your own special creations.

Chocolate
Valentine
Marquise

Serves 6–8

Ingredients:
1 ounce bittersweet or semisweet
  chocolate, cut into small pieces
Chocolate Marquise (page 165)
2 tablespoons unsweetened cocoa
  powder
Optional sauce: Crème Anglaise,
  plain or Espresso or any of the
  Fresh Cream Sauces (page 170)

Special Equipment:
7-inch heart-shaped, straight-sided
  bottomless form° with 3-inch-
  high sides the best, but a
  conventional 4-cup mold will do
Propane torch (optional)

°These bottomless forms are
  available from Parrish or Maid
  of Scandinavia (see Resources,
  page 197) if not stocked at local
  kitchenware stores. If you use a
  regular mold, choose a fairly
  plain one as the Marquise does
  not unmold perfectly and will not
  show any decorative details from
  the mold.

1. If you are using a bottomless form, trace a heart exactly the size of the form on a piece of parchment or waxed paper. Melt the ounce of chocolate. Spread it on the paper within the tracing. Tape the paper to a baking sheet to keep the chocolate heart from warping as it hardens and place the form over it. Refrigerate while you make the marquise. The thin chocolate heart on the bottom of the dessert will keep the marquise from sticking to the serving platter. If you are using a conventional mold, line it as smoothly as possible with plastic wrap; set aside. Reserve the ounce of chocolate for later use.

2. Make the Chocolate Marquise. Turn mixture immediately into prepared form or mold. Cover and chill for at least 4 hours, or until set, before unmolding to serve. Marquise may be prepared to this point, up to 2 days in advance, or frozen for 2 months.

3. **To Unmold and Serve:** If you have molded the marquise in a bottomless form, sprinkle the top lightly with cocoa sifted through a fine strainer. Remove tape, tilt the form, and peel the paper from the bottom. Place the form on a serving platter. Gently warm the sides of the mold with a hot, wrung-out wet towel or with a propane torch. Slip the mold off quickly.

If you have used a conventional mold, melt the ounce of chocolate. Spread it thinly over the top surface of the cold marquise. Chill for 10 minutes to harden. Invert mold onto serving platter. Remove mold and carefully peel plastic wrap from marquise. Dust the top with cocoa.

4. Serve cold, cut in thin slices, with the sauce of your choice.

The royalty of mousses. A Marquise is rich with butter and very, very chocolatey. The texture is stiff enough to slice and definitely to be eaten with a fork, in small servings, like a very rich and rare cake. Crème Anglaise is the classic accompaniment.

Rich masculine flavors—chestnuts and rum—make a seriously delicious chocolate cake for Dad or the main man in your life.

A Gift
for Dad

1. In a small bowl, combine rum and Simple Syrup; set aside.

2. **To Assemble the Cake:** Cut Chocolate Génoise horizontally into 3 even layers with a serrated bread knife. Place top layer, upside down, on the corrugated cardboard. Brush with rum syrup. Spread a generous ½ cup of Chestnut Buttercream evenly over layer. Brush second cake layer with rum syrup. Place it, moist side down, on the buttercream. Brush the dry side of layer with rum syrup. Spread with chestnut buttercream. Moisten top cake layer. Place it, moist side down, on second layer. Level assembled cake by pressing it firmly with the bottom of a cake pan. Check all sides to see that cake is square and symmetrical and push it into place if it is not. Trim any ragged edges, if necessary, with a serrated knife. Brush top of assembled cake with rum syrup.

3. Spread remaining chestnut buttercream smoothly over the top and sides of the cake to provide a smooth surface for the chocolate glaze. (Do not worry that cake or crumbs show, or if the buttercream coat does not look "finished.") Chill cake for at least 1 hour before glazing. Cake may be completed to this point, wrapped, and refrigerated up to 3 days ahead, or frozen for up to 3 months.

4. **To Glaze and Finish Cake:** Glaze with Sarah Bernhardt Chocolate Glaze. Skip the crumb-coat step since cake has already been spread smooth with chestnut buttercream. See Technique for Glazing with Chocolate, page 175.

5. As soon as cake is glazed, place on a rack and refrigerate. Keep refrigerated until 1 hour before serving.

6. Decorate the cake with chocolate ribbons.

Serves 12–14

For best flavor and texture, assemble cake at least one day ahead.

Ingredients:
¼ cup dark rum
⅓ cup Simple Syrup (page 171)
8-inch-square Chocolate Génoise (page 159)
Small batch Chestnut Buttercream (page 182)
Sarah Bernhardt Chocolate Glaze (page 175)
Marbled chocolate ribbons (pages 189–91)

Special Equipment:
8-inch-square piece of corrugated cardboard

Celebration Cake

Serves 24–30

Ingredients:
9-inch round Hot Milk Sponge
   Cake (page 160), baked and
   cooled
About ½ cup rum or brandy
Chocolate Ganache (page 169)
Chocolate Soufflé Pastry (page
   163), baked in 3 thin 9-inch
   round layers
Small batch Chocolate
   Buttercream, made with white
   chocolate (page 182)
1–2 teaspoons unsweetened cocoa
   powder
Chocolate Modeling Dough, made
   with white chocolate (page 192)

Special Equipment:
9-inch corrugated cake circle

- - -

I often substitute Coffee
Buttercream for white chocolate in
this cake, and I use an orange
liqueur like Curaçao or Grand
Marnier instead of rum or brandy.
I then finish the cake with dark
chocolate ribbons and a dark rose
instead of white.

1. **To Assemble the Cake:** Run a knife around the Hot Milk Sponge Cake to release it from pan. Turn it out onto a cookie sheet. Turn cake right side up. Use a long serrated knife to cut it, horizontally, into 3 even layers. Carefully set the top 2 layers aside.

2. Using a pastry brush, lightly moisten bottom layer with rum. Remove cold Chocolate Ganache from refrigerator, and beat until it stiffens and holds its shape like very thick whipped cream. (Overbeating causes granular appearance and texture and makes ganache too stiff to spread—so, easy does it.) Spread one-third of the beaten ganache evenly over moistened sponge. (If ganache is too stiff to spread, warm the spatula by dipping it in hot water and wiping it dry.)

3. Reverse one of the Chocolate Pastry rounds onto the ganache-covered sponge layer. (*Tip:* Chocolate pastry rounds are thin and delicate. Leave them on the parchment paper they were baked on. Use scissors to cut around each one leaving a paper border. Use the paper to lift, flip, and position each round as you assemble the cake. Peel the paper from each pastry only after it is in place.) Spread chocolate pastry round with ½ cup white Chocolate Buttercream.

4. Moisten the second layer of sponge with rum. Place it, moist side down, on buttercream-coated pastry layer. (If sponge layer is too delicate to moisten and flip, omit moistening and carefully move the layer into place using a rimless cookie sheet or spatula.) Brush top of sponge with rum. Spread with half of the remaining ganache. Top with a chocolate pastry round. Spread with ½ cup white chocolate buttercream.

5. Moisten the third layer of sponge. Place it, moist side down, on the buttercream. Brush the top with rum. Spread with remaining ganache. Top with third round of chocolate pastry. Sieve cocoa lightly over the top to keep it from being sticky. Cover with the 9-inch cardboard cake circle. Level the cake by pressing firmly. Examine the cake to be sure that it is symmetrical, and press where necessary to correct the shape if it is leaning. Cover and chill the cake for 20 minutes or longer to firm up for easier handling.

6. Remove chilled cake from refrigerator. Turn whole assembly upside down, using the cookie sheet to assist you, so that the top layer is now sponge cake. Trim any ragged edges with a serrated knife. Cover entire cake evenly with remaining buttercream (which eventually will be covered by chocolate ribbons). Cake may be completed to this point, wrapped well, and refrigerated up to 3 days in advance, or frozen for up to 3 months. Or you may complete the

A tour de force—
two different cakes
and two different
fillings form a
multi-layered
stack of
contrasting flavors,
textures, and
colors when sliced.
This celebration
dessert is entirely
wrapped in white
chocolate ribbons
and topped with an
outrageous cabbage
rose.

cake (see below), and then cover the cake and refrigerate it for up to 3 days in advance.

7. **To Wrap Cake with Chocolate Ribbons:** Follow the instructions on page 192 to wrap the cake with chocolate ribbons and top with a cabbage rose.

Note

The cake may be made, assembled, and frozen 3 months in advance, or it may be scheduled over the course of 5–6 days and completely assembled up to 2 days in advance of serving. If you plan to do the entire cake in one session, proceed as follows:

1. Make and refrigerate ganache first. It takes only a few minutes, but it must have time to cool and should be well chilled—several hours—before it is used.

2. Make sponge cake—it bakes in 20–30 minutes.

3. Measure ingredients for chocolate pastry while the sponge is baking. As soon as sponge is done, turn down oven and make chocolate pastry.

4. Make buttercream.

5. As soon as sponge and chocolate pastry are cool and ganache is cold, you may assemble cake and chill it while making chocolate ribbon dough.

Strawberry Basket

1. **To Make the Form:** Stack the sheets of foil and fold them together lengthwise, several times to create a 3-inch-wide strip several layers thick and still 30 inches long. Wrap the strip around the cake pan or cannister and secure it with tape so that it cannot unwrap, but do not tape foil to pan. Wrap the parchment strip around the foil with the pencil line at the upper edge. The pencil side should be against the foil so that you can see it through the paper but the pencil will not come off on the meringue. Carefully, and with minimum distortion, slip the parchment and foil form off the pan and place it on the cookie sheet lined with plain parchment paper. Adjust the form if necessary to be certain that it is still nice and round. Be sure that the foil is completely covered by the parchment.

2. **To Make the Coffee Meringue Shell:** Preheat oven to 225°. Combine egg whites and cream of tartar with coffee powder in a clean, dry mixing bowl. Beat at medium speed until soft peaks form. Slowly sprinkle in the superfine sugar, beating at high speed until meringue is very stiff. Scrape meringue into the pastry bag fitted with a decorative tip. Pipe a pattern all over the sides of parchment-lined form, reaching from the base to pencil line. See figure on page 125. All piping should touch; there must be no gaps and no parchment showing except for the ½ inch above the pencil line. (One favorite pattern is a series of simple "S" curves, zigzags, or figure-eights piped horizontally from the pencil line to the base.) If the top edge is not neat and even, finish with a neatly piped border at the pencil line. Use the same idea at the bottom edge, if desired. (Piping is much easier if you can elevate the cookie sheet and the form to eye level and rotate it on a turntable or lazy Susan as you work.)

3. Place piped shell in oven. Meanwhile, use remaining meringue to pipe or spread an 8-inch meringue disk on the second parchment-lined sheet. Bake the shell and the disk for about 2 hours, or until completely dry and crisp. (If you have a pilot light in your oven, finish the drying overnight in a turned-off oven.) Let meringue cool completely. Wrap airtight until needed. Shell may be prepared to this point 1 month or more in advance; wrap well and store at room temperature.

4. **To Assemble the Dessert:** Soften ice cream in the refrigerator for about 30 minutes, or until it can be spooned very easily but is not too mushy.

5. Unwrap meringue shell and disk. Place shell on the corrugated cardboard circle or tart pan bottom. Remove foil and parchment from shell by releasing tape and twisting foil and parchment into the center of shell to peel it away from sides. Do this very gently—meringue

Serves 12–16

Ingredients:
½ cup (3–4) egg whites, at room temperature
¼ teaspoon cream of tartar
2½ teaspoons instant coffee powder
1 cup superfine sugar
2 pints store-bought premium vanilla ice cream
1½ cups heavy cream
1½ teaspoons vanilla extract
1–2 tablespoons sugar (to taste)
2 pints fresh strawberries, rinsed and hulled (raspberries, kiwis, or other fruit can be substituted)
Chocolate Sauce (page 170) or store-bought chocolate sauce

Special Equipment:
8-inch round, straight-sided cake pan, cannister, or other similarly shaped object
Two 30-inch-long sheets of heavy-duty aluminum foil, or 3 sheets of lightweight foil
3 × 30-inch piece of parchment paper, with a heavy pencil line drawn the length of it, ½ inch from one edge
2 cookie sheets, lined with parchment paper
Pastry bag fitted with a decorative star tip (Ateco #4 closed star is a favorite)
9-inch corrugated cardboard circle or tart pan bottom

- - -

As with a hot fudge sundae with strawberries, I love this grown-up dessert for its frivolous elegance and its irresistible interplay of cold with warm and creamy with crisp.

shatters easily. Release meringue disk by sliding the flat blade of a knife between it and the parchment — do not use a prying or levering motion or disk may crack. Trim disk if necessary. Place it carefully into bottom of meringue shell.

6. Spoon all of the ice cream carefully into the meringue shell, very gently pushing and spreading with the back of the spoon to avoid cracking meringue. Use very flat spoonfuls of ice cream rather than rounded scoops so that you will not have to push hard against the meringue to flatten and spread the ice cream. The ice cream will not fill the shell all the way to the top. When all of the ice cream is distributed in the vacherin, rewrap the whole thing and freeze until hard, at least overnight. Dessert may be prepared to this point several days or 1 week in advance.

7. **To Finish and Serve the Strawberry Basket:** Forty-five to 60 minutes before serving, whip cream with the vanilla and sugar to taste. Spread the cream all over the ice cream, reaching nearly to the top of meringue shell. Arrange berries all over cream. Refrigerate up to 1 hour before serving, to soften the hard ice cream slightly.

Warm the Chocolate Sauce and pass separately.

The old-fashioned, three-day process of making a vacherin shell is eliminated by piping stiff meringue directly onto a homemade form — a simple one-step process so easy that you'll want to have meringue shells on hand throughout the berry season.

Prepare most of this "vacherin" dessert well in advance so that only the whipped cream and fresh berries need to be added before serving.

I made this ricotta-and-cream–filled layer cake for a very special Cocolat baby shower brunch. It is light and rich, and fragrant with Kahlúa and rum. If it is not for a baby shower, omit the pastel decorations and dust with cocoa and coffee, then garnish with dark chocolate shavings.

Baby Shower Cake

1. In a small bowl, combine Simple Syrup with the Kahlúa and 3 tablespoons rum. Set aside.

2. In the bowl of an electric mixer, mix cream cheese until smooth and slightly fluffy. (Do not overmix, or it will become thin and runny.) Beat in the strained ricotta. Gradually pour in heavy cream. Add confectioners' sugar, the remaining 3 tablespoons rum, and the vanilla. Beat until fluffy and stiffened like thick whipped cream. Set the filling aside.

3. Cut the 9-inch-square cardboard into an octagon by trimming 2⅝ inches in from each corner. Cut the 8-inch-square Génoise into an octagon by trimming 2⅜ inches in from each corner (see figure). Cut the octagonal cake horizontally into 2 even layers using a serrated bread knife. Place the top layer upside down on the corrugated cake board (which will be ½ inch larger than the cake, all the way around). Brush well with the rum and Kahlúa syrup.

4. Spread about 1½ cups of the filling over the moistened layer. Moisten the second cake layer with syrup. Place it, moist side down, on the first. Level the cake by pressing it with the bottom of a cake pan and be sure it is symmetrical and even on all sides. Press it where necessary to correct the shape. Moisten the top of assembled cake with remaining rum and Kahlúa syrup.

5. Spread a thick layer of filling on top of the cake. Cover the sides with a layer thick enough that the corrugated cardboard around the bottom of the cake is completely covered. Make all the surfaces as smooth as possible.

6. Use the pastry bag and tip to pipe a pretty border around the top and bottom edges. Decorate with pastel chocolate curls and ribbons. Alternatively, sift the cocoa mixture over cake. Pile dark chocolate shavings on top. Cake may be completed, covered, and refrigerated 1 day ahead.

Note

If you like this slightly Italianate filling as much as I do, you'll also enjoy trying this dessert with Chocolate or Coffee Génoise. Instead of pastel decorations, dust the dessert with a mixture of 1½ teaspoons each unsweetened cocoa powder and confectioners' sugar and ¼ teaspoon powdered instant coffee. Decorate the top with a generous handful of dark chocolate shavings.

Serves 12–16

For best flavor and texture, assemble cake at least one day ahead.

Ingredients:
3 tablespoons Simple Syrup (page 171)
3 tablespoons Kahlúa or other coffee liqueur
6 tablespoons dark rum
6 ounces cream cheese
1 cup whole-milk ricotta cheese, sieved or processed until smooth in a food processor
2 cups heavy cream
1 cup (3 ounces) confectioners' sugar
1½ teaspoons vanilla extract
8-inch-square Génoise (page 159), baked and cooled
Pastel chocolate ribbons and curls (page 192)

Special Equipment:
Pastry bag fitted with closed star tip (Ateco #4)
9-inch-square piece of corrugated cardboard

A whimsical tower of miniature help-yourself cupcakes, glazed with milk or white chocolate and set to sparkle before your eyes. The little cakes can be *Ultra Brownies*, *Petite Banana Cakes*, or yummy *Peanut Butter Minis*.

Lucy's
Birthday Cake

1. **To Prepare the Cone:** Spray paint, or wrap Styrofoam cone and the cake circle with gold or silver paper. Secure the cone to the wrapped corrugated cake circle with glue or long hairpins. (This will stabilize the tower of cupcakes and enable children, or adults, to help themselves without knocking it over.)

2. **To Prepare and Glaze the Miniature Cupcakes:** Bake a total of 70–75 cupcakes, in one flavor or a combination. Let cool completely. If you plan to glaze with white, mocha, or milk chocolate, refrigerate the cupcakes for at least 30 minutes beforehand to prevent the glaze from dripping. Do not refrigerate cupcakes if glazing with bittersweet.

3. Prepare one or more glazes. Dip the tops of chilled cupcakes into the glaze of choice; set aside.

4. **To Assemble the Tower of Cupcakes:** Have ready the toothpicks, the glazed cupcakes, and the Styrofoam cone, well secured to its cardboard base. Start attaching cupcakes at the base of the cone: One cupcake at a time, stick a toothpick into the cone and then impale a cupcake on it so that glazed top faces outward. Rotate cone as you work. Arrange the cupcake flavors randomly or in a prearranged pattern until the entire cone is covered. Stick sparklers in a few of the top cupcakes and light just before serving.

Notes

Take heed, 70 tiny cupcakes can disappear in a twinkling! Even youngsters are able to eat 2 or 3 of these delightful treats!

The recipes for Ultra Brownie Cupcakes and Peanut Butter Minis may be tripled to save time. The batter is not harmed if it sits in the saucepan while you bake each pan in succession. Petite Banana Cake batter is not quite as hardy. You will need enough muffin pans to scoop out all of the batter at once—it will be ruined if it is allowed to wait in the bowl between batches. One pan can wait for the length of time it takes to bake one batch, but probably not two. Two ovens would be handy at a time like this!

For smaller parties, shorten the Styrofoam cone by cutting it with a serrated knife about 3 inches from the bottom, or buy a shorter cone. Bake a double recipe (48 cupcakes) instead of a triple.

*Makes 70
miniature cupcakes*

Ingredients:
***A triple batch of one of the
following recipes or one of each
(recipes follow):***
— Ultra Brownie Cupcakes
— Petite Banana Cakes
— Peanut Butter Minis
***Any or none of the following
glazes:***
— White Chocolate Glaze (page 175)
— Mocha or Milk Chocolate Glaze (page 175)
— Bittersweet Chocolate Glaze (page 174)

Special Equipment:
Gold or silver spray paint or wrapping paper
Styrofoam florist's cone with a 5-inch-round base, 16 inches high (available at florist supply or craft stores)
10-inch corrugated cake circle
One or more miniature muffin pans (each with 24 mini muffin cups 2 inches in diameter at the top and 1¼ inches deep), lined with gold and/or silver miniature muffin cup liners (also called cake cases) (available at kitchenware and specialty stores)
About 70 toothpicks
Sparklers (optional)

Ingredients:
1 cup (4 ounces) sifted flour
3 tablespoons sifted unsweetened
  cocoa powder
⅛ teaspoon salt
8 ounces sweet butter, cut into
  pieces
2 ounces unsweetened chocolate, cut
  into bits
2 ounces semisweet or bittersweet
  chocolate, cut into bits
1½ cups sugar
1 teaspoon vanilla extract
4 large eggs

Ultra Brownie Cupcakes

1. Preheat oven to 350°. Sift together flour, cocoa, and salt; set aside.

2. Combine butter and chocolates in a large bowl or saucepan set in a barely simmering water bath. Stir frequently with a wooden spoon or rubber spatula until the mixture is completely melted, warm, and smooth. Or microwave on MEDIUM (50%) for about 2 minutes 15 seconds. Stir until completely smooth.

3. Off heat, whisk in the sugar and vanilla. Whisk in eggs, one at a time, until incorporated. Finally stir and whisk in the dry ingredients just until smooth. Use a spoon or pitcher to fill muffin cups nearly to the rim.

4. Bake in the lower third of the oven until a toothpick inserted in the center shows moist crumbs, 25–30 minutes. Brownies will rise beautifully and crack on the surface. Cool in the pan, on a rack. Cupcakes can be prepared up to 2 days ahead and stored in a covered container, at room temperature, or frozen for up to 2 months.

5. Serve plain, or glaze with Milk Chocolate, Mocha, or White Chocolate Glaze.

Ingredients:
1½ cups (6 ounces) sifted flour
2 teaspoons baking powder
1 teaspoon salt
½ cup sweet butter
2 cups (14 ounces) brown sugar
1 cup chunky-style peanut butter
2 teaspoons vanilla extract
2 large eggs, at room temperature

Peanut Butter Minis

1. Preheat oven to 350°. Sift together flour, baking powder, and salt; set aside.

2. In a medium saucepan, melt butter. Stir in sugar until combined. Off heat, stir in peanut butter followed by eggs, vanilla, and sifted dry ingredients. Use a spoon to fill muffin cups nearly full. Bake until a toothpick inserted in the center tests moist but not gooey, 20–25 minutes. Tops will puff up and crack, then start to settle slightly. Cool in the pan on a rack. Cupcakes can be prepared up to 2 days ahead and stored in a covered container at room temperature, or frozen for up to 2 months.

3. Serve plain, or glaze with Bittersweet, Milk Chocolate, or Mocha Glaze. I like them best plain.

Petite Banana Cakes

1. Preheat oven to 350°. Combine mashed banana, buttermilk, and vanilla in a small bowl set in a pan of hot water. Set aside until mixture is at room temperature. Meanwhile sift together cake flour, baking powder, baking soda, and salt.

2. In the bowl of an electric mixer, cream butter. Gradually add white and brown sugars until very light. One at a time, add eggs, beating until each is incorporated. Add the sifted dry ingredients in 3 parts, alternating with the banana-buttermilk mixture in 2 parts. Beat each addition only until incorporated; scrape the bowl as often as necessary. Fold in walnuts. Use a spoon or a pastry bag with a large opening to fill muffin cups about three-fourths full.

3. Bake until a toothpick inserted in the center tests dry, 20–25 minutes. Cool in the pan on a rack. Cupcakes can be prepared up to 2 days ahead and stored in a covered container in the refrigerator, or frozen for up to 2 months.

4. Serve plain, or glaze with Mocha, Milk Chocolate, or Bittersweet Chocolate Glaze.

Makes 34–36
miniature cupcakes

Ingredients:
1 cup lightly mashed ripe banana
  (about 2 large bananas)
¼ cup buttermilk
1 teaspoon vanilla extract
2¼ cups (9 ounces) sifted cake
  flour
½ teaspoon baking powder
½ teaspoon baking soda
½ teaspoon salt
4 ounces (1 stick) sweet butter
1 cup sugar
½ cup (3½ ounces) brown sugar
2 large eggs, at room temperature
1 cup (5 ounces) coarsely chopped
  walnuts

Pâté Trompé

Ingredients:
3¾ teaspoons unflavored gelatin
½ cup cold water
1 cup strong hot coffee
3 tablespoons sugar
½ cup Kahlúa or other coffee
*   liqueur*
Flavorless vegetable oil
Chocolate Marquise (page 165)
Optional:
1 ounce white chocolate, for
*   decoration*
1–2 wide strips orange zest or
*   pieces of candied orange, for*
*   decoration*
Crème Anglaise (page 170), plain
*   or orange flavored*

Special Equipment:
4-cup loaf pan
8-inch square pan or a 9-inch
*   round pan*
Parchment paper cone

1. **To Make the Coffee Gelée and Line Mold:** Sprinkle the gelatin over the cold water and allow to soften 5 minutes without stirring. Stir softened gelatin into hot coffee until dissolved. Add sugar and Kahlúa. Cool to room temperature.

2. Oil the bottom and sides of the loaf pan. Line the bottom and sides of the oiled pan with a piece of plastic wrap large enough to overhang on all sides. Smooth the plastic lining as perfectly as possible, especially on the bottom of the pan. Pour about ¼ inch of gelée in the pan. Pour the remaining gelée into the square or round cake pan. Refrigerate both pans until set. (Be sure that the loaf pan is level in the refrigerator or the thin layer of gelatin will be lopsided!) The gelée in the loaf pan will set in about 30 minutes, the rest will take 1 hour, but you will not need it until the pâté is ready to serve.

3. **To Assemble and Finish the Pâté:** When the gelée in the loaf pan is set, make the Chocolate Marquise. Turn it immediately into pan on top of the gelée. Chill for at least 4 hours, or until ready to serve.

4. To serve, invert onto serving platter or marble slab. Remove pan and carefully peel plastic wrap from pâté.

5. Decorate the top of the pâté, if desired: Use a paper cone to pipe a motif with melted white chocolate. Place bits of orange zest or candied peel to resemble the classic *Pâté en Gelée* presentation. Cut the extra pan of molded gelée into ½-inch dice with a thin sharp knife. Use a rubber spatula to scrape gelée dice from pan and heap them around unmolded pâté.

6. Serve thin slices of pâté with Crème Anglaise. Pâté may be completed and refrigerated up to 2 days ahead.

The liver pâté that everyone loves—a great April Fool's joke and a fabulous ultra-chocolate classic.

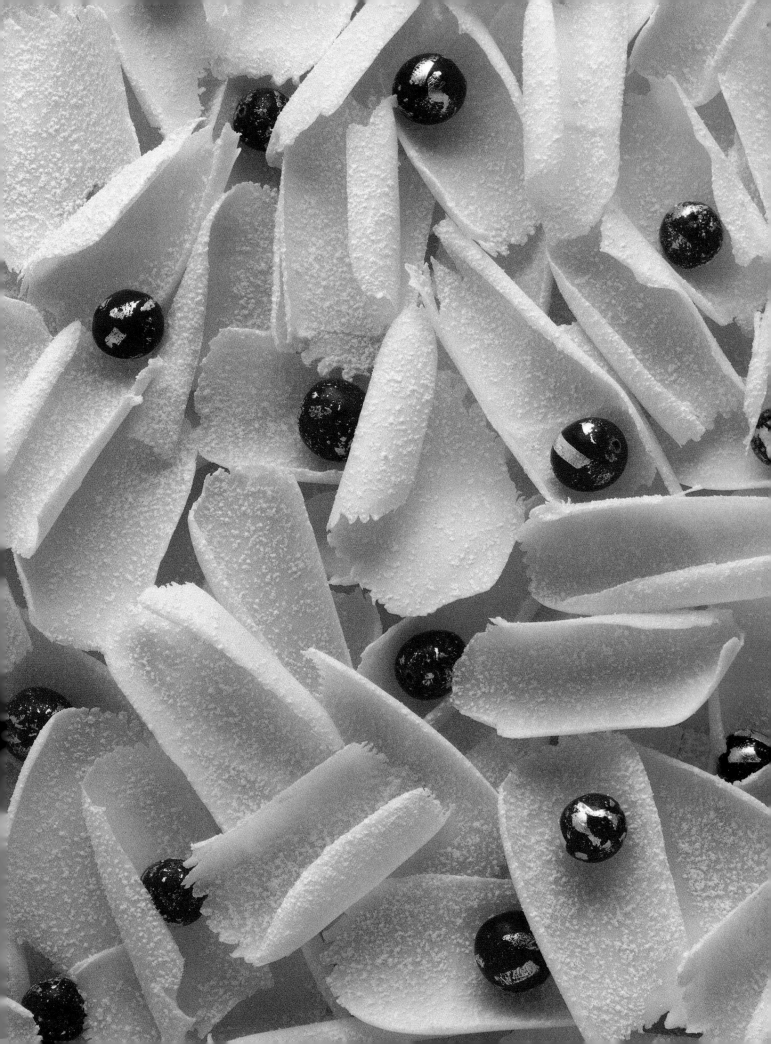

'Tis the Season

The holiday season evokes a grand nostalgia
as we unpack cherished family recipes
and traditions along with the Christmas ornaments.
It's fun to show off with a show-stopping dessert
and the dessert maker often
takes the lion's share of the kudos!

- - - - - -

The holiday season evokes a grand nostalgia as we unpack cherished family recipes and traditions along with the Christmas ornaments. ▪ ▪ ▪

Happily, these days no one bears the entire burden of the holiday cooking and baking. Joint efforts are everywhere the order of the day. With each guest contributing his or her own specialty, brand-new traditions, recipes, and rituals are added to the holiday repertoire. ▪ ▪ ▪

With only one or two dishes to contribute to the celebration, it's fun to show off with an extravagant dish or show-stopping dessert. The dessert maker often takes the lion's share of the kudos. I hope some of my favorites will inspire you. ▪ ▪ ▪

When Cocolat first began making *Bûches de Noel,* only a few customers had ever seen this stunning traditional European Yule log cake with its whimsical meringue mushrooms and chocolate bark. Today, of course, what bakery doesn't make a *bûche!* ▪ ▪ ▪

Still, the *bûche* is a potent symbol of the season for me. Every year, on the 22nd, 23rd, and 24th of December, when the Cocolat kitchen is a hive of activity, I am back in charge of *les bûches.* A friend and former employee abandons her high-tech job to decorate Yule logs with me. Spatulas flying, we catch up, gossip like mad, and tell old Cocolat stories. ▪ ▪ ▪

Nevertheless, it is time for a new twist on the old-fashioned *bûche.* Why not a frosty, frozen bittersweet chocolate parfait, shaped like a log and finished with swirls of meringue "bark," toasted golden brown and served with warm Chocolate Sauce, or Coffee Crème Anglaise? ▪ ▪ ▪

And while you're rethinking the Old Reliables, dismiss the idea of meringue mushrooms as mere *bûche* decor. These crisp sweet funghi are a delicious addition to the petit four or cookie tray. They keep marvelously and they utterly fascinate young and old. We heap them in an old-fashioned wooden produce carton called a "till," cover them with cellophane, and tie on a gold cord. Our customers can't get enough of these trompe l'oeil gifts. **- - -**

I also adore cranberries. And not just next to turkey and dressing. Cranberries are tangy and flavorful in a tempting chocolate layer cake; they offset the sweetness of white chocolate in a stunning holiday bombe. **- - -**

My favorite gifts are easy and fun to make, wrap, and give. Apricots and brandy or prunes with Armagnac in a fragrant loaf, a tin of buttery Bourbon Pecan Shortbread, or a moist ring of chocolate and fruit—each makes an enchanting and festive personal gift. **- - -**

Chocolate truffles? They launched my career! To me they are still the ultimate to-die-for chocolate indulgence. A true chocolate truffle is a rare treat indeed. It must be very fresh and made with fine chocolate, sweet butter, and/or fresh cream. Your own homemade truffles will be a revelation to you, and all who taste them. **- - -**

A gift of homemade food will never go out of style. Life in the fast lane has its welcome pauses, and fortunately for all, Christmas will always be a time for something absolutely delicious and unabashedly low-tech. **- - -**

Christmas
at the North Pole?
Or a perfect
holiday solution in
tropical climes!
Here is the classic
European Yule Log
cake transformed
into a frozen
chocolate delight,
blanketed with
swirls of snowy
toasted meringue
and served with a
favorite sauce.

Frozen Chocolate Bûche de Nöel

1. Line the mold with a piece of heavy-duty foil. Leave enough excess foil on all sides of the mold to overfill (if necessary) and to wrap after filling. Wrap cardboard in 2 thicknesses of foil. Set mold and cardboard aside.

2. **To Make the Chocolate Log:** Place a fine strainer over a clean bowl near stove. Scald milk in a heavy-bottomed, nonreactive saucepan. In a separate bowl, whisk egg yolks with granulated sugar until pale and thick. Whisk a small amount of the scalded milk into the yolk mixture to temper it. Continue to whisk while pouring the remaining hot milk into the yolks. Return the mixture to the saucepan and cook over medium heat, stirring constantly with a wooden spoon and reaching all over bottom of pan to avoid scorching. Mixture must not boil or even simmer. It will thicken slightly as it cooks. Remove from heat when custard coats the back of a spoon (at about 170°). Pour immediately into the strainer and bowl. Stir chocolates and vanilla into hot custard until dissolved. Let cool completely.

3. Whip cream just until soft peaks form; do not whip until stiff. Fold cream into cooled chocolate custard. Turn into prepared mold. Bring extended foil edges together to cover mold. Secure foil tightly around chocolate mixture, squeezing it into more of a log shape. Freeze solid until needed, or up to 1 month.

4. **To Finish with Meringue:** Beat egg whites and cream of tartar with an electric mixer on medium speed until soft peaks form. Gradually add superfine sugar, beating on high speed until meringue is stiff and glossy.

5. Unwrap frozen chocolate log. Place on the foil-wrapped cardboard.

6. Mask log completely with stiff meringue. The entire log should be covered with a thick coat of meringue, which should touch foil board all along the base of log. Use a fork to texture the meringue like tree bark and make spiral patterns to suggest stumps. The *bûche* is now ready to toast and serve. *Bûche* may be completed to this point and returned to the freezer up to 1 day in advance.

7. **To Toast and Serve:** Preheat oven to 425°. Sift the confectioners' sugar all over log. Transfer the cardboard base to a baking sheet. Bake just until golden brown, 5–10 minutes. Decorate with sprigs of holly or pine, if desired. Serve immediately with Crème Anglaise or warm Chocolate Sauce.

Serves 10–12

Ingredients:
For the Chocolate Log:
1 cup milk
5 large egg yolks
½ cup granulated sugar
9 ounces semisweet or bittersweet chocolate, cut into very small bits
1½ ounces unsweetened chocolate, cut into very small bits
1½ teaspoons vanilla extract
1½ cups heavy cream
For the Meringue:
5 egg whites, at room temperature
¼ teaspoon cream of tartar
¾ cup superfine sugar
¼ cup confectioners' sugar
Coffee or plain Crème Anglaise, or Chocolate Sauce (page 170)

Special Equipment:
6-cup nut bread mold, or Viennese cake mold for classical saddle of venison dessert (or, use the Bûche de Nöel-shaped mold available in some kitchenware shops)
Piece of corrugated cardboard cut 4 inches longer and 4 inches wider than mold
Holly or pine sprigs

- - -

For a larger party: If your oven and freezer are large enough, make two logs. Place them end to end on a double-length cardboard before spreading with meringue.

Black and White Raspberry Cake

Serves 10–12

For best flavor and texture, assemble cake at least one day ahead.

Ingredients:
4 ounces semisweet or bittersweet chocolate, cut into bits
Small batch Buttercream (page 181)
6 ounces white chocolate, cut into bits
½ cup sieved raspberry preserves
¼ cup Framboise (raspberry liqueur)
8-inch Chocolate Génoise (page 159), baked and cooled
White chocolate shavings made by shaving a block of chocolate (page 188), or scalloped shavings scraped from a pan (pages 189–91)
Handful of fresh raspberries or raspberry candies
1–2 tablespoons confectioners' sugar

Special Equipment:
8-inch corrugated cake circle

1. Combine dark chocolate with 2 tablespoons water in a small bowl. Melt gently in a barely simmering water bath. Or, microwave on MEDIUM (50%) for about 1 minute and 15 seconds. Stir until smooth; set aside to cool to lukewarm. Stir in ¼ cup plus 2 tablespoons of the Buttercream and set aside.

2. Combine white chocolate with 3 tablespoons water in a small bowl. Melt gently in a water bath which has first been brought to a simmer and then turned off for 1 minute. Or, microwave on LOW (30%) for about 1 minute and 30 seconds. Stir until smooth and remove from heat. Let white chocolate mixture cool to lukewarm. Stir into remaining buttercream; set aside.

3. **To Assemble the Cake:** Combine strained raspberry preserves with Framboise.

4. Split Chocolate Génoise horizontally into 3 layers with a serrated knife. Place top layer upside down on the corrugated cake circle. Brush liberally with raspberry syrup. Spread with half of the dark chocolate buttercream. Brush the second génoise layer with raspberry syrup. Place it, moist side down, on first layer. Spread with remaining dark chocolate buttercream. Moisten the third génoise layer with syrup. Place it, moist side down, on the second. Moisten the top with syrup.

5. Be sure assembled cake is level and even on top. If not, press gently with the bottom of a cake pan. The sides of the cake should be symmetrical—all sides should be straight up and down or equally slanted all the way around. If not, correct the leaning tower by pushing on it where necessary to slide layers into place. Ragged edges can be corrected later. Chill until firm, about 15 or 20 minutes.

6. **To Finish Cake:** Trim any ragged edges from cake with a serrated knife. Spread the top and sides of cake with white chocolate buttercream. There is no need to mask cake perfectly. Gently place white chocolate shavings in the soft buttercream all over the top and sides of the cake. Cake may be made to this point up to 3 days in advance. Refrigerate in a closed container, or freeze up to 3 months.

7. Remove from refrigerator about 1 hour in advance of serving to soften textures and enhance flavors. Place fresh or candy raspberries randomly among the shavings. Sieve confectioners' sugar gently over cake.

One Christmas we
hid a dark
chocolate and
raspberry layer
cake under a cloak
of white chocolate
and shavings.

Citrus
Tart

Serves 8–10

Ingredients:
2 cups plus 1 tablespoon sugar
2–3 bright-skinned organic°
 lemons
2 smallish bright-skinned organic°
 oranges
½ cup strained apricot preserves
3–5 tablespoons Kirsch or orange
 liqueur
½ cup Pastry Cream (page 169)
9½-inch Tart Shell (page 164),
 baked and cooled
°Poached non-organic citrus fruit
 with skins left on has a distinctly
 unpleasant chemical flavor and
 smell.

- - -

Try spreading the inside of the
baked tart shell with 2 ounces of
melted bittersweet chocolate instead
of apricot glaze. Chill for about 10
minutes to harden chocolate before
filling with pastry cream and
topping with citrus slices.

1. Combine 2 cups of the sugar with 2 cups water in a small saucepan; stir to moisten sugar. Bring to a simmer. Cover and cook for 2 minutes.

2. Meanwhile, wash and slice lemons and oranges. Cut ⅛ inch thick. You will need 12–14 good orange slices and 24–30 good lemon slices. Add half of the citrus slices to the simmering syrup and poach until tender, 15–20 minutes. Use a slotted spoon to transfer slices to a bowl. Poach remaining slices the same way. Transfer slices and syrup to bowl and let cool completely before using. Fruit may be prepared to this point, covered and refrigerated, 1–2 weeks in advance.

3. In a small saucepan, simmer apricot preserves, remaining 1 tablespoon sugar, and 2–3 tablespoons Kirsch for 1–2 minutes to make a glaze. Brush some of the glaze over the inside of the cooled tart shell. Set aside for 5–10 minutes, or until glaze is set. Reserve leftover glaze.

4. Stir remaining 1–2 tablespoons Kirsch into the Pastry Cream. Spread evenly in the glazed tart shell. Cut each orange slice in half; leave the lemon slices whole. Starting at the outer edge of tart, alternate the slices in concentric circles on top of pastry cream, overlapping slices slightly.

5. Reheat leftover apricot glaze, thinning with liqueur or water if necessary. Brush citrus slices to glaze them. Refrigerate tart unless it will be served within 2–3 hours. Tart is best served within 8 hours.

I do think that the holiday table cries out for fruit, but I don't like to use expensive fresh fruit out of season, as it often disappoints. A bright-colored, tangy fruit tart with poached citrus slices nicely fills the gap.

A show-stopping holiday dessert. Tangy cranberries and crème fraîche in a chocolate cake with a splash of orange or Kirsch.

Cranberry
Christmas Cake

1. Drain cranberries, reserving the syrup. Make liqueur syrup by combining ¼ cup reserved cranberry syrup with the Kirsch. Set aside.

2. Combine chocolate and 3 tablespoons water in small bowl. Place in a barely simmering water bath over low heat. Or, melt in a microwave on MEDIUM (50%) for about 1 minute. Stir until smooth. Let cool to room temperature; set aside.

3. **To Assemble the Cake:** Use a serrated knife to cut the Chocolate Génoise, horizontally, into 3 layers. Turn over the top layer and center it on the corrugated cake circle. (The circle will be ½ inch bigger than the cake all around—this is correct.) Brush the layer with liqueur syrup.

4. Beat ½ cup of the chilled Crème Fraîche until soft peaks form—not too stiff. Fold quickly into reserved chocolate mixture. Immediately—before the mixture has a chance to stiffen—spread the moistened génoise layer with all of the chocolate crème fraîche.

5. Moisten a second génoise layer with syrup. Place it, moist side down, over crème fraîche. Moisten the dry side of top layer with syrup. Distribute enough drained berries over layer to cover completely. (Set aside a few berries for decoration. Let them dry on a paper towel until needed.)

6. Beat remaining crème fraîche with the vanilla and about ¼ cup sugar (or to taste) until almost stiff. Spread a thick layer of whipped crème fraîche over berries. Moisten the third génoise layer with syrup. Top crème fraîche with moistened cake layer, syrup side down. Press down on the cake to compact all layers. Brush the top layer with syrup. Cake may be prepared to this point up to 36 hours in advance. Wrap well and refrigerate until needed.

7. **To Finish the Cake:** Mask the cake with stiff whipped crème fraîche, making sure to cover the excess cardboard all around the cake. Scrape the remaining crème fraîche into a pastry bag fitted with a #9 closed star tip. Pipe a border of large rosettes around the perimeter of the cake. Garnish with chocolate shavings or curls and/or the reserved dried candied cranberries. Refrigerate in a covered container up to 1 day before serving.

Serves 10–12

For best flavor and texture, assemble cake one day ahead.

Ingredients:
Candied Cranberries (page 172), prepared at least 3 days in advance
¼ cup Kirsch
5 ounces semisweet or bittersweet chocolate, cut into pieces
8-inch-round Chocolate Génoise (page 159), baked and cooled
5¼ cups chilled Crème Fraîche (page 169), prepared at least 3 days in advance
1 tablespoon vanilla extract
¼ cup sugar
Chocolate shavings or fans (optional, pages 188–91)

Special Equipment:
9-inch corrugated cake circle
Pastry bag fitted with a large closed star tip (Ateco #9)

- - -

Chestnut Variation: Substitute a can of drained broken candied chestnuts in syrup for the candied cranberries. Use rum or brandy combined with some of the chestnut syrup to moisten the cake.

A holiday vision — cranberry and raspberry pinwheels hide sumptuous white chocolate mousse scented with Kirsch.

Christmas
Bombe

1. **To Make Cranberry-Raspberry Purée:** Rinse and pick over cranberries. Combine with sugar in small nonreactive saucepan. Cover and bring to simmer over medium heat. Uncover, increase heat, and cook, stirring occasionally until about three-fourths of the berries are burst, about 5 minutes. Remove from heat. Press mixture through a medium-fine strainer or food mill along with raspberry preserves. Discard tough dry pulp and raspberry seeds. Let the purée cool completely before using. Purée may be made and refrigerated up to 1 week in advance.

2. **To Assemble and Freeze the Jelly Roll:** Reverse Hot Milk Sponge Cake onto a piece of foil; peel off parchment. Turn sponge carefully over again (use a cookie sheet to aid you if sponge is delicate) so that browned side faces up.

3. Spread all of cranberry-raspberry purée evenly over sponge. Roll up as tightly as possible to form a 16- to 17-inch-long thin jelly roll. Wrap tightly in foil. Freeze at least overnight, or up to 1 month in advance of using.

4. **To Line Bombe with Jelly-Roll Slices:** Remove frozen jelly roll from freezer and unwrap. Trim ragged ends if necessary. Use a sharp serrated knife to cut slices ¼ inch thick. Line mold with slices (see figure on this page), placing 1 slice in the center of bottom of the mold. Next fit 7 (or more) slices around the center, pushing and fitting so that no space is left between slices. Fit the next 9 (or more) slices around mold starting up the sides. Finish by fitting about 10 slices to completely line the mold, always pushing and fitting so that no space is left. Trim slices even with rim of mold if necessary, or just push them so they are flush with rim. Reserve trimmings and remaining slices; return them to freezer until needed. Set lined mold aside.

5. **To Fill the Mold:** Make the White Chocolate Mousse with Kirsch. Turn it immediately into lined mold. Level and smooth surface of mousse. Remove the remaining slices of jelly roll and trimmings from freezer. Set aside just enough slices to completely cover mousse if placed tightly together—*but do not put them in place yet.* Dice any remaining slices and any trimmings with a sharp knife. Scatter diced pieces all over mousse. Fit reserved slices closely together over scattered dice to form the bottom layer of dessert.

6. Place the corrugated cake circle (or a small plate) inside mold and press firmly to level and compact the bombe. Wrap and refrigerate for at least 4 hours before unmolding and serving. Bombe may be completed to this point up to 36 hours in advance of serving, or frozen for up to 2 months.

Serves 10–12

Ingredients:
6 ounces (½ package) fresh
*   cranberries*
¼ cup plus 2 tablespoons sugar
¼ cup raspberry preserves
Hot Milk Sponge Cake (page
*   160), baked and cooled*
White Chocolate Mousse with
*   Kirsch (page 166)*
½ cup strained apricot preserves
2–3 tablespoons minced unsalted
*   pistachios*

Special Equipment:
6-cup bombe mold or bowl with
*   similar capacity (the one I use is*
*   7¼ inches in diameter and 3½*
*   inches deep)*
7-inch round corrugated cake circle

Lemon Variation: Substitute Lemon Curd (page 169) for the cranberry purée, and use White Chocolate Mousse with lemon instead of Kirsch (page 166).

7. **To Unmold, Finish, and Serve:** Invert the mold and rap the edge sharply on counter to release dessert. Simmer strained apricot preserves in a small saucepan for 2–3 minutes to make a glaze. Use a pastry brush to paint entire dessert with glaze. Touch bottom edge of bombe with minced pistachios. Transfer to a serving platter. Refrigerate until serving.

Note

The dessert is not difficult but requires several steps that may be staged over time for your convenience. Make and freeze cranberry jelly roll up to 1 month in advance. Line mold and fill it with mousse the day before you plan to serve it. You will only need a few minutes to unmold and glaze the bombe on the day you serve it.

Chocolate
Fruit Ring

A delicious chocolate pound cake, made crunchy, sweet, and festive with dates and walnuts, is the perfect Christmas substitute for the fruitcake-weary. This is a great picnic cake, a superb gift, or a perfect defrost-in-a-hurry last-minute dessert for unexpected company.

1. Preheat oven to 350°. Spray the pan or pans with a pan release such as Pam.

2. Toss dates and nuts with 2 tablespoons of the flour. Set aside.

3. Sift together remaining flour, cocoa, baking powder, baking soda, and salt; set aside. Dissolve coffee powder in the hot water. Add to buttermilk. (This mixture should be at room temperature. If not, warm it ever so slightly in the microwave or in a bowl of hot water.)

4. In the bowl of an electric mixer, cream the butter well, gradually adding sugar and vanilla. Beat until fluffy. Add eggs, one by one, beating well after each addition. Beating at medium speed, add the dry ingredients in 3 parts, alternating with the buttermilk/coffee mixture in 2 parts. Beat after each addition just until incorporated. Fold in dates and nuts. Turn batter into the pans.

5. Bake until cakes start to shrink away from sides of pan and a toothpick or wooden skewer inserted in the center tests dry, 50–55 minutes.

6. Cool pans on a rack for about 5 minutes. While cakes are still hot, invert and rap the edge of the pans sharply to unmold. Cool on a rack. Cake is delicious fresh, but tastes best after at least a day or two. It remains remarkably delicious for about a week! Wrap cooled cake well in plastic wrap. Store and serve at room temperature, or freeze for up to 3 months. Serve plain, or dust with confectioners' sugar, or accompany with whipped cream.

Makes 2 cakes; each serves 8–10

Ingredients:
3 cups (12 ounces) coarsely chopped dates
1½ cups (7½ ounces) coarsely chopped walnuts
2¼ cups (9 ounces) sifted all-purpose flour
½ cup (2 ounces) sifted unsweetened cocoa powder
½ teaspoon baking powder
½ teaspoon baking soda
1 teaspoon salt
2 tablespoons instant coffee powder
3 tablespoons hot water
1 cup buttermilk
12 ounces sweet butter, at room temperature
2¼ cups sugar
2 teaspoons vanilla extract
6 large eggs
Confectioners' sugar (optional)
Sweetened whipped cream (optional)

Special Equipment:
Two 7- to 8-cup ring molds or loaf pans, preferably with a non-stick coating

- - -

This cake takes its flavor and character from cocoa. It is worth your while to indulge in good-quality, high-fat, Dutch-processed cocoa.

I make mushrooms uniform in size if they are to be served as cookies or petits fours. Otherwise, for decorating the traditional Bûche de Noël *or Yule Log Cake, I love a variety of sizes from tiny to large.*

Meringue Mushrooms

1. Preheat oven to 200°.

2. **To Make the Meringue and Form the Caps and Stems:** In a large bowl of an electric mixer, combine eggs whites and cream of tartar. Beat on medium speed until soft peaks form. Gradually sprinkle in sugar, beating at high speed until very stiff and dull looking.

3. Scrape mixture into pastry bag fitted with plain tip. Pipe about 65 round dome shapes for mushroom caps, and 65 pointy pyramid shapes for mushroom stems. (I usually pipe the stems, which must stand up, first, while the meringue is the stiffest.) Pipe caps and stems any size you wish. I like a variety of sizes for decorating Yule Logs or massing in baskets. Larger, uniform mushrooms make a lovely addition to the cookie platter.

4. Use a fine strainer to dust the piped caps and stems lightly with cocoa. Briskly blow or fan the caps and stems to blur cocoa and make mushrooms look more authentic.

5. Bake for up to 2 hours, or until caps and stems are perfectly dry and crisp. To test for dryness, remove 1 cap from oven; let cool and break open or bite in half. Caps and stems may be prepared, cooled completely, and stored airtight at least 1 month in advance. Or, assemble the mushrooms (see below) before storing.

6. **To Assemble the Mushrooms:** Melt the chocolate in a small bowl placed in a barely simmering water bath on low heat. Stir to hasten melting. Remove from heat when melted and smooth. Or, microwave on MEDIUM (50%) for about 2–2½ minutes. Stir until smooth.

7. Use a small sharp knife to trim off the pointed ends of the stems, creating a flat surface. Use a small knife or spatula to spread chocolate on the flat (bottom) sides of mushroom caps. Attach trimmed end of each stem to chocolate underside of each cap. (Spread chocolate on several caps first and allow the chocolate to harden partially, like glue, before affixing the stems.)

Makes about 65 mushrooms with 1¼-inch caps

Ingredients:
½ cup (3–4) egg whites, at room temperature
¼ teaspoon cream of tartar
1 cup sugar, superfine if possible
About 2 teaspoons unsweetened cocoa powder
2–3 ounces semisweet or bittersweet chocolate, cut into bits

Special Equipment:
2 cookie sheets, lined with parchment paper
Pastry bag fitted with a plain ½-inch tip (Ateco #8)

Brandied Apricot
or Prune and Armagnac
Loaf

Makes 2 cakes;
each serves 8–10

For best flavor, bake at least one
day ahead.

Ingredients:
¼ cup brandy or Armagnac
¾ cup (3½ ounces) minced dried
  apricots or prunes
3 cups (12 ounces) sifted all-
  purpose flour
½ teaspoon baking powder
½ teaspoon baking soda
½ teaspoon salt
8 ounces (2 sticks) sweet butter
2 cup sugar
2 teaspoons vanilla extract
4 large eggs, at room temperature
¾ cup buttermilk, at room
  temperature

Special Equipment:
Two 6-cup loaf pans or ring
  molds, preferrably with non-stick
  coating

1. Preheat oven to 325°. Spray pan(s) well with a pan release such as Pam. Combine liqueur with minced fruit in a small bowl; set aside. Sift together flour, baking powder, baking soda, and salt; set aside.

2. In the bowl of an electric mixer, cream butter, gradually adding sugar and vanilla. Beat until fluffy. Add eggs, one at a time, beating only until each is incorporated. In a small bowl, combine buttermilk with fruit and spirits.

3. Turn mixer to low speed and add dry ingredients, in 3 parts, alternating with buttermilk mixture. Beat only until each addition is incorporated. Turn batter into prepared pan.

4. Bake 55–65 minutes, or until cakes are well browned and shrink from sides of pans. Skewer plunged into the centers of the cakes will test clean.

5. Cool cakes in their pans on a rack for about 10 minutes. Turn out onto a rack and let cool completely. Wrap and store at room temperature overnight before serving. Cake(s) keep, well wrapped and refrigerated, for up to 5 or 6 days. Or freeze for up to 3 months. I like to serve this cake in thin slices, at room temperature. (I keep emergency loaves in the freezer. Either version is delicious with rich vanilla ice cream, and I'm not above pouring warmed caramel sauce over the apricot variation!)

Luscious, dried apricots plumped in brandy or prunes in Armagnac turn a plain buttermilk cake into a very festive gift. Perfect for brunch or teatime, it is easily partnered with whipped cream for a dressier dessert.

Bourbon Pecan Shortbread

Makes about 24 pieces

Ingredients:
8 ounces (2 sticks) sweet butter
½ cup brown sugar
scant ¼ teaspoon salt
1 tablespoon bourbon or brandy
½ teaspoon vanilla extract
2 cups (8 ounces) sifted all-purpose flour
⅔ cup (3⅓ ounces) finely chopped toasted pecans
2 teaspoons granulated sugar

Crunchy, buttery brown sugar shortbread with a splash of bourbon and toasted pecans—I couldn't get enough of this while I was pregnant, and I love it still!

1. Line the bottom and sides of an 8 × 10-inch jelly-roll or 9-inch-square pan with parchment paper so that it overhangs the pan on two sides. In the bowl of an electric mixer, cream butter with brown sugar and salt. Gradually add the bourbon and vanilla. On low speed, add the flour in large spoonfuls, followed by the pecans, mixing only until a homogenous dough forms.

2. Pat dough evenly into lined pan. Texture surface with the tines of a fork or a cake comb, if desired. Refrigerate for at least 30 minutes before baking. Dough may be made to this point, wrapped, and refrigerated up to 3 days, or frozen for up to 3 weeks.

3. Preheat oven to 325°. Remove the shortbread from the refrigerator and prick it well, all over, with a fork. Bake for 55–60 minutes, or until dark golden brown. Check after 20–30 minutes, and prick dough again if it is puffing up and away from pan.

4. Remove shortbread from oven; sprinkle lightly with the granulated sugar. Let cool completely in the pan on a rack. Remove shortbread from pan by lifting the paper liner. Use a large, sharp knife to cut into fingers or squares. Shortbread may be stored in an airtight container, at room temperature for 2–3 months.

American Chocolate Truffles

When I first began making chocolate-dipped truffles (in addition to the simple cocoa-dusted variety), I lost control of the size while trying to perfect the dipping method. The result was an alarmingly large, luscious, soft-centered, chocolate-dipped chocolate truffle. By the time I realized that the truffles were much too large, my customers were totally hooked. Since then, large chocolate truffles have become the American standard. This is a version that can easily be made at home.

1. **To Make Truffle Mixture:** Place chocolate and butter in a medium bowl; set aside. In a saucepan, bring cream to a simmer. Remove from heat and pour over chocolate and butter. Stir gently with a wooden spoon or rubber spatula until chocolate is completely melted and mixture is smooth. Do not whisk or stir briskly or the texture of the truffle will be granular instead of perfectly smooth. Stir in Grand Marnier. Strain mixture into another bowl. Let cool without stirring. Refrigerate until very firm, at least 4 hours, or longer if necessary.

2. **To Form Centers:** Scrape a small ice cream scoop or spoon across the surface of the cold truffle mixture and use your fingertips to help form 1-inch balls. Place balls in a pan and freeze, uncovered, for several hours or overnight, until very hard. Centers may be made to this point, wrapped well, and kept frozen up to 2 months.

3. **To Dip Centers:** Have ready the lined baking sheet and the large shallow pan. Melt chocolate in a clean, dry medium bowl set in a pan of barely simmering water. Or, microwave on MEDIUM (50%) for about 5 minutes. Stir frequently to hasten melting. Be sure that all utensils are dry and that no moisture is introduced into chocolate. When chocolate is smooth and melted and about 115–120°, remove from water bath, if you have used one, and *wipe the bottom of bowl dry.* Pour chocolate into the clean, dry shallow pan.

4. Stand directly in front of pan of melted chocolate. If you are right-handed, place paper-lined baking sheet to the right of melted chocolate and a pan with half of the frozen truffle centers to the left of melted chocolate. With your left hand, pick up 1 frozen truffle center and drop it into chocolate. With the side of your slightly cupped right hand, scoop lots of chocolate on top of center. Push center back and forth in melted chocolate until entirely coated. Wipe your hand on the side of the pan to remove excess chocolate. Quickly pick up the coated center with your wiped fingers and shake off excess chocolate by flicking your hand upward or to the side. Place coated truffle on paper-lined cookie sheet. Repeat dipping procedure, always using one hand to picking up frozen center and the other hand to manipulate it in the melted

Makes about
2 dozen large truffles

Ingredients:
For Truffle Centers:
10 ounces semisweet or bittersweet
chocolate, cut into bits
5 tablespoons sweet butter, cut into
bits
1 cup heavy cream
¼ cup Grand Marnier or other
liqueur of choice
For Dipping:
2 pounds semisweet or bittersweet
chocolate, cut into bits

Special Equipment:
Tiny ice cream scoop or spoon
(bowl of scoop about 1 inch
diameter)
Insta-read meat thermometer or
chocolate thermometer
Cookie sheet lined with parchment
or waxed paper
Large shallow baking pan or jelly-
roll pan

- - -

Use a hair dryer to rewarm melted
chocolate and keep it from cooling
and hardening too fast as you dip
the frozen centers. Keep the heat
away from the frozen centers!

chocolate. Work as quickly as possible. Once the truffle is coated with chocolate, don't hold it any longer than necessary, or the chocolate will harden and the truffle will stick to your hand. When you have finished dipping half of the frozen centers, remove the other half from the freezer and continue to dip. Place tray of dipped truffles in refrigerator to set coating. Once coating has set, remove truffles from paper. Store truffles in a closed container in the refrigerator for up to 2 weeks, or freeze for 3 months.

Note

There are two great secrets to these truffles. First, freezing makes it possible to dip a center that would ordinarily be too soft to dip. The center thaws and becomes incredibly soft and luscious after the coating becomes hard and crisp on the outside. Dipping in untempered° chocolate is the second trick. Untempered chocolate melts instantly in your mouth and releases an explosion of flavor. The finished truffle must be stored cold, however, to keep the untempered chocolate from blooming (discoloring).

°Do not confuse untempered chocolate with "compound coating" or imitation chocolates that do not require tempering. I use high-quality genuine chocolate, but I choose not to temper it. For further remarks about tempering and chocolate see page 25.

Classic Chocolate Truffles

I began Cocolat with these simple, classic, cocoa-dusted dark chocolate truffles. Although we've developed over a hundred variations since then, these are still my favorite! They make a rare and exquisite gift.

1. Melt chocolate with butter and ¼ cup water in a bowl set in a barely simmering water bath. Stir from time to time until mixture is melted and smooth. Or, microwave on MEDIUM (50%), stirring once or twice, for about 2 minutes. Off heat, whisk in the egg yolk just until incorporated. Do not mix or beat more than necessary. Strain truffle mixture into the lined pan and chill, without stirring, until firm, about 1 hour.

2. Remove pan from refrigerator. Unmold and cut into ¾-inch squares. (If chocolate is too firm to cut without breaking, wait 15–20 minutes to soften slightly.)

3. Put cocoa in a shallow dish. Roll truffle squares in cocoa, rounding them between the palms of your hands. Dust your hands with cocoa as necessary to keep truffles from sticking. (If the truffles are too hard to shape, wait until they soften slightly. If they are too soft, refrigerate until firmer.) Truffles look more authentic if they are a little irregular, so don't try for perfectly smooth round balls. Shake truffles gently in a dry strainer, if necessary, to remove excess cocoa.

4. Truffles may be made and stored in an airtight container in the refrigerator for 10 days, or frozen for 3 months. Remove from refrigerator about 30 minutes before serving to soften slightly. Serve heaped in a candy dish, or place each truffle in an individual fluted paper candy cup.

*Makes about
30 bite-size truffles*

Ingredients:
*8 ounces semisweet or bittersweet
    chocolate, cut into bits*
*3 ounces sweet butter, cut into
    pieces*
1 egg yolk
½ cup unsweetened cocoa powder

Special Equipment:
*5 × 9-inch loaf pan, or any
    shallow pan with a similar
    dimension, bottom and sides lined
    with parchment or waxed paper
    or foil*
*Fluted paper candy cups°
    (optional)*

*°Available from kitchenware and
    specialty stores, or by mail order
    (see Resources, page 197).*

Building
Blocks

and

Finishing
Techniques

....

Building Blocks

As much as I love the gloriously simple "one-recipe" chocolate tortes of Chapter One, these treasures represent only one small corner of the dessert chef's domain. Eventually, inevitably, I was drawn to more complex desserts — grand desserts with many layers, toothsome creations with multiple textures and contrasting flavors. To create a masterpiece was only part of the attraction. I enjoyed the prospect of learning a whole array of new recipes and techniques.

In the days when I was making desserts for the charcuterie, every Monday morning I would post a sign describing a special dessert for the following Friday. Often it was a dessert I had never made before. Thursday nights between midnight and 6 A.M. sometimes found me re-making cakes, finally getting it right. This was the beginning of my real pastry education. Somewhere between the quickly mastered chocolate torte that originally seduced me, and my first all-night baking session, a pastry chef was born.

A surprisingly small but important number of recipes form the building blocks from which thousands of classic and new desserts are created. Access to the pastry chef's domain is gained with mastery of the basics: sponges, génoises, custards, ganaches, buttercreams, mousses, meringues, caramelized nuts and liqueur syrups. With this repertoire comes the opportunity to create a symphony of flavors and textures — blending or contrasting them according to mood, desire, or occasion. Dry, crisp, light, dense, moist, cakey, creamy — this is the palette of flavors and textures with which the dessert artist paints.

The artistic metaphor may come as a surprise. Many people think that baking is less creative than other types of cooking because it is measurement-oriented and precise. It is true that no one makes génoise by throwing in the proverbial pinch of this and inspired handful of that. But, how absurd! Great chefs master basic sauces and classic techniques before they begin to invent; artists learn to draw, mix paints, use brushes, and prepare canvases. The pastry chef is no different. Creativity is spurred by a foundation of knowledge and skill.

Master the techniques and tools as you make your favorite recipes over and over. Your skill can make the difference between a dessert that is pretty good and one that is truly superb. Techniques are used again and again, just like basic recipes. If you know how to make caramel for glazing walnuts, you will not have to learn it again for making caramel sauce or praline. If you know how to beat egg whites properly, you've unlocked the secret to success for hundreds of recipes!

With the building blocks, you will be able to create your own desserts. Whether or not you keep a freezer full of cake layers, buttercreams, meringues, caramelized nuts and other components — select the texture and flavors for your dessert by consulting an imaginary larder. Draw a cross-section diagram of the dessert and label all of the layers so that you can envision how it will be assembled. Draw several alternatives and see which one, after all, seems the most appealing. If you are like me, you'll find that you can begin to "taste" a cake once you've sketched it!

GÉNOISE

Makes one 8- or 9-inch round cake,
8-inch square, 11 × 17- or 12 × 16-inch sheet,
or one 6-cup dome

Génoise is the classic, plain butter sponge cake. Its open-grained texture makes it a perfect vehicle for moistening with liqueurs and filling with delicate, rich buttercreams.

3 tablespoons hot clarified° sweet butter (4 tablespoons solid butter yields
3 tablespoons clarified)
1 teaspoon vanilla extract
1 cup (3½ ounces) sifted cake or pastry flour
⅔ cup sugar
4 large eggs
° To clarify: Melt butter gently, without stirring. Skim off foam and use
only the clear yellow oil (butter fat). Discard the milk solids and the
thin milky-looking liquid at the bottom of the container.
Special Equipment:
8- or 9-inch round cake pan, 8-inch square pan, 11 × 17- or 12 × 16-inch
jelly-roll or half-sheet pan, or 6-cup dome or bombe mold
Electric mixer with whisk attachment, if there is a choice

1. Preheat oven to 350°. Prepare pans: Line bottoms of round or square pans with parchment or waxed paper. Line bottom of jelly-roll pan with parchment paper long enough to hang over at 2 opposite ends. Spray dome or bombe mold with pan release such as Pam.

2. Combine clarified butter and vanilla in a small bowl. Keep hot until needed. Rewarm for a few seconds just before using, if necessary—this is important!

3. Combine flour with 3 tablespoons of the sugar. Sift together twice; return to sifter and set aside.

4. In a large heatproof mixing bowl, use a hand-held whisk to combine eggs and remaining sugar. Place bowl in or over a saucepan containing 1–2 inches of barely simmering water. Heat the eggs to lukewarm (check by touching), whisking occasionally. (Alternatively, you may skip the water bath and simply hold the bowl of eggs over a stove burner and whisk vigorously for about 1 minute, until the eggs are warm. This is the quickest, easiest way, but you must whisk eggs continuously to keep them from starting to scramble.)

5. Remove bowl from heat. Beat egg mixture at high speed with an electric mixer until it has cooled, tripled in bulk, and resembles softly whipped cream.

6. Sift about one-third of the combined flour and sugar over whipped eggs. Use your largest rubber spatula to fold the mixture, by hand, quickly but gently until combined. Fold in half of the remaining flour and sugar; fold in the rest. Scoop about 1 cup of batter into another bowl and combine with the hot butter and vanilla, folding with a smaller rubber spatula. When completely combined, use the large spatula to fold butter mixture

completely into batter. Turn batter into pan.

7. Bake until cake shrinks slightly from the edges and top springs back when pressed with fingers: 20–25 minutes for an 8-inch square or 9-inch round pan; 25–30 minutes for an 8-inch round; 15–20 minutes for a jelly-roll sheet; and 40–45 minutes for a bombe mold.

8. The bombe-shaped génoise should be turned out of the pan onto a rack after about 5 minutes of cooling. Run a small knife or spatula around the upper edges first, if necessary, and/or rap the side of the pan sharply, to release. Other shapes may be cooled completely in the pan on a rack. If you have baked a jelly-roll sheet that will be rolled, cover the hot pan, as it comes from the oven, with a sheet of foil. This will steam it slightly and keep it flexible for rolling later on.

9. When cake is cool, run a small knife or spatula around edges to release before unmolding. Always be sure cakes are completely cool before assembling, filling, or frosting. Unmolded génoise may be wrapped well and refrigerated 2 days ahead of using. They may be frozen for up to 3 months.

COFFEE GÉNOISE

Follow the method for plain Génoise, but first dissolve 1 tablespoon powdered instant coffee in 1 teaspoon of water combined with the vanilla. Add it to the clarified butter before proceeding.

CHOCOLATE GÉNOISE

3 tablespoons hot clarified sweet butter (4 tablespoons sweet butter yields
3 tablespoons clarified)
1 teaspoon vanilla extract
½ cup plus 1 tablespoon (2 ounces) sifted cake or pastry flour
⅓ cup plus 1 tablespoon (1½ ounces) sifted unsweetened cocoa powder
4 large eggs
⅔ cup sugar

Follow the method for plain Génoise with 2 modifications: Sift flour and cocoa together twice; warm the eggs with *all* of the sugar.

GÉNOISE TIPS

Mixing Techniques/Avoiding Trouble: For the plain Génoise, I sift some of the sugar with the flour to aerate and separate the grains of flour. This enables the flour to be folded quickly and easily into the delicate egg foam and reduces the risk of having tiny hard flour balls in an otherwise perfect génoise. For the Chocolate Génoise, sifting the cocoa together with the flour accomplishes the same end, so it is not necessary to sift the flour with the sugar.

Combining some of the batter with the hot butter and vanilla before folding the entire batter together is critical. The butter is first absorbed into a small amount of batter, so it is easier to fold into the rest of the batter. Melted butter otherwise has a tendency sink to the bottom of the pan while baking, and form a hard rubbery bottom on the cake.

HOT MILK SPONGE CAKE

Makes one 8- or 9-inch round cake, 8-inch square,
one 11 × 17- or 12 × 16-inch sheet, or one 6-cup dome

I use this sponge cake interchangeably with génoise. It has a closer grain and slightly moister texture, and makes a nice change. It rolls beautifully, staying flexible even after it has cooled flat in the pan. The inclusion of baking powder makes it less delicate in mixing and folding, thus more foolproof than génoise.

¼ cup milk
2 tablespoons sweet butter, cut into small pieces
¾ cup (2⅔ ounces) sifted cake flour
1 teaspoon baking powder
¾ cup sugar
3 large eggs
3 egg yolks
Special Equipment:
8- or 9-inch round cake pan, 8-inch square pan, 11 × 17- or 12 × 16-inch
*   jelly-roll or half-sheet pan, or 6-cup dome or bombe mold*
Electric mixer with whisk attachment, if there is a choice

1. Preheat oven to 400° for jelly-roll sheet or to 350° for other pan sizes. Line the bottom only of round or square pans with a round or square piece of parchment or waxed paper. Line bottom of jelly-roll or half-sheet with parchment or waxed paper so that the paper overhangs the pan at 2 opposite ends. Spray dome or bombe mold with a pan release like Pam.

2. Heat milk with butter in small saucepan over medium heat until butter melts. Reduce heat to low and keep hot, but do not simmer.

3. Sift flour with baking powder twice. Return to sifter and set aside. In a large heatproof bowl, use a hand-held whisk to combine sugar, whole eggs, and egg yolks. Set bowl over or in a pan of barely simmering water. Heat mixture, whisking occasionally, until lukewarm to the touch. (Alternatively, omit water bath and hold bowl directly over a stove burner, whisking vigorously for about 1 minute until eggs are warm. This is the quickest, easiest method, but you must whisk eggs continuously to keep them from starting to scramble.)

4. Transfer bowl to electric mixer and beat at high speed until mixture has cooled, tripled in volume, and has the consistency of thick whipped cream.

5. Sift one-third of flour mixture over batter and fold in gently by hand, using the largest rubber spatula you have. Fold in half of remaining flour; then fold in remainder of flour.

6. Pour the hot milk and butter into batter and fold well, scraping the bottom each time and bringing the batter up the sides of the bowl until you can no longer see traces of liquid. Turn batter into prepared pan.

7. Bake until cake is browned, starts to shrink from the sides of the pan, and springs back when lightly pressed, about 10 minutes at 400° for a jelly-roll pan; 20–35 minutes at 350° for square or round pans; up to 45 minutes in a dome or bombe mold.

8. Except for the dome or bombe shape, cool cake in the pan on a rack. When cakes are cool, run a small knife or spatula around the edges to release before unmolding. Dome should cool for 5 minutes in the pan. Then slide a small knife around the top edge, if necessary, to release; invert and rap the pan against the counter to unmold. Cool on a rack. Always be sure cakes are completely cool before assembling, filling, or frosting. Unmolded sponge cakes may be wrapped well and refrigerated 1–2 days ahead of using. They may be frozen for up to 3 months.

Notes

—Sponge batter is thicker and more stable than génoise. It is not necessary to use the flour and sugar sifting technique, or the butter and batter technique that I use for génoise.
—Unlike génoise, the sponge sheet is very flexible. It is not necessary to wrap or steam it in order to roll it after it is cool.
—Sponge baked in a thin sheet usually forms a golden brown "skin" on the surface. The skin may be left on or scraped off. I usually take it off only if it is blistered and loose by slipping a long serrated knife between the skin and the cake. Alternatively, the sponge sheet can be inverted on a sheet of plastic wrap while it is still very slightly warm. When cool and ready to use, turn it right side up. When the plastic wrap is peeled away, the skin will come with it!

LADYFINGERS

Makes enough to line one 8-inch mold or eight 3-inch petite charlottes
¾ cup (2⅔ ounces) sifted cake flour
3 large eggs, separated
½ cup granulated or superfine sugar
1 teaspoon vanilla extract
⅛ teaspoon cream of tartar
¼ cup confectioners' sugar
Special Equipment:
For an 8-inch Charlotte:
Pastry bag fitted with a plain tip, Ateco #9 (⅝-inch opening)
Large baking sheet
Parchment paper to line the baking sheet, traced with a 6 × 12-inch
*   rectangle and one or two 7-inch circles, depending on dessert recipe*
8-inch springform pan or cheesecake pan with removable bottom

For 8 Petite Charlottes:

Pastry bag fitted with a plain tip, Ateco #8 (½-inch opening)

2 baking sheets (one must be at least 16 inches long)

Parchment paper to line baking sheets: one traced with 4 rectangular bands, each 16 inches long and 2 inches wide (spaced ½ inch apart), the second traced with 8 circles, each 2¼ inches in diameter.

Cardboard mailing tube, 3 inches in diameter and at least 16 inches long

1. Preheat oven to 400°. Turn traced parchments upside down on baking sheets so that the tracing can be seen, but so that the pencil or ink will not transfer onto the ladyfingers.

2. Place the sifted flour in a strainer, set over a small bowl. In a large bowl, whisk egg yolks with ¼ cup granulated sugar and the vanilla by hand, until pale and thick.

3. In a separate clean, dry mixing bowl, beat egg whites and cream of tartar at medium speed until soft peaks form. Gradually sprinkle in the remaining ¼ cup granulated sugar, beating at high speed until stiff but not dry. By hand, with the largest rubber spatula you own, fold one-third of the egg whites into the yolk mixture to lighten it. Scrape half of the remaining whites onto the batter and sift half of the flour over them. Carefully fold in whites and flour to retain stiffness and volume. Repeat the process, scraping the remaining whites onto the batter, sifting in the rest of the flour, and folding again. Scrape the batter into the pastry bag.

4. **To Pipe Ladyfingers for an 8-inch Charlotte:** Place parchment-lined baking sheet in front of you. Pipe parallel ladyfingers quite close to each other—only ¼ to ⅜ inches apart—within the rectangular guideline traced on the parchment. Each one will be about 6 inches long. Ladyfingers may be piped straight

or slanted at an angle, depending on the desired effect.

Ladyfingers will spread and touch each other during baking. This is correct. Make one or two disks, or layers, by piping or spreading remaining batter within traced 7-inch circles. Sift the confectioners' sugar over ladyfingers and disks. Bake for 10–12 minutes, or until golden. Cool in the pan on a rack. Ladyfingers may be made a day in advance. Wrap and store at room temperature, or freeze for up to 3 months. To continue recipe, skip to Step 7.

5. **To Pipe Ladyfingers for 8 Petite Charlottes:** Place baking sheet lined with banded parchment in front of you. Pipe 4 separate rows of zigzags within the rectangular bands.

Zigzags should have about ¼ inch of open space between them; as they bake, they will puff up and attach to one another. Dust with the confectioners' sugar. Bake for 8–10 minutes, until golden. Meanwhile, pipe remaining batter in 8 spirals to form 2¼-inch disks on the second parchment-lined baking sheet. Dust with confectioners' sugar and set aside. As soon as the first sheet is baked, remove it from the oven. Bake second sheet for about the same time. Cool ladyfingers in their pans on a rack. To continue recipe, skip to Step 8.

6. To Pipe Individual Ladyfingers: Line a baking sheet with parchment. Pipe batter into any size and length desired. For individual ladyfingers that are dryer and crisper, reduce oven temperature to 350° and bake 10–15 minutes, or until golden brown. Place the pan on a rack to cool.

7. To Line the Mold for an 8-inch Charlotte: Have ready the 8-inch springform or cheesecake pan and the baked, cooled ladyfingers still attached to the parchment paper. Cut the 12-inch strip of attached ladyfingers lengthwise in half to make two 12-inch strips each 3 inches wide.

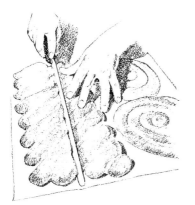

Turn ladyfingers upside down. Peel away parchment paper. Line the inside sides of the pan with the strips of attached ladyfingers

by fitting first one strip (cut side of the strip against the bottom of pan, rounded ends of the ladyfingers pointing upward) and then the second, around the inside of the pan. The curved surface of the ladyfingers should touch the sides of the pan while the flat surface faces inward. Trim if necessary to make a tight fit where the 2 strips meet each other. (The ladyfingers will usually flex and curve where each one joins the other. If they are very crisp and tend to break apart, turn to the charlotte recipe that you are

making and brush the back, flat sides of the ladyfinger strips with the liquor mixture *before* lining the mold. Moistening the ladyfingers may help to soften the strips. In any case, if the ladyfingers break apart, go ahead and line the pan with them anyway—when the filling is poured the ladyfingers will be held nicely in place.)

Line the bottom of the mold with the 7-inch ladyfinger disk, trimmed to fit if necessary. Reserve the second ladyfinger disk, if you have made one, to use as a second layer inside the charlotte (see individual recipe).

8. To Line the Molds for 8 Petite Charlottes: Have ready the baked and cooled ladyfingers and the mailing tube. To make eight 3-inch charlotte molds: Using a sharp serrated knife or single-edged razor blade, cut mailing tube into 8 lengths, each 2 inches long. Cut strips of parchment or waxed paper to line the inside sides of the little molds (this will keep the ladyfingers from actually touching the cardboard and enable you to re-use the molds in the future). Leave the ladyfingers attached to the parchment. Cut each 16-inch ladyfinger zigzag into two 8-inch lengths. Turn upside down and peel away parchment. Lift each 8-inch strip, and curl it to fit inside the cardboard tubes,

curved sides against sides of cardboard mold and flat surfaces facing inward. Trim if necessary to make a tight fit. The ladyfingers will usually flex and curve where each one joins the other. (If they are very crisp and tend to break, turn to the charlotte recipe you are making and brush the flat sides of the ladyfinger strips with the liquor mixture *before* lining the mold. Moistening the ladyfingers may help to soften the strips. In any case, if the ladyfingers break, go ahead and line the pan with them anyway—when the filling is poured the ladyfingers will be held nicely in place.) When all of the molds are lined, fit the bottoms with the ladyfinger disks trimmed to fit snugly.

CHOCOLATE LADYFINGERS

½ cup plus 3 tablespoons (2⅓ ounces) sifted cake flour

2 tablespoons (½ ounce) sifted unsweetened cocoa powder

3 large eggs, separated

⅔ cup granulated or superfine sugar

1 teaspoon vanilla extract

⅛ teaspoon cream of tartar

Additional unsweetened cocoa powder for dusting (optional)

Resift flour and cocoa together twice. Follow the master recipe, but instead of ¼ cup, whisk ⅓ cup granulated sugar with egg yolks. Use the remaining ⅓ cup in step 3. You may sift a little extra cocoa over baked, cooled ladyfingers, if desired.

CHOCOLATE SOUFFLÉ PASTRY

Makes one thin 11 × 17- or 12 × 16-inch sheet or three thin 9-inch
*   rounds*

6 ounces semisweet or bittersweet chocolate, cut into small pieces

2 teaspoons instant coffee powder (not freeze-dried), dissolved in 3
*   tablespoons hot water*

1 teaspoon vanilla extract

6 large eggs

¼ teaspoon cream of tartar

¾ cup sugar

3–4 tablespoons unsweetened cocoa powder, for dusting

Special Equipment:

11 × 17- or 12 × 16-inch jelly-roll or half-sheet pan lined with parchment
*   or waxed paper cut long enough to hang over opposite ends, or cookie*
*   sheets lined with parchment traced with three 9-inch circles*

1. Preheat oven to 375°. Have the baking sheets lined as instructed. Turn traced parchments upside down so that tracing can be seen, but so that pencil or ink will not transfer onto pastry.

2. Melt chocolate with coffee in a small bowl set in a pan of barely simmering water. Stir frequently until completely melted and smooth. Or, microwave on MEDIUM (50%) for about 1 minute and 15 seconds. Stir until smooth. Stir in vanilla. Set aside and keep warm.

3. Separate eggs. Place egg whites and cream of tartar in a clean, dry mixing bowl. Beat egg whites on medium speed until soft peaks form. Gradually sprinkle in the sugar, beating at high speed until whites are stiff but not dry.

4. Whisk egg yolks into melted chocolate mixture. Fold one-fourth of egg whites into chocolate mixture to lighten it. Add remaining egg whites and fold gently but completely. Spread batter evenly in prepared pan. (If you are baking 9-inch rounds, divide batter equally among traced circles and spread evenly. You must spread all 3 rounds right away, but they can be baked in 2 or 3 shifts if your oven is not big enough.)

5. Bake for 10 minutes. Reduce oven temperature to 350°.

Bake for 5 minutes, until the pastry is firm to the touch. Cool pastry completely in the pan on a rack. Pastry may be completed, left in the pan, covered well, and refrigerated up to 2 days ahead, or it may be frozen for up to 3 months.

6. To unmold, follow individual recipe instructions. Otherwise run a small knife or metal spatula around edges of pastry to release it from pan. Dust a sheet of foil with sifted cocoa. Invert pan onto foil. Remove pan and peel off the paper.

MERINGUE LAYERS

Makes two 8- or 9-inch layers

3 egg whites, at room temperature

⅛ teaspoon cream of tartar

¾ cup sugar (superfine, if possible)

Special Equipment:

Baking sheet lined with a sheet of parchment paper traced heavily with
*   two 8- or 9-inch circles (see individual recipe)*

Pastry bag fitted with a plain Ateco #5 tip (optional)

1. Preheat oven to 250°. Turn the parchment paper upside down on baking sheet so that tracing can still be seen but pencil or ink will not transfer onto meringue.

2. Combine egg whites and cream of tartar in a clean, dry mixing bowl. Beat at medium speed until soft peaks form. Gradually sprinkle in sugar, beating at high speed until meringue is very stiff.

3. Scrape meringue into the pastry bag. Starting from center of each traced circle, pipe a widening spiral of meringue until it fills in whole circle. Or, omit pastry bag and spread meringue in the circles with a metal spatula.

4. Bake for 1–2 hours, or until meringue layers are perfectly light, dry, and crisp. If possible, allow meringues to cool in turned-off oven with door closed. If meringues are not light, perfectly dry, and crisp, bake in a 200° oven until they are. Meringues may be made, cooled completely, and stored airtight at room temperature for up to 2 months.

COFFEE MERINGUE LAYERS

Follow the master recipe above, but stir 2 teaspoons powdered instant coffee into the sugar before sprinkling it over egg whites.

AZTEC MERINGUE LAYERS

Makes two 9-inch layers

⅓ cup (1⅓ ounces) finely ground pecans

1 teaspoon instant coffee powder

1 teaspoon flour

¼ teaspoon ground cinnamon

3 egg whites, at room temperature

⅛ teaspoon cream of tartar

¾ cup superfine sugar

Special Equipment:

Baking sheet lined with a sheet of parchment paper traced with two 9-inch circles

Pastry bag fitted with Ateco #3 plain tip (optional)

1. Preheat oven to 250°. Turn traced parchment upside down on baking sheet so that tracing can still be seen, but so that the pencil or ink will not transfer onto meringues.

2. Combine pecans, instant coffee, flour, and cinnamon; set aside.

3. In a clean, dry mixing bowl, combine egg whites and cream of tartar. Beat at medium speed until soft peaks form. Slowly sprinkle in sugar, beating at high speed until meringue is very stiff.

4. Fold pecan mixture into meringue. Scrape into pastry bag. Fill in traced rounds by piping spirals of meringue, starting at the center of the circle and working toward the edges. Or, skip the pastry bag and divide meringue equally between the 2 circles, spreading it as evenly as possible with a spatula.

5. Bake meringue layers for about 1 hour. Turn heat off and leave meringue in the oven (do not open the door) for as long as possible, until meringues are completely dry and crisp. If they are not, bake in 200° oven until they are. Slide a spatula gently under cooled meringue layers to release. Cooled meringue can be stored airtight for 2 months at room temperature.

COFFEE-ALMOND MERINGUE

Makes two 9-inch layers

Follow recipe and instructions for Aztec Meringue, substituting ground almonds (either blanched or with skins left on) for pecans, increasing instant coffee powder to 1½ teaspoons, and deleting cinnamon.

CHOCOLATE TART PASTRY

Makes enough for one 9½-inch fluted tart shell or one cheesecake crust

3 ounces sweet butter

½ cup sugar

¾ teaspoon vanilla extract

⅛ teaspoon salt

¼ cup plus 2 tablespoons (1½ ounces) sifted unsweetened cocoa powder

¾ cup (3 ounces) pastry or all-purpose flour

Special Equipment:

9½-inch fluted tart pan with removeable bottom

1. **To Make Dough in a Food Processor:** Combine butter, sugar, vanilla, and salt. Process until mixture is creamy. Add cocoa and process until mixture is a dark, smooth paste. Add flour and pulse just until incorporated but still crumbly. For cheesecake crust proceed with recipe instructions, page 67. For tart

crust, pulse a few more times to form a dough and proceed with steps 2–4.

To Make Dough with an Electric Mixer: Cream together butter, sugar, vanilla, and salt just until smooth. Add cocoa and mix just to a dark, smooth paste. Add flour and mix just until barely incorporated but still crumbly. For cheesecake crust proceed with recipe instructions, page 67. For tart crust, mix a few seconds longer to form a dough and proceed with steps 2–4.

2. Turn dough out onto a piece of plastic wrap and press into a large flat disk. Wrap and refrigerate at least 45 minutes, or until ready to use. Pastry may be completed to this point up to 3 days ahead, or frozen for up to 6 months.

3. **To Line Pan and Bake Tart Shell:** Remove chilled dough from refrigerator. If it is hard, let stand for 20–30 minutes, or until it is rollable but still firm. Roll out dough between 2 pieces of plastic wrap until about ⅛ inch thick and roughly 11 inches in diameter. Peel away top sheet of plastic, pick up the bottom sheet, and invert dough into tart pan. Line pan with dough, using plastic wrap on top side to ease dough carefully into corners. Pinch off dough at upper rim. (If dough becomes too soft to handle, stop and refrigerate it for 5–10 minutes before continuing.) Peel away plastic wrap; check to see that pan is evenly lined, patching and correcting as necessary. Cover and refrigerate the tart shell for at least 30 minutes before baking. Tart shell may be made to this point up to 3 days in advance (unless dough was already stored for 3 days) or frozen for up to 6 months unless it was previously frozen.

4. Preheat oven to 375°. Prick bottom of tart pastry all over with a fork. Bake for 12–14 minutes, until it is set around edges but may still look slightly wet or undone in the center— this is OK. Cool on a rack. Always be sure that tart shells are completely cool before glazing, assembling, or filling.

SWEET TART PASTRY

Makes enough pastry for two 9½-inch single-crust tarts

1 whole egg or 2 yolks

½ teaspoon vanilla extract

¼ cup sugar

Grated zest of 1 lemon (optional)

2⅔ cups (11 ounces) all-purpose or pastry flour

⅛ teaspoon salt

8 ounces (2 sticks) sweet butter, cold and firm, but not hard

Special Equipment:

Two 9½-inch fluted tart pans with removable bottoms

1. In a bowl, mix the egg, vanilla, sugar, and lemon zest with a fork; set aside.

2. **To Make the Pastry in a Food Processor:** Combine flour and salt in food processor fitted with a metal blade. Process for a second or two just to distribute salt. Cut butter into small

pieces. Add to processor and pulse on and off until butter and flour resemble coarse meal. Dribble in egg mixture and pulse on and off till the dough starts to gather into a mass.

To Make Pastry in Electric Mixer: Stir flour and salt together in the mixer bowl. Make a well in the center. Cut the butter into small pieces. Place pieces in the well and pour egg mixture over it. Mix at medium-slow speed until dough starts to gather into a mass.

3. Remove dough and push together into a mass. Divide into 2 equal pieces. Press each into a flat disk. Wrap each disk in plastic wrap; refrigerate until ready to use, or at least 45 minutes, before rolling. Pastry may be completed to this point 2 days ahead, or frozen for up to 6 months.

4. **To Line Pan and Bake Tart Shell:** Roll out pastry between 2 sheets of plastic wrap until about ⅛ inch thick and roughly 11 inches in diameter. (If dough is too cold to roll, wait a few minutes until it softens. Avoid pounding, working, or kneading it.)

Once rolled, peel away top sheet of plastic. Use bottom sheet to lift pastry and invert it into tart pan. Line pan with pastry, using sheet of plastic on top to help with this process. Do not stretch dough; ease it carefully into corners. Pinch off dough at upper rim of pan. Peel away plastic wrap and check to see that sides of tart shell are even. Patch as necessary by pressing excess bits of dough in place. (If pastry becomes too soft to handle at any point, or if plastic wrap won't peel away, stop and refrigerate pan and dough until you can handle it. Once chilled, the plastic will readily peel away.) Chill lined pan for at least 30 minutes.

5. Preheat oven to 400°.

6. Prick bottom of chilled shell all over with a fork. Bake for 15–20 minutes, until golden brown. Check the pastry after 7 or 8 minutes; if the bottom has puffed up, prick again with a fork or skewer to deflate it. Cool tart shell on a rack. Always be sure that shell is absolutely cool before glazing, filling, or assembling in any way.

CHOCOLATE MARQUISE

Makes about 4 cups

Don't ask me why this very rich, buttery chocolate mousse is especially delicious served cold, in thin slices, as opposed to being eaten with a spoon. It just is. And, I wouldn't be surprised if crème anglaise weren't invented just to accompany it, although I also serve it with a quicker Fresh Cream Sauce (page 170) or just plain whipped cream.

Chocolate Marquise is a great standby. It is almost too easy to make and indescribably elegant to eat. I use it as the base for my Tricolor Mousse, as well as the Valentine Marquise, and Pâté Trompé.

10 ounces semisweet or bittersweet chocolate, cut into bits
4 ounces (1 stick) sweet butter, cut into small pieces
2 teaspoons powdered (not freeze-dried) instant coffee, dissolved in 2 teaspoons water
4 large eggs, separated
⅛ teaspoon cream of tartar
2 tablespoons sugar

1. Melt chocolate and butter together in a medium bowl placed in a pan of barely simmering water. Or, melt in a microwave on MEDIUM (50%) for about 2 minutes and 30 seconds. Stir from time to time to hasten melting. When chocolate is melted and smooth, whisk in dissolved coffee powder and egg yolks. Remove from heat and set aside.

2. In a clean, dry mixing bowl, beat egg whites and cream of tartar at medium speed until soft peaks form. Gradually sprinkle in the sugar, beating at high speed until stiff but not dry. Fold one-fourth of eggs whites into chocolate mixture to lighten it. Fold remaining whites into mixture until completely incorporated. Scrape mousse immediately into prepared mold (see individual recipes). Refrigerate for at least 4 hours to set before unmolding. Marquise may be completed, covered, and refrigerated 2 days ahead of serving, or it may be frozen for up to 2 months.

CHOCOLATE VELVET MOUSSE

Makes about 4½ cups

Yet another favorite mousse, with a texture all its own. This one, without butter, is lightened with egg whites and made rich with cream. It is stiff enough to slice and stars in Chocolate Ruffle Torte, Chocolate Banana Charlotte, etc.

12 ounces semisweet or bittersweet chocolate, cut into bits
2 teaspoons powdered instant coffee (not freeze-dried), dissolved in ¼ cup water
¼ cup Curacao or rum
2 egg yolks
4 egg whites, at room temperature
¼ teaspoon cream of tartar
2 tablespoons sugar
½ cup heavy cream

1. Melt chocolate, dissolved coffee, and Curaçao in a medium bowl set in a barely simmering pan of water. Stir frequently to hasten melting. Or, melt in a microwave on MEDIUM (50%) for about 2 minutes and 15 seconds. Stir until smooth. When mixture is warm and smooth, whisk in egg yolks and combine well. Remove from heat and set aside.

2. In a clean, dry mixing bowl, beat egg whites and cream of tartar on medium speed until soft peaks form. Gradually sprinkle in 2 tablespoons sugar, beating on high speed until stiff but not dry. Fold one-fourth of the egg whites into chocolate

mixture to lighten it. Scrape all of the remaining whites on top of mousse and set aside while you beat the cream. Beat cream until it holds its shape softly (do not beat until stiff).

3. Scrape whipped cream over egg whites and chocolate. Fold together just until incorporated. Turn the mousse immediately into lined mold (see individual recipes).

WHITE CHOCOLATE MOUSSE
Makes about 4 cups

My favorite creamy, rich white chocolate mousse is soft enough to eat with a spoon from a pretty dessert dish, but firm enough to slice when assembled into a dramatic dessert. For a lighter, more ethereal version for spooning only, see White Chocolate Mousse II (below).

9 ounces white chocolate°, cut into very small pieces

1½ cups heavy cream

°*Use Nestlé's, Tobler, Lindt, or another high-quality brand—do not use white compound, summer coating, or any other "white chocolate" that is not made with cocoa butter. See White Chocolate, page 29.*

1. Place chocolate and ¼ cup plus 1 tablespoon water in a medium-size heatproof bowl. Bring 1 inch of water to a simmer in a wide skillet. Turn the heat off and wait 30 seconds. Set bowl of chocolate in pan of hot water. Stir white chocolate mixture constantly until melted and smooth. Or, melt in a microwave on LOW (30%) for about 2 minutes. Stir until smooth and completely melted. (White chocolate is very fragile and burns easily. Do not turn the heat on again under the skillet unless absolutely necessary.) Let cool away from heat until a small dab on your upper lip feels slightly cool, about 85°.

2. Whip the cream until soft peaks form—not too stiff. Carefully fold cream into cooled white chocolate mixture; the mousse will seem very soft. Scrape mousse immediately into lined mold, mousse glasses, or onto or into the dessert that it will enhance. (Mousse sets quickly and should not be spread or manipulated too much after it is completed.) Cover and refrigerate up to 2 days, or freeze for up to 2 months.

Kirsch or Liqueur Variation: Substitute 3 tablespoons Kirschwasser or other liqueur for 3 tablespoons of the water. Melt the chocolate with the Kirsch and remaining 2 tablespoons water.

WHITE CHOCOLATE MOUSSE II
Makes about 6 cups

A lighter textured mousse for filling chocolate dessert cups or eating from pretty dessert glasses with fresh berries. This one is not stiff enough to slice.

9 ounces white chocolate°, very finely chopped

5 tablespoons water, or 2 tablespoons water mixed with 3 tablespoons liqueur

1½ cups heavy cream

3 egg whites, at room temperature

⅛ teaspoon cream of tartar

°*Use Nestlé's, Tobler, Lindt, or another high-quality brand—do not use white compound, summer coating, or any other "white chocolate" that is not made with cocoa butter. See White Chocolate, page 29.*

1. Place chocolate and water in a medium-size heatproof bowl. Bring 1 inch of water to a simmer in a wide skillet. Turn the heat off and wait 30 seconds. Set bowl of chocolate in hot water. Stir white chocolate mixture constantly until melted and smooth. Or, melt in a microwave on LOW (30%) for about 2 minutes. Stir until smooth and completely melted. (White chocolate is very fragile and burns easily. Do not turn the heat on again under the skillet unless absolutely necessary.) Remove chocolate from heat and let cool until a small dab on your upper lip feels slightly cool, about 85°.

2. Meanwhile, whip the cream until soft peaks form—not too stiff. Set aside.

3. In a clean, dry mixing bowl, beat egg whites and cream of tartar until stiff but not dry. Fold one-fourth of beaten egg whites into cooled white chocolate. Scrape remaining egg whites and whipped cream on top of white chocolate mixture. Fold together until combined. Turn the mousse immediately into dessert glasses or chocolate dessert cups (page 105). Cover and refrigerate for up to 1 day in advance.

MOCHA MOUSSE
Makes about 4 cups

This is one of the nicest milk chocolate desserts that I know. It is a delicious mousse all by itself, and an absolutely wonderful ingredient in more elaborate desserts like the Tricolor Mousse, page 54.

9 ounces milk chocolate°, cut into very small pieces

4–5°° teaspoons powdered instant coffee (not freeze-dried), dissolved in ¼ cup plus 1 tablespoon water

1½ cups heavy cream

°*The flavor of this mousse relies on only two ingredients, one of which is the chocolate. Don't cut corners. Choose a brand of milk chocolate that you especially enjoy nibbling! I like Callebaut, Lindt, Tobler, or Valrhona.*

°°*Use the smaller amount of coffee if the mousse is to be eaten alone, as a mousse. Use the greater amount of coffee if the mousse will be used with other stronger elements in a dessert such as Tricolor Mousse, page 54. In any case, remember that different brands of milk chocolate vary in flavor so the amount of coffee that will be perfect will also vary. The first time you taste this mousse, ask yourself whether the flavor of the coffee is just right, or whether a small adjustment should be made next time.*

1. Place chocolate and coffee in a medium-size heatproof bowl. Bring 1 inch of water to a simmer in a wide skillet. Turn the heat off and wait 30 seconds. Set bowl of chocolate in pan of hot water. Stir chocolate mixture constantly until melted and smooth. Or, melt in a microwave on LOW (30%) for about 2 minutes and 30 seconds. Stir until smooth and completely melted. (Milk chocolate is very fragile and burns easily. Do not turn the heat on again under the skillet unless absolutely necessary.) Remove chocolate from heat and let cool until a small dab on your upper lip feels slightly cool, about 85°.

2. Whip cream until soft peaks form—not too stiff. Fold carefully into cooled milk chocolate mixture; the mousse should seem very soft. Scrape mousse immediately into lined mold, mousse glasses, or onto or into the dessert that it will enhance. Mousse sets quickly and should not be spread or manipulated too much after it is completed. Cover and refrigerate up to 2 days, or freeze for up to 2 months.

LEMON MOUSSE

Makes 7 cups
1¾–2¼* teaspoons unflavored gelatin
½ cup fresh lemon juice
Grated zest of 1 lemon
1 cup sugar
4 large eggs, separated
1 teaspoon vanilla extract
¼ teaspoon cream of tartar
1 cup heavy cream
*Use 2¼ teaspoons if the mousse must be stiff enough to unmold and slice (see Lemon Bombe, page 70). Use the smaller amount of gelatin if mousse will be served in glasses and eaten with a spoon.

1. Sprinkle gelatin over 3 tablespoons cold water in a small container. Set aside for at least 5 minutes, without stirring, to soften gelatin.

2. Bring lemon juice, zest, and ½ cup sugar to a simmer in a small nonreactive saucepan.

3. Place egg yolks in a small bowl. Slowly pour hot lemon mixture over them, whisking constantly. Return mixture to the saucepan and cook over gentle heat, stirring constantly and reaching all over the bottom of the pan to avoid scorching. Cook and stir until mixture just begins to simmer. Remove from heat. Pour through a strainer into a clean bowl. (If you prefer flecks of lemon zest in your mousse, do not strain.) Whisk in softened gelatin and vanilla. Let cool to room temperature before completing mousse.

4. In a clean, dry mixing bowl, beat egg whites and cream of tartar on medium speed until soft peaks form. Gradually sprinkle remaining ½ cup sugar over whites, beating on high speed until whites are stiff but not dry. Fold one-fourth of beaten whites into lemon mixture. Scrape remaining whites on top of mixture; set aside while you beat cream.

5. Immediately beat cream in the same bowl used for egg whites. Beat until soft peaks form (do not overbeat or mousse will have a granular texture). Fold beaten cream and egg whites into lemon mixture until completely combined. Turn mousse immediately into dessert glasses or prepared dessert mold (as for Lemon Bombe, page 70). Cover and refrigerate.

BAVARIAN CREAMS

Two things contribute to the success of a Bavarian cream: First, it is essential that the cream be softly whipped, not stiff, when it is folded into the custard base. Otherwise, the folding process will continue to stiffen the cream until it is overbeaten, and the Bavarian cream will have a granular texture. Second, the custard base must be at the correct temperature and consistency when the cream is folded into it. If the base is warm, the whipped cream will melt and lose body. If the base is cool but has not begun to thicken from the gelatin, it will be thin and prone to sink to the bottom of the bowl as you try to fold the cream into it. Whipped cream should be folded into the Bavarian when the base is cold and thickened—just beginning to set from the gelatin.

The custard base cools fastest in a stainless bowl set into a larger bowl of ice and water, in the refrigerator. Whisk frequently, scraping the cold sides of the bowl to redistribute the mixture and keep it from setting around the edge. It may be ready in as little as 10 minutes; it will take longer if the bowl is crockery or glass. Meanwhile, whip the cream and have it ready in the refrigerator—so it need only be given a few last strokes with a whisk before folding.

If the custard base chills for too long, it will set. If this happens, do not try to fold the cream into it anyway. Instead, set the bowl of jelled custard in a barely simmering water bath for a few seconds and whisk the mixture continuously to melt the gelatin slightly and soften the custard.

VANILLA BAVARIAN CREAM

Makes 4½–5 cups
1¾ teaspoons unflavored gelatin
1 cup milk
4 egg yolks
¼ cup plus 2 tablespoons sugar
1¼ cups heavy cream
2 teaspoons vanilla extract

1. Sprinkle gelatin over 3 tablespoons cold water in a small container. Let stand for at least 5 minutes to soften gelatin, or until needed.

2. In a small nonreactive saucepan, scald milk over medium-low heat.

3. Meanwhile, beat egg yolks with sugar until pale and thick. Dribble hot milk over yolk mixture, whisking constantly, until all milk has been added. Return mixture to the saucepan and cook over medium-low heat, stirring contantly with a wooden spoon and reaching all over bottom of pan to avoid scorching. Cook only until custard coats the spoon slightly (about 175° to 180°); do not allow to simmer or boil.

4. As soon as custard has reached the proper consistency, pour through a strainer into a clean bowl set in a larger bowl of ice water. Whisk in softened gelatin and vanilla. Let mixture cool in ice water, in the refrigerator, stirring frequently, until cold, thick, and syrupy but not yet set, 10 minutes or more. (See Bavarian Creams, page 167.)

5. In a mixing bowl, beat cream until soft peaks form (do not beat cream stiff or Bavarian will be granular). Fold into custard. Immediately turn the Bavarian into prepared charlotte(s) or dessert glasses. Cover and refrigerate.

COFFEE BAVARIAN CREAM

Follow recipe for Vanilla Bavarian Cream, but substitute 2½ teaspoons powdered (not freeze-dried) instant coffee, dissolved in 2 teaspoons water, for the vanilla.

CARAMEL BAVARIAN CREAM

Makes about 5 cups
2 teaspoons unflavored gelatin
4 egg yolks
⅔ cup sugar
1¾ cups heavy cream
1 cup milk
½ teaspoon vanilla extract
1 tablespoon plus 1 teaspoon rum (preferably dark)

1. Sprinkle gelatin over 3 tablespoons cold water in a small container. Let stand for at least 5 minutes to soften gelatin, or until needed.

2. Meanwhile, in a medium bowl, whisk egg yolks and ⅓ cup sugar until pale and thick. Set aside.

3. In a small saucepan, scald ½ cup cream. Set aside.

4. Caramelize the sugar: In a 1½–2 quart saucepan, combine the remaining ⅓ cup sugar with 2 tablespoons water. Stir to moisten the sugar. Cover and bring to a simmer. Uncover and wash down any sugar crystals clinging to sides of pan with a pastry brush dipped in water. Cover and cook for 2 minutes to dissolve sugar. Uncover and cook, without stirring, until the syrup turns a pale amber. (The color of the syrup is deceptive in the saucepan. Spoon a drop or two, periodically, onto a white saucer to judge the color more accurately.) Watch carefully.

Swirl pan gently, and continue to cook and test until drops of syrup are medium dark amber in color. Off heat, immediately pour the hot cream into caramel, stirring briskly with a whisk. Caramel will bubble up and steam dramatically. Be careful, but keep stirring, reaching all over the bottom of the pan until caramel completely dissolves into cream. Add milk to caramel sauce and bring to a simmer over medium heat.

5. Whisk a small amount of hot caramel mixture into beaten yolks and sugar. Continue adding sauce to yolks, whisking constantly. Return mixture to saucepan, and cook over medium heat, stirring constantly with a wooden spoon, until the mixture thickens slightly, about 175° to 180°. Do not allow to simmer or boil.

6. Pour custard immediately through a fine strainer into a clean bowl set in a larger bowl of ice water. Stir in softened gelatin until dissolved. Stir in vanilla and rum. Cool mixture in ice water, in the refrigerator, stirring frequently, until cold, thick, and syrupy but not yet set, 10 minutes or more. (See Bavarian Creams, page 167).

7. Beat remaining 1¼ cups cream until soft peaks form (do not beat stiff or Bavarian will be granular). Fold into caramel custard. Immediately turn Bavarian into prepared charlotte(s) or dessert glasses. Cover and refrigerate.

BANANA BAVARIAN CREAM

Makes 4½–5 cups
2 teaspoons unflavored gelatin
¾ cup puréed, very ripe banana
2 tablespoons dark rum
½ teaspoon vanilla extract
¾ cup milk
4 egg yolks
⅓ cup granulated sugar
2 tablespoons brown sugar
1¼ cups heavy cream

1. Sprinkle gelatin over 3 tablespoons cold water in a small container. Let stand for at least 5 minutes to soften gelatin, or until needed.

2. Combine bananas with rum and vanilla and set aside until needed.

3. In a small nonreactive saucepan, scald milk over medium-low heat.

4. Meanwhile, in a bowl, beat yolks with both sugars until pale and thick. Dribble hot milk over yolk mixture, whisking constantly, until all the milk has been added. Return mixture to saucepan and cook over medium-low heat, stirring contantly with a wooden spoon and reaching all over bottom of pan to avoid scorching. Cook only until mixture coats the spoon slightly (about 175 to 180°); do not allow to simmer or boil.

5. As soon as custard has reached the proper consistency, pour through a strainer into a clean bowl set into a larger bowl of ice water. Whisk in softened gelatin, stirring well to dissolve. Stir banana mixture. Cool the mixture in ice water, in the refrigerator, stirring frequently, until cold, thick, and syrupy but not yet set, 10 minutes or more. (See Bavarian Creams, page 167.)

6. Beat cream until soft peaks form (do not beat stiff or Bavarian will be granular). Fold into custard. Immediately turn the Bavarian into prepared charlotte(s) or dessert glasses.

CHOCOLATE GANACHE

Makes about 3 cups
2 cups heavy cream
8 ounces semisweet or bittersweet chocolate, finely chopped

1. Heat cream in a heavy-bottomed medium saucepan over medium-high heat until it simmers. Remove from heat. Add chocolate all at once and stir until partially melted. Let stand for 15–20 minutes to complete melting. Stir mixture again until smooth and all chocolate particles are melted. Let cool.

2. Cover surface of chocolate mixture with waxed paper or plastic wrap to prevent skin from forming. Refrigerate ganache until extremely cold, at least 5–6 hours before using. Ganache can be prepared and refrigerated up to 4 days ahead.

Notes

— Ganache is beaten before it is used in a cake or dessert. Like cream, it must be very cold or it will break down when whipped.
— If you have a choice, use the paddle attachment to your mixer when beating ganache—the finished texture is a little nicer.
— Ganache stiffens considerably when beaten and begins to harden, so it must be spread immediately. To avoid problems, follow the exact sequence of instructions in each individual recipe for beating and using ganache. If the ganache is too stiff to spread, use a spatula that has been warmed by dipping in hot water and then dried. Then, next time, beat the ganache just a bit less.
— Do not overbeat ganache. Overbeaten ganache becomes buttery and granular like overbeaten whipped cream.

PASTRY CREAM

Makes 1⅓ cups
or enough for two 9½-inch tarts
3 tablespoons sugar
1½ tablespoons flour
1½ tablespoons cornstarch
3 egg yolks
1 cup milk
½ teaspoon vanilla extract

Notes

— Pastry cream may be flavored in a variety of ways. Stir in liqueur, instant coffee powder dissolved in a bit of water, grated citrus zest, praline powder, etc., to taste.

1. In a mixing bowl, sift together sugar, flour, and cornstarch. Add egg yolks and whisk by hand or with an electric mixer, until pale and light.

2. Scald the milk in a medium nonreactive saucepan. Pour hot milk gradually over yolk mixture, whisking constantly until all the milk is added. Return mixture to saucepan and cook on medium heat, stirring constantly, reaching all over the bottom and sides of the pan, until custard thickens and starts to simmer. Simmer gently, stirring constantly for about 1 minute, to cook the flour. Remove from heat. Strain immediately into a clean bowl. Stir in vanilla. Let cool completely before using. Store covered in the refrigerator for up to 3 days.

LEMON CURD

Makes 1¾ cups
3 large eggs
½ cup lemon juice
Grated peel of 1 lemon
½ cup sugar
6 tablespoons butter, cut into pieces

1. Whisk eggs and set aside.

2. In a small nonreactive saucepan, combine lemon juice, grated peel, sugar, and butter. Heat to a simmer over medium heat. Pour hot liquid gradually over eggs, whisking continuously until all of the liquid is combined with the eggs. Return the mixture to the saucepan and whisk over medium heat until thick and barely beginning to simmer. Remove from heat and strain into a clean container to cool. Lemon curd may be prepared, covered, and refrigerated, up to 1 week in advance.

CRÈME FRAÎCHE

Makes about 5⅓ cups

Crème fraîche should be started at least 48 hours in advance, as the thickening time varies, and for many recipes the cream needs several hours of chilling before use. Some chefs use sour cream instead of buttermilk. More sour cream per cup of heavy cream is required to start the culture, so the resulting crème fraîche is not as rich and will not whip as beautifully.
5 cups heavy cream (not sterilized or "ultra-pasteurized")
5 tablespoons buttermilk

1. Warm the cream to baby bottle temperature, about 105°. Off heat, stir in the buttermilk and allow the mixture to stand in a warm place, loosely covered, until thickened and slightly nutty flavored. This may take as little as 12 or as long as 36 hours. Stir and taste it every 6 to 8 hours. Do not let it

mature too long or it will take on an unpleasant astringent flavor. Chill several hours before using. Crème fraîche may be made and stored in the refrigerator for up to 10 days.

CRÈME ANGLAISE
Makes 2²/₃ cups
2 cups milk
4 egg yolks
½ cup sugar
1 tablespoon vanilla extract
Alternate flavorings: 1 teaspoon vanilla extract plus 1 tablespoon powdered instant coffee, or a teaspoon of a freshly ground espresso, liqueur of choice, or freshly grated citrus zest

1. Have ready, near the stove, a medium-fine strainer set over a clean medium-size bowl placed in a bowl of ice water.

2. In a heavy, nonreactive medium saucepan, scald milk.

3. In a bowl, whisk yolks, gradually adding sugar until mixture is pale and thick. Pour scalded milk gradually into yolk mixture, whisking° constantly until all the milk is added. Return mixture to saucepan and cook over medium heat, stirring constantly with a wooden spoon, reaching all over the bottom of pan to avoid scorching. Sauce must not boil or even simmer. It will thicken slightly as it cooks. Remove from heat when sauce coats spoon lightly (about 175–180°) and pour it immediately into the ready strainer and bowl. Allow to cool completely, then stir in vanilla or other flavorings. Sauce may be completed and refrigerated one day ahead.

°Keep the whisk in contact with the bottom of the bowl as you mix, to avoid making foam or froth. Foam makes it hard to see whether or not the sauce is starting to simmer!

FRESH CREAM SAUCES
Makes 2 cups

Basically these sauces are glorious fakes—they look, taste, and act like sauces but they are simply under-whipped cream with flavorings. They are easier and faster than crème anglaise. Serve one of these with Chocolate Marquise (page 165). They are also good with the chocolate tortes in Chapter 4, when you don't feel like finishing them with chocolate glaze! Everyone should know how to cheat....
2 cups heavy cream
3–4 tablespoons sugar
1 teaspoon vanilla extract, or 3–4 tablespoons crème de menthe, Grand Marnier, Amaretto°, Frangelico°, or other liqueur of your choice

°*I sometimes add ¼ cup or more finely minced toasted almonds to Amaretto-flavored sauce, toasted hazelnuts to Frangelico-flavored sauce, etc.*

1. Whip cream, sugar, and flavorings until cream is past the foamy stage and has just begun to thicken. Correct flavoring and sweetness. Sauce should be a voluptuous, thick liquid rather than a fluffy topping. To serve, either pass the sauce separately or sauce each individual dessert plate and place the dessert serving on or next to the pool of sauce. Sauce may be completed a few hours ahead. Liquid will separate from the cream and need to be reincorporated with a few strokes of the whisk.

CARAMEL SAUCE
Makes 2 cups
1 cup heavy cream
1³/₄ cups sugar
5 tablespoons cold sweet butter, cut into pieces
1 teaspoon vanilla extract
⅛ teaspoon salt
1 tablespoon or more (to taste) rum, bourbon, or brandy

1. In a small saucepan, scald cream. Keep hot until needed.

2. Combine sugar with ½ cup water in a 2½–3-quart saucepan. Stir to moisten all of the sugar. Cover and bring to a simmer. Uncover and wash down any sugar crystals clinging to sides of pan with a pastry brush or paper towel dipped in water. Increase heat and simmer uncovered without stirring until syrup begins to color. Watch pan carefully, swirling it from time to time until syrup turns a medium amber color. (It is easiest to judge the color if you drip a few drops on a white plate.)

3. The moment the caramel has reached the proper color, turn off heat and immediately add cream in a steady stream, stirring briskly with a wire whisk. Caramel and cream will bubble up and steam dramatically. Be careful, but keep stirring. Continue to whisk, reaching all over the bottom and corners of the pan, until caramel is completely dissolved and combined with cream.

4. Stir in pieces of butter until melted and completely combined. Stir in vanilla, salt, and optional rum or brandy to taste. Caramel sauce may be stored, covered, in the refrigerator for 3 months or more. Reheat gently to serve, if desired.

CHOCOLATE SAUCE
Makes 1½ cups

This simple chocolate sauce shows off a good-quality semisweet or bittersweet chocolate.
10 ounces bittersweet or semisweet chocolate, cut into small pieces
½ cup milk or more, to thin if necessary
½ teaspoon vanilla extract

1. In a small bowl, combine chocolate and milk and melt gently in a barely simmering water bath, or microwave on MEDIUM (50%) for about 2 minutes. Stir until smooth. Add

additional tablespoons of milk as necessary if sauce looks either curdled or too thick. Remove from heat and stir in vanilla. Use warm sauce immediately or set aside until needed and rewarm briefly. Sauce may be prepared and refrigerated, covered, up to 1 week in advance.

2. To serve, spoon warm sauce on plate next to dessert.

RASPBERRY SAUCE

Makes 2–2½ cups
Two 10–12-ounce packages of frozen raspberries
2–3 tablespoons confectioners' sugar (optional)

1. Thaw raspberries without heating them. Drain and reserve the juice.

2. Purée the raspberries in a food processor or blender. Pass the purée through a strainer to remove the seeds. Add some or all of the reserved juice to the purée, depending on how thin you would like it to be. Taste and sweeten, if desired. (I like this sauce to be quite tart and tangy.) Refrigerate until needed. Sauce may be prepared and refrigerated up to 3 days in advance, or frozen for 6 months or longer. Never heat the sauce, even to thaw it.

3. To serve, spoon sauce onto plate next to dessert.

SAUCE BIJOU

Makes 2 cups

A sparkling ruby-red, tangy raw cranberry-raspberry dessert sauce. The ultimate holiday dessert sauce to serve with Chocolate Decadence. . . .

12 ounces raw cranberries, fresh or frozen
¾ cup red seedless or strained raspberry preserves
¾ cup sugar

1. Wash and pick over cranberries. Drain and combine with sugar in the bowl of a food processor or blender. Purée as finely as possible.

2. Press the purée through a medium-fine strainer to remove the toughest skins. You will end up with about ⅓ cup tough dry pulp and skins to discard. Stir strained raspberry preserves into purée. Sauce may be prepared and refrigerated for at least 3 weeks, or frozen for 6 months or longer. Never heat sauce, even to thaw.

3. To serve, spoon sauce onto plate next to dessert.

ORANGE SAUCE

Make 2 cups
4 cups fresh orange juice
¾ cup sugar
3 teaspoons arrowroot, dissolved in 2 teaspoons water
1 tablespoon fresh lemon juice

1 teaspoon grated lemon zest
2 teaspoons greated orange zest
Candied orange zests (page 173; optional), for garnish

1. In a medium-large, nonreactive saucepan over medium heat, reduce orange juice to 2 cups.

2. Add sugar and dissolved arrowroot to reduced orange juice. Simmer for 1 minute, until mixture is very slightly thickened.

3. Cool. Add lemon juice and lemon and orange zests. Cover and refrigerate until needed. Sauce will be thin. Sauce keeps, refrigerated, for at least 3 weeks.

4. To serve, spoon sauce onto plates next to dessert and decorate with candied orange zests, if desired.

BLUEBERRY SAUCE

Makes 2 cups
16 ounces blueberries, fresh or frozen
2 tablespoons fresh lemon juice, or more to taste
½ cup sugar, or more to taste

1. Combine ingredients in a medium saucepan. Cover and cook over medium heat until berry juices are released, about 1–2 minutes. Stir to moisten all of the berries, cover again, and cook 3 more minutes. Uncover and cook just until the mixture has come to a full rolling boil. Boil for 1 minute. Cool.

2. Adjust flavor with additional teaspoons of sugar and/or drops of lemon juice.

3. Serve as a compotelike sauce, or purée in a food processor (and strain, if desired) for a more uniform consistency. Sauce may be made and refrigerated in a covered container a week ahead, or frozen for 6 months or longer.

SIMPLE SYRUP

Makes about 2 cups
2 cups sugar
½ teaspoon cream of tartar

In a small saucepan, stir together sugar, cream of tartar, and 1 cup water until sugar is completely moistened. Wipe the sides of the pot with a wet pastry brush or paper towel to remove sugar crystals. Cover and bring to a simmer over medium heat. Simmer, covered, for 2 minutes without stirring. Uncover and let cool. Simple syrup keeps, covered, at room temperature, for at least 2–3 weeks, or refrigerated for 6 months or more.

PRALINE

Makes 1⅓ cups

Use this marvelous ingredient, in powdered or crunchy form, to flavor buttercream, to garnish a dessert, or to add texture to a caramel sauce. Or, sprinkle over a dish of ice cream. Each different nut praline seems to taste better than the next.

½ cup sugar

⅛ teaspoon cream of tartar

¾ cup (4 ounces) coarsely chopped toasted hazelnuts (skins removed) or toasted almonds, or untoasted walnuts or pecans

Special Equipment:

Baking sheet or marble slab

Sheet of parchment paper or foil

1. Place parchment or foil on a marble slab or baking sheet.

2. In a medium saucepan off heat, stir together sugar, cream of tartar, and ¼ cup water until sugar is completely moistened. Cover and bring to a simmer over medium heat. Continue to simmer, covered, for 2–3 minutes. Uncover and wash down the sides of the pan with a wet pastry brush. Continue to cook until syrup is light amber. (The color of the syrup is deceptive in the saucepan. Spoon a drop or two of syrup onto a white plate from time to time until the color looks right.)

3. Add chopped nuts. Stir gently with a wooden spoon to coat nuts. Use the wooden spoon to turn the syrup-coated nuts in the pan until the syrup is a deep amber. Remove from heat. Immediately scrape nut mixture onto the parchment paper and spread thinly.

4. Let praline cool completely. Break into pieces. In a food processor or blender, pulverize coarsely or grind to a powder, as desired. Praline may be completed and stored in an airtight container in the refrigerator for at least 2 months, or frozen for up to 6 months.

CARAMELIZED NUTS

Makes 30–40 caramelized nuts

Like sparkling amber jewels, these shiny caramel-clad nuts dress up my favorite nut tortes and layer cakes.

½ cup sugar

Walnut halves, whole almonds, hazelnuts, or pecans individually skewered on 9-inch wooden barbeque skewers

Special Equipment:

Lightweight 3- to 4-cup saucepan

Cake pan or bowl to prop up the skewered nuts after glazing

1. Ready a bowl of ice water and be sure to skewer the nuts before the caramel is cooked.

2. Place sugar and ¼ cup water in the saucepan. Off heat, stir until sugar is completely moistened. (Do not stir again during the cooking; stirring creates air bubbles that may crystalize the syrup.) Cover and bring to a simmer over medium heat. Uncover and wash down the sides of the pan with a wet pastry brush. Cover and cook for 2 minutes to dissolve the sugar completely. Uncover and cook until the syrup turns a pale amber. (The color of the syrup is deceptive in the saucepan. The color is more

accurately judged by periodically spooning a drop or two of the syrup onto a white saucer.) Swirl the pan gently, continuing to cook, and test the color until syrup darkens to a medium amber.

3. Remove the saucepan from the heat and immediately plunge the bottom into a bowl of ice water for a few moments to stop the caramel from boiling and continuing to darken.

4. Remove the caramel from the ice water, and tilt the pan at a 45° angle to facilitate dipping. Dip the skewered nuts, one by one, into the hot caramel and prop them up on the edge of a cake pan or bowl to cool and harden.

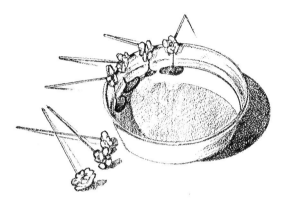

5. When the caramel is cool and hard, snip off any caramel drips or "tails" with a pair of scissors. Store glazed nuts in an airtight container until ready to use.

CANDIED CRANBERRIES

Makes about 1½ cups cranberries in about 1½ cups syrup

Tangy bright red berries partner chocolate and crème fraîche in Cranberry Christmas Cake (page 145). Use them to make a "fresh" fruit tart in the middle of winter, or substitute for fresh berries wherever you like. The syrup makes a delicious soda.

2 cups cranberries, rinsed and picked over

1¼ cups sugar

Special Equipment:

Heatproof nonreactive 6- to 8-cup bowl

A plate that fits inside the bowl

Covered pot or steamer large enough to contain the bowl (above)

1. Place cranberries in the heatproof bowl; set aside. Bring about 2 inches of water to a simmer in the steamer.

2. Meanwhile, combine sugar and ¾ cup water in a small saucepan. Stir just to moisten sugar. Cover and bring to a boil. Pour boiling syrup over cranberries; weigh them down with the plate.

3. Set the bowl of berries in the steamer. Cover and steam over medium heat for 45 minutes.

4. Remove and let berries and syrup cool without stirring. Cover bowl and leave in a warm, dry room for 3 or 4 days. The syrup will become slightly jellied. Berries to be used for garnish can be drained and allowed to dry on a rack. Leave the rest in the syrup and refrigerate until ready to use. Berries can be prepared and refrigerated up to 2 weeks in advance.

CANDIED CITRUS ZESTS

Brightly colored candied zests make an extra-pretty garnish for citrus desserts.

1–2 bright-skinned oranges, lemons, or limes, preferably organic
½ cup sugar

1. Use a vegetable peeler to remove the zest (colored part of the skin only) from the fruit in pieces as long and wide as possible. To obtain the longest and widest pieces, hold the fruit against the counter and start peeling from the stem end toward the opposite end of the fruit. Bear down firmly with the peeler and move the blade back and forth (as though you were cutting with a knife) ever so slightly as you work your way from one end of the fruit to the other.

2. Pile 2–3 pieces of zest one on top of another. Slice diagonally into fine julienne about 1½–2 inches long. Shorten or lengthen the julienne by varying the angle of your diagonal slice.

3. Combine sugar and ¼ cup water in a small saucepan. Stir just to moisten sugar. Cover and bring to a simmer. Simmer for about 30 seconds, just to dissolve sugar. Add the julienned zest, cover, and simmer for 2 minutes. Remove from the heat. Uncover and let the zest cool in the syrup. Candied zests can be made and stored in the syrup in a jar, in the refrigerator, for at least 3 months. Remove from syrup and drain on a paper towel before using.

Finishing Techniques

The traditional style of American cake decorating relies on the ubiquitous pastry bag and lavish quantities of frosting. Instead, I was out to master the sleek and shiny chocolate glaze, the smooth thin coat of rich buttercream, the fine hand with piping. Ruffles, and ribbons of pure chocolate, were the stuff of dreams.

My one-week stage at the Ecole Lenôtre in 1973 exposed me briefly to many of the techniques I needed. Most importantly, it set the visual standard for my aspirations. Then I practiced.

In this chapter you will find the fruits of my practice and the knowledge I have gained in training others over the years. I have attempted to make these professional techniques approachable by describing procedures in detail so that you will know, literally, where to stand and how to hold the spatula, what a glaze or buttercream will look and feel like, and how and when to alter the consistency or temperature as necessary. The troubleshooting notes and tips included in this chapter will help you evaluate your results and improve the next time. I also suggest "practicing" some techniques first—on the back of cake pans or on a sheet of waxed paper—without wasting ingredients or ruining a dessert.

Even the simplest Special Effects are guaranteed to bring out the show-off in anyone. You will find decorating with piping or stencils easy—I urge you to try your hand. Chocolate ruffles and cigarettes take more time to learn. Why not treat yourself to an afternoon, with no other distractions, to learn and practice this technique? You will be rewarded with a new skill as well as with dozens of chocolate decorations ranging from cigarettes, curls, and fans, to abstract shapes of all kinds. Store them in the refrigerator or freezer (they are best done in advance anyway) for decorating a future show-stopping dessert, or simply to garnish a dish of ice cream with panache.

So, gather your tools and clear your counter. You are about to embark on a most satisfying mission.

MAKING AND WORKING WITH CHOCOLATE GLAZE

Beautifully glazed tortes are not difficult to achieve, but they require a little attention to detail. The torte must be at the proper temperature and it must be leveled and crumb-coated. The glaze must be warmed to the correct temperature and manipulated as little as possible. The recipes below are my favorites. Detailed procedures and troubleshooting notes follow.

About Glazing Cold Cakes and Room-Temperature Cakes

Before glazing any cake, torte, or pastry, check the recipe to see how it is stored and served. Many chocolate tortes keep well and taste best at room temperature. In order for the glaze on these cakes to stay shiny, they should be at room temperature before they are glazed, and they must remain unrefrigerated afterwards. Cakes and desserts that are perishable and must be stored cold should be well chilled *before* they are glazed. They should be refrigerated again immediately after glazing to keep the glaze from streaking or graying! I developed Sarah Bernhardt Chocolate Glaze (page 175) especially for cold desserts. It is thinner and does not become too brittle when chilled. I use it for desserts such as Sarah Bernhardts, Lutèce, and A Gift for Dad. Do not glaze cakes or desserts while still frozen.

BITTERSWEET CHOCOLATE GLAZE
Makes enough for an 8- to 10-inch torte

This is the simplest, most classic chocolate glaze. Use it on tortes that are stored and served at room temperature.

6 ounces bittersweet or semisweet chocolate, cut into pieces
4 ounces (1 stick) sweet butter, cut into pieces
1 tablespoon light corn syrup

1. Place chocolate, butter, and corn syrup in a small bowl. Melt gently in a water bath over low heat, stirring frequently until almost completely melted. Do not overheat the glaze; there is no need to warm it above 120°. Remove glaze from water bath and set aside to finish melting, stirring once or twice until glaze is perfectly smooth. Or, melt in a microwave on MEDIUM (50%) for about 2 minutes. Stir mixture gently with a spatula or a wooden spoon until completely smooth; do not whisk or beat. Follow procedure for Glazing with Chocolate, page 175. Use glaze at 90°–92°. Leave torte at room temperature after glazing.

Chocolate Honey Glaze Variation

Follow the instructions for making Bittersweet Chocolate Glaze, but substitute 2–3 tablespoons honey (to taste) for the corn syrup.

SARAH BERNHARDT CHOCOLATE GLAZE

Makes enough for an 8- to 10-inch cake or torte,
or 20–24 Sarah Bernhardts

Use this glaze for cakes and pastries that are stored and served chilled. If used at the proper temperature, poured onto a cold dessert, and refrigerated immediately afterwards, it will remain dark and shiny. It becomes even shinier if the cold dessert is removed from the refrigerator for up to 1 hour before serving!

8 ounces semisweet or bittersweet chocolate, cut into bits
6 ounces sweet butter
1 tablespoon light corn syrup

Follow the procedure above for making Bittersweet Chocolate Glaze, adding 5 teaspoons of water to the ingredients in Step 1. Be sure that dessert is well chilled (but not frozen) before glazing. To glaze, skip over the leveling and crumb-coating step (pages 175–76) and pick up the instructions for glazing with Bittersweet Chocolate Glaze on page 176. Use glaze at 88°–90°. Refrigerate dessert immediately after glazing.

MOCHA GLAZE

Makes enough for an 8- to 10-inch torte

Wonderfully rich mocha flavor. Coffee takes the edge off the sweet milk chocolate perfectly. This glaze is especially delicious with the Mocha Pecan Torte (page 48). It also makes a great eclair glaze. Omit the coffee and use it to glaze Chocolate Brownie Cupcakes for a child's party (see Lucy's Birthday Cake, page 129). Milk chocolate glaze is thicker and stickier than dark chocolate. It covers the top of a torte thickly enough to make crumb coating unnecessary (unless the torte is badly cracked), although the sides will still look imperfect. This is fine if you cover the sides of the torte with chopped nuts after glazing. Otherwise, plan to crumb-coat so that the glazed sides of the torte will look smooth and finished.

10 ounces milk chocolate, cut into tiny bits
¾ cup heavy cream
1 tablespoon light corn syrup
1 tablespoon plus 1 teaspoon powdered instant coffee or espresso, dissolved
*   in a few drops of water*

Place chocolate in a bowl and set aside. In a saucepan, bring cream and corn syrup to a simmer. Stir in dissolved coffee. Pour over chocolate and stir until completely smooth and all of the chocolate is melted. Follow the procedure for Glazing with Chocolate. Use glaze at 100°.

WHITE CHOCOLATE GLAZE

Makes enough for an 8- to 10-inch torte

White Chocolate Glaze partners fruit and chocolate combinations, such as Italian-Cherry Torte, beautifully. The sweet white chocolate picks up the sweetness and offsets the tartness of the fruit. White Chocolate Glaze, like the Mocha Glaze, is thick and sticky; plan to press nuts or chocolate shavings against less-than-perfect sides. White Chocolate Glaze requires an extra-thick crumb-coat so that the dark cake will not show through the white glaze.

10 ounces white chocolate, cut into tiny bits
½ cup heavy cream
1 tablespoon light corn syrup

Place chocolate in a bowl and set aside. In a saucepan, bring cream and corn syrup to a simmer. Remove from heat. Pour over chocolate and stir until completely smooth and all of the chocolate is melted. Follow the procedure for Glazing with Chocolate. Use glaze at 100°.

THE TECHNIQUE FOR GLAZING WITH CHOCOLATE

Special Equipment:
Metal icing spatula with 8-inch blade
A flat platter, lazy Susan, or decorator's turntable or a potter's
*   banding wheel*

To Level and Unmold the Torte

Most chocolate tortes rise like a soufflé while baking, then fall in the center as they cool, leaving a faintly crusty higher rim around the edges of the torte. Before glazing, the torte must be leveled to get rid of the "sunken in the center" look and inverted so that the bottom, which rests against the flat bottom of the pan, will become the perfectly flat top of the finished torte.

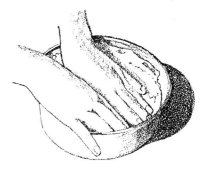

Level the torte *before* removing it from the pan as follows. Run a small metal spatula or knife between the edges of the torte and the sides of the pan to release it. Press the raised edges of the torte down with your fingers until it is level with the center. Place a cardboard cake circle on the torte. If you have used a springform or cheesecake pan, release the sides and invert the torte so that the bottom becomes the top, then remove the pan bottom and paper liner. If you have not used a pan with removeable sides, invert it and rap gently against the counter until the torte slips out. Remove the pan and the paper liner from the bottom of the torte. If the torte is uneven or still appears slightly sunken in the middle, level it again by pressing the top firmly with the bottom of the empty cake pan. The torte is now ready to crumb-coat and glaze.

Buttercream-filled layer cakes finished with chocolate glaze, such as Lutèce or A Gift for Dad, are leveled and made symmetrical in the assembly process described in their respective recipes, so they do not require the special preparations described above. They also are usually covered with smooth buttercream on the outside in preparation for glazing, so they do not require any additional crumb coating. Do be sure to chill these cakes before glazing and use Sarah Bernhardt Chocolate Glaze, page 175. Follow glazing instructions as for Bittersweet Chocolate Glaze.

To Crumb-Coat the Torte

The "crumb coat" is a thin layer of cooled glaze spread over the torte to smooth the surface, fill the cracks, and "glue" on loose crumbs before the final glaze is poured over the cake. Like spackling a wall before painting, crumb-coating makes it possible to pour a thin, perfect coat of glaze over the torte without showing any of the imperfections that might lurk beneath the surface. The crumb coat for each glaze is handled a little bit differently. Before proceeding, have ready the prepared torte— baked, cooled completely, leveled, and unmolded onto a corrugated cardboard.

With Bittersweet Glaze: Make glaze according to the recipe and cool, without stirring, until it is nearly set and has the consistency of easily spreadable frosting. About one-quarter of the cooled glaze will be used for crumb-coating; the rest will be re-melted and used to glaze the torte. I usually make the glaze and set it aside before I bake the torte so it will be ready for crumb coating by the time the torte is cool. If it becomes *too* stiff to spread easily, soften it slightly, stirring gently, for a few seconds in the water bath, but don't let it return to its fluid state. If you do not make the glaze in advance, you may speed the cooling process by pouring about one-fourth of the fresh glaze into a shallow pan where it will cool faster.

Using a metal icing spatula, spread about one-fourth of the cooled glaze in a thin layer all over the torte. Smooth the rough surfaces of the torte, securing loose crumbs, and filling any cracks. This crumb coat will not be glossy or attractive. Its sole purpose is to provide a smooth, even undercoat for the final glaze. Be careful not to get any crumbs in the remaining, unused glaze.

Refrigerate the torte for about 10 minutes, or just until the crumb coat is set. Do not leave the torte in the refrigerator for more than 10 minutes—if it becomes cold through and through, it will dull the final glaze.

With Mocha or White Chocolate Glaze: Make glaze according to recipe and cool. Cooled glaze will be thick and sticky. Pour about one-fourth of it into another bowl. Beat it with a wooden spoon over a bowl of ice and water until it stiffens slightly and becomes a creamy, spreadable mass. (If it becomes too stiff to spread, rewarm it slightly in a water bath.) Proceed to crumb-coat as for Bittersweet Glaze. (Unless the torte is badly cracked, crumb-coating with Mocha Glaze may be omitted if you plan to press chopped nuts against the sides of the dessert.)

To Glaze the Torte

With Bittersweet Glaze: Rewarm the remaining cooled glaze (if necessary) by placing the bowl in a barely simmering water bath for a few seconds, stirring gently until the glaze is perfectly smooth, 90°–92° (88°–90° for Sarah Bernhardt Glaze) and the consistency of heavy cream. Or, rewarm slightly in the microwave. (Do not overheat; glaze will dull and/or streak as it dries on the torte; its too-thin consistency will coat the torte poorly and look drippy on the sides. If you accidentally overwarm the glaze, wait until it is the right temperature again before you pour it over the torte.)

If there are crumbs or air bubbles in the glaze, pour glaze through a very fine strainer just before pouring it over the cake.

Center the crumb-coated torte on a platter or turntable. Have ready a clean, dry metal icing spatula. Pour all of the glaze in a puddle in the center of the top of the torte. Working quickly, use just 2 or 3 spatula strokes to spread the glaze over the top of the torte so that it runs over all sides of the torte. This is easiest if you rotate the turntable or platter as you spread.

If there are any bare spots on the sides of the cake, use the spatula to scoop up excess glaze and touch it to the bare spots to cover them. Tiny bare spots can be fixed by dipping a finger into the excess glaze and touching the bare spots. The idea is to be sure that the glaze goes on the torte while it is still fluid because the best-looking glaze is *poured*, not spread. If necessary, jiggle or rap the turntable gently to settle any uneven glaze. If you attempt to respread or resmooth glaze once it is poured and starting to set, the finished torte will show spatula marks and dull streaks.

With Mocha or White Chocolate Glaze: Follow the procedure above, but rewarm glaze to 100° before pouring. These glazes will have a heavy, syrupy consistency and it will be hard to get perfect sides.

Once the torte is glazed, slide a wide spatula under it and remove it to a rack to dry at room temperature (unless it is meant to be a cold cake—then you must refrigerate it). Keep the torte as level as possible while you lift it so that the wet glaze on top won't shift before it has set. (If you leave the torte on the turntable or the platter, it will dry in its own puddle of excess glaze and the edges will be damaged when you try to pry it loose.) Glaze will set in 10–20 minutes. If you plan to decorate the sides of the torte with nuts, be sure to do this before the glaze has completely dried. Store room-temperature desserts at room temperature, cold desserts in the refrigerator.

Glazing is simpler than it sounds. If you feel insecure about getting it right the first time, practice by glazing the back of a clean cake pan (omitting the crumb-coat step). The practice glaze need not be wasted. Scrape it off with a rubber spatula, rewarm and reuse it. Do this two or three times to get used to the proper temperature, the way the glaze flows, and how best to get the torte entirely covered with the fewest spatula strokes. I do this whenever I'm trying out a new technique or decorating idea.

TROUBLESHOOTING

Glazed torte looks dull and streaky:
—Glaze was overheated and poured while still too warm.
—Glaze was too cool when poured, and/or you spread it with the spatula while it was drying on the torte.
—Torte meant to be at room temperature was cold when glaze was poured, or cake meant to be cold was at room temperature when glaze was poured.
(Bittersweet) Glaze looks drippy on the sides of the torte:
—Glaze was too warm, and coated cake too thinly.
—Torte was cold and glaze was too cool, so glaze started to set before it could completely cover the torte.
Glaze on torte has lots of air bubbles:
—Glaze was stirred or whisked too vigorously—straining through a fine strainer could correct this. Next time stir gently. Mocha and White Chocolate Glaze are prone to air bubbles regardless. Gentle handling reduces but may not eliminate bubbles.
Torte buckled and glaze cracked when torte was transferred to the rack or to a serving dish:
—You didn't use a cardboard cake circle under the torte to keep it rigid.
Torte was cracked, sunken, and uneven before glazing and all of these imperfections still showed after the torte was glazed:
—You didn't allow the torte to cool in the pan and/or you didn't

level it correctly before removing it from the pan
—You didn't crumb-coat before glazing.

FINISHING TOUCHES

A glazed torte is perfectly beautiful without added decoration, but sometimes you will wish to add a finishing touch:

To Cover the Sides of Torte with Chopped or Shaved Toasted Nuts

Do this while the glaze is still tacky, just before it is completely dry. Lift the torte off the rack and hold it in the palm of your left hand (if you are right-handed). The cardboard cake circle will support the torte and keep it from buckling. Tilt the torte over a platter of nuts. Scoop the nuts into the palm of your free hand and press them carefully against the sides of the torte. Rotate torte and continue to press nuts around the sides.

To Pipe a Decorative Chocolate Motif onto the Torte

See Piping with Melted Chocolate, page 185. The subtlest effect is achieved by piping white chocolate on white glaze, dark chocolate on dark glaze, etc. Pipe contrasting chocolates for a more striking effect. Try piping two different chocolates on one torte for variety.

To Gild the Torte with Gold or Silver

Decorate the torte with edible gold or silver shot or the gold- or silver-covered almonds called dragées. (Both are available from cake decorating stores or by mail from Maid of Scandinavia, page 197.) Or randomly place tiny flecks of edible real gold or silver leaf, available at Indian grocery stores or art supply stores.

MARBLED GLAZE

A pattern of chocolate is piped on wet chocolate glaze and a fine artist's brush or wooden skewer is drawn through the pattern before the glaze is set. Different effects are achieved depending on the pattern piped and the brush strokes drawn through it.

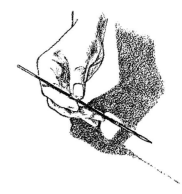

The usual pattern for piping is either horizontal lines piped across the cake

or a spiral piped from the center of the cake to the outer edge.

I make these patterns more interesting by using two different chocolates, piping the second chocolate in between the lines of the first so that the colors alternate or make a double spiral.

A common marbling technique is simply a series of parallel brush strokes drawn back and forth across the cake perpendicular to the parallel chocolate piping. The popular spider web marble is achieved by drawing the brush through the spiral piping from the center of the cake to the outer edge, alternating with stokes drawn from the outer edge to the center. Mocha Pecan Torte (page 48) is finished with this technique.

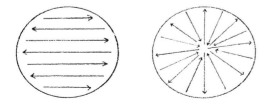

More unique marbling is achieved with more unusual piping and brush strokes. I pipe a loose loopy scribble all over the cake, first with milk chocolate and then with white chocolate overlapping the milk chocolate.

I then use a series of bisecting strokes, drawing the brush across the edges of the cake, letting each stroke cross over the previous one, continuing around the cake, moving gradually in toward the center.

The Queen of Sheba torte (page 46) is finished with this technique. I also use this bisecting stroke on the piped spiral pattern. After you have tried one or two of these marbling schemes, you will want to dream up your own combinations. *Before pouring the glaze onto the torte, have ready:*
—1 ounce each melted white, milk, or dark chocolate (or use two) in one or more paper cones
—a fine artist's brush with bristles about ¾-inch long (#0 or #1), or a thin wooden skewer
—a decorating turntable or potter's banding wheel

Decide which marbling motif you will use. Practice piping the pattern on the back of a pan, if desired, and be sure that you understand how to draw the brush *before* you glaze the torte. You will not have time to stop and figure this out afterwards! On the other hand, do not worry about perfection or absolute accuracy in either piping the pattern or marbling it. Even if your piping looks amateurish and messy and your marbling random, you will be amazed and delighted with the final results.

When you are ready, glaze the torte on a platter or turntable as described. When the top and sides are completely glazed, leave the torte on the turntable. Immediately pipe the chocolate or chocolates quickly onto the wet glaze in the chosen pattern. Use a very light brush or skewer stroke to marble the chocolate while the glaze is still wet. Remove the torte onto a rack, as described, until set or until tacky enough to cover the sides with nuts, if you wish.

FROSTING WITH WHIPPED CREAM

Whipped cream is the freshest-tasting, most pleasing accompaniment to a rich chocolate dessert that I can think of.

About the Cream

Use heavy whipping cream. It should contain 38–40 percent butterfat. Pure, fresh, pasteurized dairy cream is the best and most delicious. If posssible, avoid cream that is labeled "ultrapasteurized" or "sterilized." This cream has an unfortunate canned taste because it has been processed to make it last for a long time without spoiling.

I do not add gelatin or any kind of thickener or stabilizer to whipped cream. If the dessert is not to be served immediately, refrigerate it. Once the cream has firmed in the refrigerator, the dessert can stand up perfectly for an hour or two unrefrigerated—on display, or on the road—before serving.

I like to frost with whipped cream on the same day I will serve the dessert. In a pinch, however, you may frost up to 24 hours in advance of serving. In any case, cover the frosted cake with a dome or seal it in a plastic container to prevent the cream from picking up flavors and odors from the refrigerator.

Cream whips to its fullest volume and best texture if it is very cold. If it is not cold enough, it will break down—stay soft and look curdled—when you whip it. The extra precaution of chilling the bowl and the beater is a good idea if the kitchen or the weather is warm.

TIPS FOR WHIPPED CREAM FROSTING

Whipped cream is frequently overwhipped during the act of frosting a cake. This happens because the cream, whipped stiff in the first place, continues to stiffen as you manipulate it with the spatula. As you smooth and spread the cream over and over again to make it perfect, it becomes overwhipped. It looks granular and ragged instead of smooth and moist. The solution is to underwhip the cream just a little. By the time the cake is covered and the cream has been spread to your satisfaction, the cream will be stiff enough.

When whipped cream is to be used as a frosting, I always use a cardboard cake circle 1 inch in diameter larger than the actual cake size. The extra half-inch all around the bottom of the cake is a perfect support for the whipped cream. I slant the frosted sides of the cake so that the shape of the cake becomes

slightly pyramidal. This shape is more pleasing to me than the more common tall fat cylinder shape. The spatula rests against the edge of the cardboard circle fully ½ inch away from the cake, so it is easier to achieve a smooth frosted surface without patches of bare cake showing through. The cardboard also absorbs moisture that may "weep" from the whipped cream as it stands. Most important of all, though, the pyramid prevents the whipped cream from sagging under its own weight—especially if you frost with lots and lots and lots of whipped cream (see Chocolate Decadence, page 45, and Diabolo, page 42)!

THE TECHNIQUE FOR FROSTING WITH WHIPPED CREAM

For each cup of cream use ½ teaspoon vanilla extract and 1–3 tablespoons granulated sugar (to taste). Add the vanilla to the cream when you start to beat. Sprinkle the sugar in after the cream has started to thicken. You will need 2–4 cups of cream, depending on the dessert to be frosted and the desired effect (see individual recipes).

Special Equipment:
Metal icing spatula with an 8-inch blade
Cake decorator's turntable or a potter's banding wheel
Pastry bag and tip, if you plan to pipe a border
Pitcher of hot water
Cake or torte on a cardboard cake circle 1 inch larger than the dessert
Whipped cream, not too stiff (it will continue to stiffen as you spread it)

1. Center cake on its cardboard in the center of decorating turntable. Heap about 1 cup (or more, if frosting is to be extra thick) of whipped cream on top of cake. Spread cream level and flat using the icing spatula, shimmying it slightly to push excess cream over edges of cake. To smooth the top, scrape spatula against edge of the bowl to remove excess cream. Dip spatula in hot water and wipe dry. Hold it stationary, against the top of the cake at a slight angle, with the end of the blade in the center while you turn the decorating turntable counterclockwise.

Adjust the pressure of the spatula while you rotate the turntable until the surface is smooth. Excess cream will extend over edge of cake.

2. Scoop up a large dollop of cream on the end of the spatula. Apply the cream to the left side of the cake (if you are right-handed), always holding the spatula vertically—handle side up—next to the cake.

Shimmy the spatula as you spread the dollop smooth, filling in the entire space between the edge of the cardboard and the top edge of the cake. Continue to rotate the turntable, scoop up dollops of cream, and spread the sides of the cake in this manner. When the sides are covered, scrape spatula against the side of the bowl to remove excess cream. Dip spatula in hot water and wipe dry. Smooth sides by holding the spatula (always vertically and on the left side, if you are right-handed) at a slight angle, against the cake while rotating turntable. A ridge of cream will build up around the top edge of cake—this is normal.

3. To smooth the ridge of cream on top of the cake, hold spatula horizontally at a 10° angle behind the cake. Pull spatula toward you, smoothing the ridge of cream just to the center of the cake. (Do not continue to pull the spatula all the way across the cake or you will create another ridge of cream overhanging the side!)

Scrape the spatula, dip it in hot water, and wipe it dry. Rotate the cake nearly a quarter of a turn and smooth the next section of cream into the center. Continue to smooth the top of the cake in this manner, remembering to scrape, dip, and wipe the spatula between each stroke.

4. To decorate with a pastry bag, scrape leftover whipped cream into a large pastry bag with a decorative tip such as the Ateco closed star #7 or #9 for large rosettes or borders or closed star #4 for a daintier edging. Decorate the top edge with a series of rosettes or a continuous border (see Cranberry Christmas Cake, page 145) formed by holding the tip of the pastry bag at a 45° angle with the top of the cake and tracing a continuous coil as you go around the top edge of the cake.

MAKING AND WORKING WITH BUTTERCREAM

Sooner or later you may want to make a cake and finish it with the old-fashioned elegance of classic buttercream. An expertly masked cake, subtly textured on top or sides and ringed with a dainty piped border, is a thing of grace and beauty. Fresh flowers can add softness and romance.

Finishing a cake with buttercream is different from frosting an American cake with swirls of thick, fluffy frosting. The cake is rich to start with, and the buttercream is richer. We use it sparingly. The idea is to mask the cake with a very thin coat of smooth or textured buttercream prefacing a dainty border, chocolate piping, fresh flowers, etc. The challenge? How to put that buttercream on thinly and smoothly without flaws, crooked cakes, or stray crumbs. There will be no forgiving billows of frosting, swirls, or frills to hide behind!

Making and using buttercream can be tricky if you are new to it, but a little knowledge goes a very long way. Expertise in handling a spatula comes with practice, practice, practice. The illustrated instructions that follow will get you started. Pay careful attention to the sequence of steps, the position of the spatula, and the tips about scraping, warming, and wiping the spatula blade between strokes. You will be surprised at the difference these details can make!

BUTTERCREAM

Small batch makes 1½ cups,
large batch makes 2 cups

For Small Batch:

½ cup sugar

¼ cup water

2 pinches of cream of tartar

1 large egg

6 ounces sweet butter, slightly softened

For Large Batch:

⅔ cup sugar

⅓ cup water

⅛ teaspoon cream of tartar

1 large whole egg

1 egg yolk

8 ounces sweet butter, slightly softened

1. In a small (3- to 4-cup) saucepan, combine sugar, water, and cream of tartar. Stir to wet sugar. Cover and bring to a simmer over medium heat. Simmer, covered, without stirring, for about 1 minute to dissolve sugar. Uncover and wash down the sides of the saucepan with a wet pastry brush. Cook until syrup registers 242° (the upper end of the soft-ball stage) on a candy thermometer. Or, cook just until you can blow a bubble (resembling a soap bubble) by dipping a slotted spoon into the syrup, holding it up, and blowing gently but steadily through it.

2. Meanwhile, in the bowl of an electric mixer, beat egg (or egg and egg yolk) until pale and thick; set aside. Just before syrup reaches 242°, begin beating eggs again on medium speed, using the paddle attachment°, if you have one. When the syrup registers 242°, remove it from the heat, pour syrup in a thin, steady stream over the eggs and syrup, beating constantly. To avoid splashing hot syrup on yourself or all around the sides of the bowl, pour it next to the beaters, close to the edge of the bowl. Continue beating until mixture cools to room temperature.

°Buttercream spreads smoother and with fewer air bubbles, if it is made with the paddle attachment (if you have a choice) instead of the whisk, which beats more air into it. Paddle or whisk, avoid beating longer than necessary once the buttercream reaches the desired consistency.

Cut butter into 1-tablespoon lumps. Add butter, a few pieces at a time, continuing to beat until smooth and spreadable. Flavor as desired. Buttercream may be made several days ahead and stored in the refrigerator, or frozen for up to 3 months. The recipe can be doubled without a problem.

To Reconstitute Cold or Frozen Buttercream

If you are using a microwave, chop frozen buttercream into chunks and soften on LOW (30%) until you can stir it smooth with a rubber spatula. Buttercream that is cold but not frozen can be softened on MEDIUM (50%) for about 25 seconds for a small batch, 30–35 seconds for a large batch. Stir or beat until smooth. If softening buttercream using a water bath, chop buttercream into chunks and place in a bowl set in a barely simmering pan of water. Allow some of the buttercream to melt, then beat with an electric mixer to the desired consistency. If lumps remain or buttercream is still too cold or curdled, return bowl to the water bath for a few seconds longer before rebeating.

TROUBLESHOOTING

Three things can go wrong, or appear to go wrong, with buttercream: crystallization of the sugar syrup, curdling of the buttercream when butter is added, and buttercream that is too runny. These are all easy problems to avoid or correct.

Crystallized Syrup: Air bubbles and/or undissolved grains of sugar introduced into the syrup toward the end of cooking can result in crystallization. This is easily avoided.

—Use a small saucepan, as specified, for a small quantity of syrup. If the syrup is too shallow (because the pan is too big), the water may evaporate too quickly before all of the sugar is dissolved in the syrup. Besides, it is hard to get a good thermometer reading in very shallow syrup.

—Do not stir the syrup as it cooks. Even gentle stirring can create air bubbles that may cause crystallization.

—Wash the sides of the pot with a wet pastry brush to coax stray sugar crystals into the syrup to dissolve before it's too late.

Curdling: Hot syrup will not curdle or cook the egg(s) as long as they have been beaten in advance and are being beaten as the syrup is poured over them. Curdling is caused by adding butter that is significantly colder than the egg mixture. Buttercream is an emulsion—it curdles or breaks, like a delicate sauce, if the temperature of its components are too different from one another. Curdled or broken buttercream is self-correcting. Continue to beat and the butter will gradually warm up as the egg mixture cools down. When both are about the same temperature, the buttercream will magically smooth out.

If the butter added was *very* cold, the beating and smoothing out may take unnecessarily long and/or the buttercream may be too stiff even when smooth. To uncurdle the buttercream faster or to soften it when it is too stiff, place the bowl in a pan of barely simmering water for a few seconds while stirring vigorously with a rubber spatula until smooth.

Buttercream left untouched for awhile may seem to lose its smoothness when spread. It may seem to be full of tiny air bubbles or slightly curdled. Stir briskly with a rubber spatula to smooth it again.

Runny, Liquid, or Too-Soft Buttercream: If very soft butter is added to a still-warm egg-and-syrup mixture, the resulting buttercream will be quite liquid. The same thing will happen if you warm the buttercream too much in an attempt to soften it. In either case runny or too-soft buttercream is easy to fix. Refrigerate to chill it slightly before beating again with a rubber spatula or mixer. When you start to beat the partially chilled mixture, it may curdle at first, but it will smooth out. If you chilled it too long you may have to warm it again (see above) in a water bath before it will beat smooth.

Each chef has his or her own preference about the ideal consistency for buttercream. With experience you will also know what you like best. I like a fairly stiff buttercream for filling cake layers, crumb-coating, and piping crisp, well-defined decorative borders. But I find soft buttercream (similar to the consistency of homemade mayonnaise) best for a smooth finishing coat. Adjust the softness or stiffness of buttercream by slight warming or chilling as described above. Do this as much or as little as needed, and as often as required to keep the buttercream at the desired consistency.

CHOCOLATE BUTTERCREAM

For Small Batch:

10 ounces semisweet, bittersweet, milk, or white chocolate, cut into small bits

¼ cup plus 1 tablespoon water

For Large Batch:

13 ounces semisweet, bittersweet, milk, or white chocolate, cut into small bits

¼ cup plus 3 tablespoons water

1. Combine chocolate and water in small bowl placed in a saucepan of barely simmering water. Stir chocolate frequently to hasten melting. Or, melt the chocolate and water gently in a microwave on MEDIUM (50%) for 1 minute and 45–50 seconds for dark chocolate, on LOW (30%) for about 2 minutes for milk or white chocolate. Remove from heat and stir until smooth. Cool to barely lukewarm, if necessary.

2. Combine chocolate mixture with buttercream, stirring with a rubber spatula only until incorporated. *Note:* If you beat chocolate buttercream, it will become increasingly pale in color, as air is incorporated into it.

COFFEE BUTTERCREAM

Dissolve 1½ teaspoons instant coffee powder or instant espresso in ¾ teaspoon warm water for a small batch of buttercream, or use 2 teaspoons instant coffee in 1 teaspoon water for a large batch. Stir coffee mixture into buttercream. Taste and add more dissolved coffee if you prefer a stronger flavor.

LIQUEUR-FLAVORED BUTTERCREAM

Adding liquor or liqueurs, or any liquid, to buttercream must be done judiciously. Too much liquid will cause the buttercream to break or curdle irretrievably. You may achieve a delicate liquor flavor by adding up to ¼ cup liqueur to a small batch of buttercream or ⅓ cup to a large batch. You will need to stir the buttercream vigorously from time to time to resmooth it, as the liquid makes it less stable. More liquid may be added if the buttercream has chocolate in it (chocolate stabilizes buttercream so that it can handle more liquid without breaking). If additional or stronger liquor flavoring is desired, brush liquor directly on the cake layers in addition to flavoring the buttercream.

CHESTNUT BUTTERCREAM

Add up to ½ cup canned sweetened chestnut purée (also called chestnut spread) or to taste, per cup of plain Buttercream. A little dark rum enhances the flavor as well.

NUT BUTTERCREAM

Add ground or chopped nuts to plain Buttercream, to taste. Toasted nuts usually give the best flavor.

PRALINE BUTTERCREAM

Add praline powder—pulverized caramelized nuts of any kind (page 171)—to plain or Chocolate Buttercream. Or pulverize the praline until it forms a paste. Stir or beat the paste into the buttercream.

THE TECHNIQUE FOR FINISHING WITH BUTTERCREAM

Follow individual recipes for assembling (cutting layers and filling) cakes on cardboard circles, making sure they are symmetrical and level on top. Chill the assembled cake for at least 20 minutes to firm (use the freezer if you are in a hurry) before continuing.

Trimming and Crumb-Coating

If the sides of the assembled cake are very ragged and/or some of the layers stick out more than the others, trim them even with a serrated knife. Trimming is easier if the cake has been chilled beforehand. Use a metal icing spatula to spread a small amount of buttercream around the top and sides of the cake. This is the crumb coat. It will not look attractive and you will probably be able to see the cake through the buttercream. The purpose is simply to secure all loose crumbs and seal and smooth the porous surface of the cake before the final finishing.

Do not get any crumbs from the cake into the bowl of buttercream—they will drive you crazy later on. As a precaution remove a small quantity of buttercream to a separate bowl first, and spread the crumb coat from this bowl.

For best results chill the crumb-coated cake until the buttercream is firm, 20 minutes or longer. Use the freezer if you are in a hurry.

Masking the Cake

Stir the remaining buttercream smooth with a rubber spatula, softening it if necessary, as described above. It should spread easily and smoothly.

Have ready a metal icing spatula with an 8-inch blade, a pitcher of hot water at least 8 inches tall (or 12 inches tall if you plan to texture the top of your cake), a clean towel that has been wet and well wrung out, and a folded *dry* towel (or several thicknesses of dry paper towel) anchored on the counter near you so that you can, with one hand, wipe your spatula against it. I anchor mine by putting one edge of the towel under my mixer or decorating turntable. If you plan to comb the sides of the cake you will need a cake comb or a serrated knife with a straight—not curved—blade. If you plan to texture the top of the cake, you will need a serrated bread knife with a 12-inch straight—not curved—blade.

1. Place the chilled, crumb-coated cake in the center of a decorating turntable. Spread the sides of the cake with buttercream first. Always work on the left side of the cake holding the spatula vertically—handle side up—with your right hand, if you are right-handed. Scoop some buttercream on the end of the spatula and apply it to the left side of the cake, holding the spatula upside down in a vertical position. Shimmy or pivot the blade back and forth as you spread the buttercream, rotating the cake as necessary with your left hand. Repeat the scooping, spreading, and shimmying routine until the sides of the cake are covered with buttercream. A ridge of buttercream will build up around the top edge of the cake. This is normal.

2. To smooth the sides, scrape off excess buttercream from the spatula against the inside of the buttercream bowl. Dip the spatula in the hot water and wipe it on the damp towel. Hold the warmed spatula vertically, but stationary, against the left side of the cake while you turn the wheel with your left hand.

3. Place a large dollop of buttercream on top of the cake and spread it roughly over the top. To smooth the top, scrape off excess buttercream from the spatula, dip it in hot water, and wipe it with the damp towel. Hold the spatula stationary, against the top of the cake at a slight angle, with the end of the blade in the center of the cake while you turn the decorating turntable counterclockwise.

Adjust the pressure of the spatula while you rotate the turntable until the surface is smooth. Continue to rotate as you carefully pull the spatula toward you and off of the cake. Excess buttercream will extend over the edge of the cake. This is fine. If you plan to texture the top of the cake with a serrated knife, continue with Step 4; otherwise, skip to Step 5.

4. Remove the cake from the wheel, and place it on the counter directly in front of you. Dip the serrated knife into the hot water and wipe it with the damp towel. Hold the warmed knife with two hands, at the back of the cake, and pull it toward you, across the freshly buttercreamed surface at a slight angle with the surface of the cake. Use a wavy or zigzag stroke as you pull the blade.

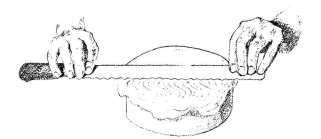

Do not worry about any buttercream that hangs over the edge of the cake!

5. Slide the spatula under the cake and lift it onto the fingers of your left hand (if you are right-handed). Hold the cake, balanced on your fingers, in front of your face. Scrape the spatula clean against the sides of the buttercream bowl, dip it in hot water, and wipe it *dry* against the folded *dry* towel. Hold the spatula vertically, with the blade pointing up, next to the right side of the cake. Keep the spatula vertical while you work. Smooth the excess buttercream that hangs over the edges of the cake by pulling it down against the sides of the cake with the flat of the spatula blade. Start near the spatula handle. Pull, simultaneously, down and part way around the sides of the cake.

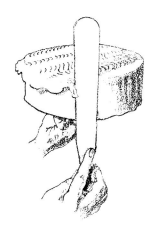

After each and every pulling and smoothing stroke, rotate the cake about one-eighth turn counterclockwise; scrape the spatula clean, dip it in hot water, wipe it against the *dry* towel, and repeat the process until the sides of the cake are neat and smooth.

6. To texture the sides of the cake, return the cake to the center of the decorating turntable. Dip a cake comb or serrated knife into the hot water and wipe it on the damp towel. Turn the wheel with the left hand while you hold the comb or knife against the cake with your right hand.

Alternatively, zigzag the comb against the sides of the cake as for Aztec Layer Cake, page 83.

Practicing to Perfect the Method

Before trying to texture the top of a cake for the first time, practice on the back of a clean cake pan. Tape the pan to the counter in front of you so that it won't slide (since it is not as heavy as a cake!) toward you as you pull the knife blade. You may need to try several times to get the right angle and pressure on the blade.

Practice piping with a pastry bag and decorative tips. Pipe on waxed paper or on the back of a clean cake pan. Buttercream may be scraped off and used again. Use small dainty tips for buttercream borders. Try to keep each shell or rosette equal in size by using equal pressure each time you squeeze the bag. Never fill a pastry bag more than two-thirds full. If the borders look soft and limp, chill the buttercream slightly to stiffen it.

For a serious practice session there is no need to make a batch of buttercream. Instead, buy a box of instant mashed potatoes and mix them up so they are soft enough to pipe. Then, practice away by the hour, adding water as necessary to keep the potatoes from drying out!

Final Touches

After the cake is neatly masked, use excess buttercream to pipe a decorative border around the cake with a pastry bag and small decorative closed star tip (#27, #1, or #2) or small plain tip with a ⅛-inch opening. A star tip border is prettiest if the buttercream is somewhat stiff (see Pavé d'Amour, page 91, and Marjolaine, page 89). The plain "roped" border on page 76 (Grand Marnier Cake) is made with softer buttercream. Use melted chocolate to pipe a birthday greeting or make lacy filigree or crosshatching (see page 185, Piping with Melted Chocolate).

If you wish to stencil the cake, chill it first to firm the buttercream (see Tips for Using Stencils, pages 186–88).

If you wish to press chopped nuts or chocolate shavings against the sides of the cake, do this before the buttercream is chilled so that the nuts or shavings will adhere to the soft buttercream.

PIPING WITH MELTED CHOCOLATE

Piping a motif or writing in fancy script with a fine line of chocolate is one of the most satisfying and elegant finishing touches that I know. Imagine a lacy filigree border, a birthday greeting all in curlicues, or a sinuous spray of tendrils and vines framing a cluster of fresh blush pink roses.

Perhaps you think that wonderful borders, curlicues, and handsome script are best left to the artists and professionals among us. But this is decidedly not so. My own handwriting is atrocious, and I can't draw—but I can pipe, and even write, quite elegantly with chocolate. Even your first efforts will surprise you, and the results of just a little practice will please and delight you. Personally, I find piping with chocolate more fun and infinitely more rewarding than working with a pastry bag full of frosting and a whole army of star tips.

Melting the chocolate is a cinch (read Melting Chocolate, page 25) and learning to fold the paper cone may take you as long as 5 minutes! After that, a bit of practice is the thing.

1. Melt 1–2 ounces of chocolate in a small container.

2. Cut an 8 × 12-inch piece of parchment paper or waxed paper. Fold across opposite corners to form a right triangle. Hold the triangle on the counter with your left hand (if you are right-handed). Slide a sharp knife between the folds and cut along the fold into 2 right triangles.

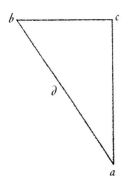

3. Fold each triangle into a cone: Hold a triangle in your left hand with your thumb at the center of the hypotenuse, point (d). Grasp point (b) with your other hand and roll it toward point (c) to form a cone.

Be certain that the tip of the cone remains completely closed. Continue to roll the cone toward point (a), and fold the tip at point (a) over and into the open end of the cone to secure it.

The idea is to be able to fold the paper so that the cone does not come apart when you put it down. At first you may find this a bit awkward. Use some tape, if necessary, and master the finer points of cone-making later. Right now you want to get on to the business of piping chocolate!

4. Prop the cone up in a very narrow-mouthed jar (like a spice jar) or anchor it in a cup of sugar so that it stands up by itself.

5. Scrape melted chocolate into the cone, filling it only about halfway. If you have melted the chocolate in a water bath, be sure to wipe the bottom of the container dry so that drops of water will not fall into the cone with the chocolate. Water will thicken the chocolate and cause gritty lumps that are impossible to pipe.

6. Fold the open end of the cone two or three times, like a toothpaste tube, to seal in the chocolate.

7. Snip the tip of the cone with a sharp pair of scissors to make a small opening. Do not make the opening so big that the chocolate flows out when you are not pressing on the back of the cone.

8. Use two hands to pipe. Hold the cone in your right hand (if you are right-handed), so that your thumb can squeeze the back to push out the chocolate. Your left hand simply steadies the cone as you guide it with your right hand.

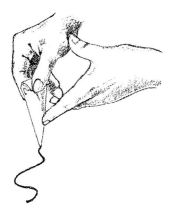

There are two piping methods. Try them both, and choose the one that suits you best. I find that I have more control and can pipe smoother loops and curls using Method One.

Method One: Hold the cone about 1 inch above the dessert and allow the chocolate to fall onto the surface as you squeeze and guide the cone.

Method Two: Hold the cone barely touching the surface of the dessert and pipe directly on it.

TIPS FOR PIPING WITH CHOCOLATE

The tip of the cone should be totally closed before you fill it. This way you can cut it open just as much or as little as you like.

Keep the paper at the back of the cone folded up tightly against the chocolate.

An opening that is too big is hard to control, but a very, very fine line is also difficult because it shows the slightest waver and smallest imperfection in your stroke. Experiment to find the opening that suits your own pace.

Practice on waxed paper or the back of a cake pan.

Chocolate in cones tends to cool and stiffen. Make 2 cones and keep one on a plate in a pilot-lit oven while practicing with the first. When the first cone starts to cool off, trade cones, placing the cool one in the oven to rewarm it. If your oven doesn't have a pilot light, use the microwave to reheat cones (on LOW [30%] for 5–10 seconds) or keep the second cone in a folded heating pad! Sometimes a cone can be rewarmed by waving it quickly and carefully back and forth about 5 inches above a lit stove burner.

Practice fancy motifs from books, hand-drawn designs, and other sources by piping on a sheet of waxed paper placed over the real thing.

Do not overheat the chocolate. Dark chocolate need not be hotter than 120°. Milk and white chocolate should be 100°–110°.

Chocolate chips do not make good piping chocolate.

TROUBLESHOOTING

The chocolate comes out too fast:
—The opening is too big and/or you are squeezing too hard.
The chocolate comes out too slowly, or hardly at all:
—The opening may not be large enough, or it may be blocked with a bit of unmelted chocolate or grit; try pinching the end to eject it. The chocolate may have cooled and become too thick. Put it in a microwave on LOW (30%) for 5–10 seconds.
The chocolate comes out of the cone in loops instead of a steady, even flow; it is impossible to draw a smooth or controlled line:
—There may be an obstruction. It could be an unmelted grain of chocolate or grit, or the cone is imperfectly folded and part of the paper is obstructing the opening. You may have snipped the cone with dull scissors leaving a ragged edge. Try pinching the tip to eject a possible obstruction. Try snipping off a tiny bit more of the cone to create a slightly larger opening. Be sure the chocolate it still melted and fluid. If all else fails, make a new cone, squeeze the chocolate into it and try again.
The cone works fine, but I can't seem to stop the chocolate exactly when and where I want. I always end up with an extra "tail" at the end of each motif or word:
—Stop squeezing a second or two before the end of your design.
—At the same time, lower your tip so that it actually touchs the surface of the dessert at the exact point that you wish to stop, as though you were making a dot. Instead of a "tail" at the end of your figure, you will have a neat, slightly rounded end.

STENCILS

A stencil is an easy way to finish a dessert in a unique and personalized way. Cocoa, confectioners' sugar, ground cinnamon, pulverized nuts, and grated chocolate make wonderful dusting materials, alone or in combination.

Stenciling offers the opportunity to play with different textures and colors. You may stencil a velvety matte-cocoa design on the contrasting surface of a satiny truffle tart. Or, dust the entire surface of a torte with cocoa, and then stencil a pattern in confectioners' sugar.

A store-bought doily makes an obvious and easy stencil, but your own homemade stencil offers many more distinctive, dramatic possibilities, as well as a chance for you to be creative. Clean lines, fabulous optical effects, and striking goemetric patterns are all doable—and much easier than you think. It may take a little time to draw and cut a stencil, but once made, you will use it over and over again. (See photo on page 10.)

TO MAKE STENCILS

Special Equipment:

Pencil

Pair of scissors

X-acto knife

Piece of lightweight cardboard, square or round, at least 1 inch bigger on all sides than the dessert you will decorate (This will be your stencil cardboard. It should have at least one smooth or shiny side, if possible. You may cut up a gift box with a shiny surface, use the cardboard foil top from a frozen food container, or purchase a piece of acetate or waxed stencil board from an art supply store. Failing these, an ordinary manila file folder is about the right weight and usually smooth enough to do the job.)

An additional piece of cardboard or stiff paper is helpful for making a template

Ruler, compass, or square may be useful depending on the type of design you choose

Surface that you can cut on

On the stencil cardboard, trace a circle about ½ inch greater in diameter than the dessert to be decorated. You will design and cut out your stencil within this circle.

Repetitive Waves, Curves, and Zigzags: These are my favorites, and you'll be amazed by how easy it is to create these designs.

First, make a template by drawing a freeform wavy pattern or a zigzag (use a straight edge to help you) across a piece of scrap cardboard at least as long as the diameter of your stencil. Cut along the line you have drawn.

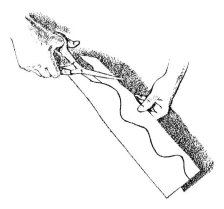

Place the cut edge of the template on the circle you have traced on your stencil cardboard. Run a pencil along the edge to transfer the design. Slide the template below the original position and trace the edge of the template again, parallel to the first tracing.

Continue to do this until the circle is entirely filled. Cut along each of the lines with an X-acto knife, then cut between every other line so that you can remove alternating pieces.

Radiating Patterns: Make a template by drawing a simple curve or S-shape across a piece of scrap cardboard at least as long as the radius of your stencil. Cut along the curve you have drawn. Place one end of the template in the center of the stencil and trace along the cut edge to the edge of the circle. Hold the end of the template in the center of the circle while you pivot the other end away from the first tracing. Retrace the curve over and over again, each time holding the template in the center and pivoting the other end along the edge of the circle until the entire circle is covered with an *even number* of curvy spokes.

Cut carefully along the lines with an X-acto knife, then cut between every other line along the edge of the circle so that you can remove alternating spokes.

Multiple Stencils: Design more than one stencil and use them in succession with different tones of dusting material, such as cocoa *and* confectioners' sugar. Or dust the entire dessert with one dusting material, set a stencil over it and dust with a second dusting material, then remove the first stencil, set a second stencil in place, and dust with a third dusting material. (See Aztec Layer Cake on page 83.)

TIPS FOR USING STENCILS

— If your dusting material is a fine powder, such as cocoa, confectioners' sugar, or ground cinnamon, use a *very fine* strainer or sieve so that you can control how fast and how heavily the dusting material comes out. Be sure it is large enough so that the dusting material does not spill out while you are dusting.

— If the dusting material is coarse—like ground nuts—use a sieve with a coarse mesh or sprinkle the nuts with your fingers. Try grating chocolate directly over the stencil. It probably will not pass through a sieve and it definitely will melt if you try to sprinkle it with your fingers.

— First put the dusting material in a strainer or sieve and try dusting a plate or piece of waxed paper to make sure you have control. *Do not shake the strainer*—this causes the dusting material to come out too heavily in one place. Instead, hold the strainer a few inches above the stencil with one hand and gently tap the side with the other hand. Move the strainer over the stencil tapping gently until the entire stencil is covered. You control how heavily the dusting material falls from the strainer by the gentleness of your taps. For even coverage, dust lightly everywhere, and then redust—always lightly—until you have the coverage you want.

— Practice using your stencil before decorating a dessert with it. Lay the stencil, smooth side down (if there is a choice), on a piece of waxed or parchment paper and dust the top. Remove stencil carefully. If you have never used a stencil before, you may find that either you are dusting too heavily—which causes the dusting material to pile up and later fall or blow over and smudge the design—or you are not lifting the stencil off gently enough—which also damages the design. Your practice run will enable you to correct your technique before you actually decorate your dessert.

If you are satisfied with your design and technique, clean the stencil before dusting the actual dessert. To do this, hold the stencil vertically over a piece of waxed paper on the counter. Tap the edge against the counter to remove most of the dusting material. Wipe the under (smooth) side of the stencil clean with a dry tissue.

— If the dessert that you plan to decorate is dry and not at all sticky, there should be no problem with laying the clean stencil directly on it before dusting. A light dusting will adhere nicely, even to a dry surface. A moist or sticky dessert is another story. A stencil may cause damage if it touches the moist surface. In this case you have two options: Prop up the stencil, about ¼ inch above the dessert, or ask a friend to hold the stencil as steadily as possible while you dust it. Easier still, dust the entire surface of the dessert first with one dusting material, then lay the stencil on the dusted surface and redust with a second material in a contrasting color. Whether the dessert is dry or moist, avoid

dusting too heavily or dusting material will blow over and blur the design.

CHOCOLATE SHAVINGS, CIGARETTES, RIBBONS, AND FANS

Lavish chocolate ruffles with delicate deckled edges crown show-stopping desserts; two- and three-toned cigarettes add panache to a special-occasion cake; curly trompe l'oeil ribbons create endless possibilities, as do myriad abstract chocolate shapes produced "by accident" as one works with the chocolate.

The simplest shavings are no more difficult than scraping a sharp knife across a piece of chocolate. The most dramatic shapes—fans, cigarettes, and ribbons—take a bit more time and patience to master.

Fortunately, these very special finishing touches can be made weeks in advance. Store them in the refrigerator, between sheets of waxed paper, in an airtight container. Keep a supply on hand to decorate a store-bought dessert, fresh fruit, or ice cream.

TO MAKE SHAVINGS FROM A BLOCK OF CHOCOLATE

The easiest shavings are made simply by scraping a sharp knife against a bar of chocolate.

These shavings are very fine and melt easily if touched with warm hands. Instead, handle them with a metal spatula. Shovel them up gently and put them aside for later use, or transfer them directly onto the dessert they will decorate.

Larger curls and shavings can be made using a 5- or 10-pound block of chocolate, a chef's knife, and an old gooseneck desk or clamp lamp with a 60-watt bulb. (If such large pieces of chocolate are impractical for you, try the alternate technique for making chocolate curls, fans, etc., from the back of a cookie sheet on page 189.)

Place the chocolate block in a shallow pan. Use the lamp to warm the surface of the block and soften it slightly. Position the lamp about 12 inches from the block of chocolate, moving it from time to time and adjusting the distance if necessary, to warm the block only slightly but evenly all over without melting it. Test the block by rubbing the heel of your hand over it—it should start to feel slightly oily but not yet sticky. When you are ready to make curls, place the pan of chocolate perpendicular to the edge of the counter in front of you. Lean against the counter to brace the pan with your body. Grasp the knife with both hands and hold it horizontally in front of you. Pull the blade firmly toward you, scraping the chocolate off the block at about a 90° angle.

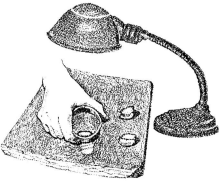

If the chocolate splinters, the block needs a few more minutes under the lamp to soften it. If the chocolate melts or gums up against the knife, it is too soft—turn the lamp off for a few minutes and let the chocolate harden.

Round curls and shavings are made by scraping the softened block with a round cookie cutter instead of a knife.

The softness of the chocolate and the angle and pressure of the knife determine the shape and size of the shaving or curl. Firm pressure on a soft block results in big, sturdy curls; less pressure against a harder block gives thinner, more fragile results.

After you have scraped off the softened surface of the block you may need to rewarm it in order to continue. Remember to adjust or turn off the lamp as necessary while you work.

TO MAKE CHOCOLATE CIGARETTES, RIBBONS, FANS, AND CURLS ON THE BACK OF A COOKIE SHEET

To make more sophisticated shapes—ruffles, ribbons, and cigarettes—melted chocolate is spread on warmed pans, chilled to set, then scraped off at just the right moment. Curls, shavings, and abstract shapes can be formed this way as well.

Pick a cool day to do this work. If it is your first attempt or if you are planning to make lots of chocolate shapes, allow plenty of time and spread chocolate on as many pans as you can find. You will get plenty of practice without having to stop and re-melt, re-spread, and re-chill pans. Clear enough space in the refrigerator to hold several cookie sheets spread with melted chocolate. With a little experience, you will be able to make wonderful chocolate decorations in much less time, using many fewer pans! Save and store your best results in the refrigerator or freezer. Mistakes, unwanted shapes, and scraps may be saved and re-melted for use in a cake batter or glaze.

Special Equipment:
Offset metal spatula for spreading melted chocolate on pans
8-inch metal icing spatula with a very flexible blade (I test all the blades in the store by flexing them)
2 or more heavy-duty, unwarped, undented cookie sheets with smooth surfaces (I use the backs of my half-sheet [12 × 16-inch] pans. Do not use pans with special coatings or non-stick surfaces. The process of making curls and cigarettes will scrape or damage special pan coatings and probably integrate bits of it into your chocolate decorations. If your pans have sides, use the backs.)
Water bath (pan of barely simmering water) or a microwave oven to melt and keep chocolate warm

To Melt and Spread the Chocolate

For Solid Decorations: 1. Melt about 6 ounces of chocolate for each 12 × 16-inch pan you intend to use. You may use dark, milk, or white chocolate.

2. Warm the back of a pan or cookie sheet by holding it about 6 inches above a stove burner and moving it back and forth until it is very warm all over but not hot enough to burn your fingers.

3. Use an offset spatula to spread melted chocolate evenly, about ¹⁄₁₆ inch thick, over the warmed pan.

Refrigerate pan to harden chocolate. To spread additional pans, warm another cookie sheet and repeat the spreading and chilling step described above. Continue until you have spread as many pans as you wish. Leave the chocolate-covered pans in the refrigerator until they are completely hardened, at least 20 minutes or up to several hours.

For Striped Decorations: Melt 6 ounces of chocolate for each stripe color you intend to use—dark, milk, and/or white chocolate. Fill large parchment-paper decorating cones with melted chocolate. Warm pans as described in Step 2 above. Snip the tips of the cones enough so that you can pipe ¼-inch-thick lines of chocolate down the length of the pan about ¼ inch apart.

Use an offset spatula to spread the lines of chocolate so that they flatten out and touch each other. Chill pans. Continue with Step 4.

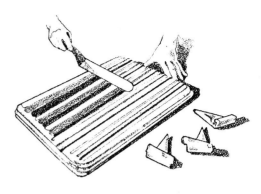

For Marbled Decorations: Use 2 contrasting chocolates, such as white and dark, or milk and white, etc. Decide which of the chocolates will be the dominant color. For each sheet pan, melt 6 ounces of the dominant chocolate and 1 ounce of the other chocolate for marbling. Fill a paper cone (page 185) with the marbling chocolate. Warm pans as described in Step 2 above. Pipe a random scribbly pattern on a warmed pan.

Immediately pour about 6 ounces of the other chocolate over the scribble and spread it evenly all over the sheet, covering the scribble. (The marbling will not show until you scrape your decorations and turn them over.) Chill pans. Continue with Step 4.

4. Remove one pan at a time and let the chocolate warm up at room temperature until it is soft enough to scrape according to the instructions below. If it cracks and splinters as you scrape, it is still too cold—wait a few minutes longer. If the chocolate gums up or melts against the spatula, it is too soft and should be returned to the refrigerator briefly. *Most difficulties are caused by chocolate that is too soft or not soft enough. Don't fight it. Sheets can be re-chilled over and over again, or allowed to soften longer at room temperature, as necessary.* If the temperature of the chocolate is perfect but you still can't get the shape you want, try altering the angle of the spatula blade as you scrape the chocolate. Once you have a feel for this, you may remove more than one pan at a time—or remove them at short intervals depending on the warmth of the room and the speed with which you work.

5. Place finished shapes on a cold pan lined with parchment or waxed paper and refrigerate as soon as possible. If shapes start to melt, work with 2 pans, rotating one in and one out of the refrigerator as needed to hold your finished work.

6. Save and store your best results. Mistakes, unwanted shapes, and scraps can be saved to remelt for future use.

To Form the Decorations

Each shape is formed by scraping the chocolate from the pan with a different angle and/or stroke of the spatula.

Cigarettes: Brace the pan against your body, perpendicular to the edge of the counter in front of you. Start about 2 inches above the lower left corner of the pan if you are right-handed. Hold the metal spatula blade with two hands, horizontally, in front of you and pull the blade toward you, scraping the chocolate off the pan at about a 45° angle for an inch or two until it forms a cigarette. Work your way from the bottom of the pan toward the top, forming each cigarette behind the last. If you have spread the pan with 2- or 3-tone stripes of chocolate, scrape cigarettes parallel with stripes.

Scalloped Shavings: To form shallow, boat-shaped shavings (as for Black and White Raspberry Cake, page 140), proceed as for cigarettes but scrape the spatula at a 10° angle with the pan instead of 45°. As you gain facility, try sliding the spatula slightly to the right and back again as you scrape, to vary the shape of the decoration.

Flat and Curly Ribbons: Brace the pan of chocolate against your body, perpendicular to the edge of the counter in front of you. Start at the upper-left-hand corner of the pan if you are right-handed. Hold the spatula blade horizontally and bend it slightly with two hands. Pull blade toward you, pressing the bent part of the blade against the chocolate at about a 10° angle. The blade will actually slide under the chocolate, peeling it off the pan to form a ribbon with beautiful deckled edges.

Depending on the angle of the blade and the temperature of the chocolate, the ribbon will lie flat or curl. You may uncurl it with your fingers if you need flat pieces, or use it curled. The softer the chocolate, the more it will curl. The width of the ribbon is determined by how sharply the blade is bent as it contacts the cookie sheet. If you have marbled the chocolate in the pans, turn the ribbons over to reveal marbling.

Fans: Brace the pan of chocolate against your body, perpendicular to the edge of the counter in front of you. Start at the upper left hand corner of the pan if you are right-handed. Hold the spatula blade with two hands with the right hand above the left. Pull the spatula toward you so that it describes the shape of a fan. This is accomplished by pulling the right hand toward you at a faster rate than the left. The right-hand side of the spatula blade should form a loose, open ruffle of chocolate. The left hand will move only a short distance toward you, acting as a pivot to gather the ruffled chocolate tightly on the left side. The spatula blade should scrape the chocolate off the pan at about a 10° angle. The results should resemble a fan with a beautiful deckled edge. If you have spread the 2- or 3-tone stripes of chocolate, scrape fans across or parallel to stripes, depending on desired effect. If you have marbled the chocolate on the pan, turn fans over to reveal design. With practice you may be able to make 10–15 good-size fans from each 12 × 16-inch baking sheet.

Pastel Decorations

Pastel or colored shapes are made by mixing melted white chocolate with specially formulated powdered food colors that dissolve in chocolate. *Do not use regular household liquid food coloring because the water or liquid content of these colors will cause the chocolate to seize.* Powdered food colors are available at cake decorating shops and by mail order (see Resources, page 197). Proceed as for making cigarettes, ribbons, or fans.

WRAPPING A CAKE IN CHOCOLATE RIBBONS AND MAKING A CHOCOLATE CABBAGE ROSE

This is my favorite way to turn almost any cake into a very special party dessert. Festive, dramatic, unusual—we use it for weddings, anniversaries, and galas of any kind. Basically the technique involves running pieces of white or dark chocolate "dough" through a pasta machine to form wide ribbons. The cake is wrapped in the ribbons and the remaining "dough" is turned into a dramatic oversized cabbage rose for the top of the cake.

CHOCOLATE MODELING DOUGH

Makes enough for one 9-inch Celebration Cake

14 ounces semisweet or bittersweet chocolate, cut into bits, or white chocolate, very finely chopped

⅓ cup light corn syrup

Special Equipment:

Electric pasta machine

Old-fashioned gooseneck desk lamp (with an ordinary 60-watt light bulb), to help keep the dough warm as you work (optional, but helpful)

Tray lined with waxed paper

Bowl (about 7 inches in diameter and 3½–4 inches tall) lined with a long piece of plastic wrap so that ends hang over the sides of the bowl

1. **To Make the Dough:** Combine 12 ounces of the chocolate with the corn syrup in a small bowl. Stir to moisten the chocolate. For dark chocolate dough, melt in a barely simmering water bath over low heat. Stir frequently to hasten melting. Or microwave on MEDIUM (50%) for about 2½–3 minutes. For white chocolate dough, melt in a water bath which has first been brought to a simmer and then turned off for 30 seconds. Or, microwave on LOW (30%) for about 2½–3 minutes. Stir just until mixture is combined. It may look curdled and broken; this is all right.

2. Pour mixture onto a marble surface or a plate. Let dark chocolate dough rest until it begins to harden. It firms up on the outside surface first, so scrape it up and knead it once or twice now and then as it hardens. The dough is ready to use when it is the consistency of firm Playdough as you knead it. If it is too soft and gooey, let it rest again until harder, then knead again. Let white chocolate dough rest, without handling, several hours or

overnight before kneading. It may seem hard and crumbly at first. Knead it firmly, breaking it apart and pushing it together with the heel of your hand, until smooth and pliable.

Chocolate dough softens and hardens readily. Manipulation and the warmth of your hands and/or a warm lamp keep the dough soft; letting it stand, untouched, on a cool surface causes it to harden. Keep this knowledge in mind, along with the desk lamp, as you work with the dough. In general, white chocolate dough is more sensitive to heat and manipulation than dark. Dough may be used right away or wrapped airtight for later use. It keeps for at least 1 month, well wrapped, at room temperature. Prepared in advance, dough will harden and must be reworked. To rework, knead with your hands until pliable and smooth. If it is much too hard to knead, cut into thin slices and place under a lamp or in an oven with a pilot light until slightly softened so that you can knead it. Or, soften slices *very* slightly in the microwave on LOW (30%) for 10 seconds at a time, until just soft enough to manipulate in your hands. Err on the conservative side; if the dough becomes too warm, it will "break" and the cocoa butter will start to separate from it. You will have to let it set until hardened and try to reknead it until smooth—a very tricky proposition.

3. **To Make Chocolate Ribbons:** Break off and knead pieces of dough to form fifteen to twenty 1-inch balls. Flatten each one into a disk that is about 2 inches in diameter. Run each disk, in succession, through the pasta machine at a setting that will flatten and elongate the disks just a little. (My machine has settings #1 through #6, so I start with setting #5½ or #6, which is the widest.) Lay the flattened pieces on the waxed paper–lined tray. Reset the machine to flatten the dough even more (I use #3½ or #4 this time) and run each of the pieces through again. (Always start with the first piece from the last run and end with the last piece from the last run.) Ribbons may be layered between sheets of waxed paper to save space. Reset the machine for the third time (I use #2 or #2½) to make the thinnest possible ribbon that won't break or disintegrate. Ribbons should be at least 15–16 inches long. You will cut each in half when the cake is wrapped. Ribbons may have a ragged edge; this is fine.

If the ribbons become too cold and brittle between runs through the machine, divide them into 2 groups and run only half at a time through each successive setting, then go back and do the other half. This will reduce the time between handling each piece of dough and keep them from getting too cold. You may use the lamp judiciously to warm the work area gently and/or burnish the pieces of dough with the heel of your hand to warm them. If the dough gets too soft, let it rest longer between runs. Do not try to run one piece of dough successively through each of the machine settings without letting it rest in between—it will soften too much from handling and stick to the machine.

4. **To Wrap the Cake:** Take the cake from the refrigerator. Mark the center of the top of the cake by sticking a toothpick in it. Cut one of the chocolate ribbons in half and place the tapered end of one piece at the toothpick and drape the rest of the ribbon over the edge of the cake and down the sides to the bottom edge of the cake. Place the other piece of ribbon, partially overlapping the first, always with the tapered end at the toothpick and the wider, cut end hanging over the cake. Continue to cut and drape the ribbons, working around the cake. Ribbons will stick to the buttercream a bit more as you work because the buttercream will soften. Try to slip the last ribbon partway under the first—I usually tuck a thin strip of waxed paper partially under the very first chocolate ribbon at the start to keep it from sticking to the buttercream, then I slide it out and slip the last ribbon in its place. Trim ribbons at the bottom edge of the cake, if necessary. Remove the toothpick and return the wrapped cake to the refrigerator. Save any trimmings not contaminated by buttercream, and knead them with extra ribbons into the remaining chocolate dough.

5. **To Make a Cabbage Rose:** Break the remaining dough into 9 pieces and knead and roll into balls about 1½ inches in diameter. Use a rolling pin to flatten each one between waxed paper or plastic wrap into a thin, approximately oval sheet about 7 inches long and 5–6 inches wide. Set aside.

6. Melt the remaining 2 ounces chocolate. Pour about 1 tablespoonful of it into the center at the bottom of the plastic-lined bowl to act as a base for the outer petals of the rose. Pick up and peel the plastic wrap from one of the oval sheets. Gather it along one of the long edges to form a large freeform petal. Press the gathered edge partway into the melted chocolate at the bottom of the bowl. Form the second oval sheet into a similar petal and press it next to and somewhat overlapping the first.

Continue to form petals with 5 of the ovals, placing them around the sides of the bowl. Use additional melted chocolate as necessary to make the petals stick to the base of the bowl. The fifth petal should be tucked slightly behind the first. Form the next 3 ovals into petals and use them for interior petals. Form a center for the giant rose by rolling up or pleating the last oval sheet into a loose trumpet shape. Dip the end in the remaining melted chocolate and push it into the center of the rose with a chopstick or the handle of a spoon. Cover the rose with plastic wrap and chill to set the melted chocolate base and to firm the petals. Rose may be stored this way until the cake is served or displayed.

7. **To Put the Rose on the Cake:** Uncover the rose. Lift it out of the bowl by pulling up on the overhanging ends of the plastic wrap.

Secure the rose to the top of the cake with a little melted chocolate. Unless it is a very hot day, the cake can be displayed for 3–5 hours, if necessary.

Equipment

Every chef and cook has a favorite battery of equipment, without which life in the kitchen would be incomplete. In addition to the usual measuring cups (dry and liquid) and spoons, whisks, saucepans, and bowls, here is my personal list of "necessities." I even travel with some of them—like a security blanket—if I am teaching in an unfamiliar kitchen.

Heavy-Duty Mixer

I like a serious mixer. KitchenAid (models K5A, K5SF, KSM5, or K45) is my own favorite. Buy an extra bowl or two, so that you will not have to transfer mixtures and wash the bowl when you beat egg whites or when a recipe requires beating two different mixtures. This mixer comes with a wire whisk—for beating egg whites, cream, génoise batters, and any mixture that must have lots of air beaten into it—as well as a sturdy flat beater called a paddle or leaf beater, used for creaming butter and beating stiff batters. It comes with a dough hook for kneading yeast doughs. A copper liner for beating egg whites is available from Williams-Sonoma stores (see Resources, page 197).

Food Processor

Food processors are marvelous for pulverizing nuts, reducing granulated sugar to superfine for meringues, making purées, mixing tart doughs, grinding praline, etc.

Microwave Oven

I was not an early convert, but the microwave is now a very good friend. Use it to melt and remelt chocolate quickly and cleanly, defrost and/or soften butter, warm glazes almost instantly, toast nuts, instantly restore frozen buttercream to working consistency, and much, much more.

Cake Pans/Regular Sizes

I use heavy-duty professional pans with straight sides, most commonly 8-inch and 9-inch round pans that are 2 inches deep. These are available from restaurant supply or kitchenware shops. An 8-inch square (2 inches deep) is a useful alternative to a 9-inch round pan, as both have about the same capacity.

Dessert Rings and Springform and Cheesecake Pans

Dessert rings are bottomless, straight-sided forms, used for molding my favorite architectural desserts. Dessert rings are widely available in France, but not in the U.S. They are imported in many sizes by Bridge Kitchenware Corp. and may be purchased by mail order (see Resources, page 197). Some kitchenware stores carry an expandable ring with diameters from 7 to 14 inches. If you fall in love with "designer desserts" such as the Strawberry Carrousel, Apricot Soufflé, or Tricolor Mousse, you will find that a dessert ring is a special joy to work with. It is easy to have a sheet metal shop fabricate a couple of them for you out of 18- or 20-gauge stainless steel. You will probably be inspired to create some new desserts just as an excuse to use your dessert rings more often. A ring that is 8 inches in diameter and 3 inches deep will do the job for the desserts in this book. A straight-sided loose-bottom pan, also called a cheesecake pan, 8 inches round and 3 inches deep (available from Parrish or Maid of Scandinavia [see Resources, page 197]) can be used in almost the same way. A dessert made in a dessert ring is unmolded by warming the ring with a torch or hot towel and slipping the ring *upward* and off the dessert. The cheesecake pan must be propped up on a cannister or a large food can before warming, then the sides of the pan are pulled *down* and off the dessert. A conventional springform pan can also be used, but the sides do not come off quite as cleanly, so you will usually have to smooth them with a spatula.

Baking Sheets and Jelly-Roll Pans

I prefer heavy-duty professional aluminum baking sheets because they do not warp or bend. The "half-sheet" size measures 12×16 inches on the bottom inside and is 1 inch deep. These can be used as jelly-roll pans in place of the standard home size (11×17 inches), or as cookie sheets, or to make chocolate ruffles and cigarettes and curls (see page 189). Do not mistake these pans for the 8×12-inch pans referred to as "half-sheets" by some kitchenware catalogues.

If you don't use professional-weight "half-sheet" pans as cookie sheets, buy the heaviest aluminum cookie sheet you can find. Toroware makes good ones. I don't use the ones with the special Teflon or Silverstone coatings because I use parchment paper liners for baking and because these coated pans are not suitable for making chocolate cigarettes, curls, etc.

Parchment Paper

Parchment paper comes in rolls for home use. (If you have access to bakery suppliers, you may buy it in large sheets and in precut circles for lining cake pans.)

Thermometers

Candy Thermometer: Use a candy or sugar thermometer for sugar syrups, or use the shortcut slotted spoon technique to determine the soft-ball stage, buttercream recipe, page 181.

Insta-Read Meat Thermometer: This is a sturdy, inexpensive dial thermometer made by Taylor with a range from 0° to 220°. It is perfect when making delicate custards like crème anglaise, for getting the temperature of chocolate glaze just right, and for anything else that you do with chocolate. (Taylor also makes a chocolate thermometer with a range from 40° to 125°. It's excellent for chocolate but does not have a high enough range for custards.)

Oven Thermometer: Use an oven thermometer every now and again to see that your oven is really achieving 350° when the dial says it is!

Pastry Brushes

Keep a couple of natural boar's bristle brushes on hand for dessert making. Never, never let them touch barbecue marinades and/or garlic! A 1-inch brush and one 1½ or 2 inches wide will cover most contingencies from brushing syrup on cake layers to glazing fruit tarts or lattice crusts.

Fluted 9½-Inch Tart Pan, with Removeable Bottom

These are my favorite pans for tarts of all kinds.

Rubber Spatulas

Have on hand at least one large professional-size rubber spatula as well as the standard home size and a mini. The largest one is the very best thing for folding delicate, airy batters and scraping larger bowls. If you have no specialty kitchen shop near you, check the phone book for restaurant supply stores; most will let anyone come in and buy. A mini spatula is very handy for scraping small quantities of melted chocolate from small containers. I use the largest and the mini most of all.

Icing Spatula

An icing spatula should be made of stainless steel with an 8-inch blade that is rounded at the end. A stiff blade is best for most frosting and glazing techniques. I also like to have at least one with a very flexible blade for making chocolate ruffles, fans, and cigarettes. The best spatulas are made by Wearever, Dexter, and Ateco, and are available at restaurant supply stores and cookware and cake-decorating specialty stores. I always ask to see a whole boxful, and then I flex each and every one of them to find a stiff one and a flexible one. The salesperson will tell you that they are all the same stiffness, but usually this is not so. Less expensive, usually more flexible, spatulas are available in the kitchen section of housewares and hardware stores.

Offset Spatula

This is a stainless-steel spatula with a bend at the base of the blade near the handle. The blade should be at least 8 inches, but preferably 12 inches after the bend. This is the best thing for spreading a mixture thinly and evenly over a large surface—like cake batter into a jelly-roll pan or melted chocolate onto the back of a pan to make chocolate fans and shavings.

Wooden Barbecue Skewers

Wooden skewers are inexpensive and come in packages of several dozen. I like the ones that are at least 9 inches long. For testing cakes for doneness, they are cleaner than broom straws and longer than toothpicks. I dislike the thin metal skewers that are sold as cake testers, because nothing sticks to them and it is hard to tell whether the skewer is wet or dry. Batter sticks readily to a wood skewer so you can see the exact consistency of the interior of the cake. Plunge the skewer into the cake at a wide angle to test more than just one little place in the center of the cake.

Skewers are perfect for caramelizing nuts (page 172). Skewers are the next best thing to a fine artist's brush for marbling chocolate glaze (page 177).

Although wooden skewers are made to discard, you may rinse and re-use them.

Cake Decorating Turntable

A cake decorating turntable is a heavy, well-balanced lazy Susan used to help you frost and decorate cakes. They are available at restaurant supply and kitchenware stores. If you love to make and decorate cakes, you should have one. The lightweight plastic ones are very inexpensive but not very satisfying to work with. The heavy-duty metal ones made by Ateco are a joy, but the expense may not seem justified unless you use it regularly and/or just love good tools. I have found one alternative. For nearly half the price of a good decorating turntable, you may purchase a banding wheel from a ceramics supply shop. Ceramicists use them for decorating. They are nicely weighted and heavy. Get one that is at least 12 inches in diameter.

Whether you buy a decorating turntable or a ceramics banding wheel, be sure that you never, ever, submerge it in water. The stem must not be allowed to rust or corrode or your wheel will not spin freely. Lubricate the stem now and then with mineral oil.

Eight-Ounce Glass Jelly Jars

These are very inexpensive. I buy a case of 12 and use them for melting small quantities of chocolate, butter, etc. They can go into the microwave or water bath. I also use them to store small quantities in the refrigerator or freezer. The jelly jars keep my 1-cup measuring cups and my small china bowls from becoming lost in the fridge and freezer for long periods of time.

Artist's Brushes

A fine artist's brush, size 0 or 1 with ¾-inch-long bristles, is the ideal tool for marbling glazes (see page 177).

Medium and Fine Strainers

I like a medium strainer better than a sifter for flour and dry ingredients because it can be operated with one hand and it shakes out and cleans easily. A fine strainer is ideal for dusting cocoa or confectioners' sugar over a stencil and for straining ganaches and glazes.

Scissors

Keep a pair in the kitchen for cutting parchment paper, etc.

Ruler

A plastic kitchen ruler is handy for drawing templates for ladyfingers, cutting parchment paper strips to make chocolate bands for wrapping desserts, dividing a sheet of sponge cake into exactly the right proportions, measuring pans, cutting a cake or torte into perfect individual squares, measuring the thickness or diameter of rolled-out pastry doughs, and so on. Plastic cleans easily. I love the transparent rulers that are 2 inches wide and marked with a grid. They are made for printers and are available in art supply stores.

Serrated Bread Knife

A serrated bread knife with a 12-inch blade is the best. Use it for cutting thin cake layers as well as texturing the buttercream or mousse on top of cakes or desserts.

Scale

A scale is the most convenient way to measure flour, dry ingredients, and nuts, since it enables you to weigh before sifting or grinding. This saves bowls, and measuring cups, and mess on the counter. It also saves the guesswork of wondering, for example, how many cups of nut pieces equal 2 cups of ground nuts.

You will also want a scale if you buy chocolate in 10-pound blocks, since the block will not be marked into convenient, 1-ounce segments!

Light- or Medium-Weight 3- to 4-Cup Saucepan

I make small batches of caramelized sugar (for caramelizing nuts, etc.) in a small lightweight saucepan instead of the heavyweight "professional" copper pot made expressly for this purpose! This is contrary to advice you will get elsewhere, but I swear by it. A small batch of caramel burns easily in a heavy pan, because the pan stays hot and the caramel continues to cook after you remove it from the heat. A light pan offers more control, as it cools almost immediately when it is removed from the heat and plunged into cold water.

X-acto or Utility Knife

This type of knife is handy for cutting stencils.

Pastry Bags and Tips

If possible, avoid the traditional cloth pastry bags and look for a French brand called IMPER. These wash easily and dry without becoming stiff and smelly. They also hold moisture so that whipped cream does not weep through them while you are decorating. (See Resources, page 197.) A 16- to 18-inch bag is handy for piping lots of whipped cream or forming ladyfingers or macaroons. A 10- to 12-inch bag is good for smaller work such as piping decorative borders of buttercream.

You will want an assortment of pastry tips for forming batters or cookie doughs, and for decorating. The recipes in this book use the following Ateco brand tips: closed star tips #4, #5, #7, #8, #9, #26, and #27; plain round tips #8 and #9.

Propane Torch

This is handy for unmolding desserts made in dessert rings, warming pans for making chocolate decorations, and caramelizing meringue. I like the type with the automatic trigger. Buy these at any hardware store.

Resources

Equipment and ingredients for baking are available from these special sources. Many of them have mail-order catalogues.

SPECIALITY HOUSES

Bridge Kitchenware Corp.
214 East 52nd Street
New York, NY 10022
(212) 688-4220
A legendary (enormous) selection of domestic and imported kitchenware for home and professional use. Bridge has stainless-steel dessert rings in myriad sizes and stocks my favorite IMPER pastry bags from France.

Cocolat
2547 Ninth Street
Berkeley, CA 94710
(415) 843-1182
My own selection of chocolate for dessert making—white, milk, and bittersweet, as well as my favorite DeZaan cocoa.

Maid of Scandinavia
3244 Raleigh Avenue
Minneapolis, MN 55416
1-800-328-6722
An incredible assortment of pans, equipment, supplies, and novelties for the dessert maker and cake decorator. Also chocolate molds and candy-making equipment, colored candy foils, fluted candy and petit four cups, and doilies. Lindt and Callebaut chocolate. Powdered food colors suitable for coloring white chocolate. Copper bowls for KitchenAid mixers.

Parrish
314 West 58th Street
Los Angeles, CA 90037
(213) 750-7650
A paradise for cake makers and decorators. A selection similar to Maid of Scandinavia. Mail-order catalogue available.

Post Haste
PO Box 743
Camarillo, CA 93010
Mail-order source for expandable dessert rings.

S.E. Rycoff
761 Terminal Street
Los Angeles, CA 90021
(213) 622-4131
Imported and domestic ingredients. Callebaut chocolate. Mail-order catalogue available.

Summit Cookware
PO Box 994
San Mateo, CA 94403
Mail-order source for copper bowls to fit KitchenAid mixers.

Torn Ranch
1122 Fourth Street
San Rafael, CA 94901
(415) 459-1660
All kinds of nuts and dried fruits.

Albert Uster
Addresses in Oakland, California; Kansas City, Missouri; and Gaithersburg, Maryland.
Call for further information
1-800-231-8154
Imported ingredients and professional baking and candy-making equipment. Catalogue available. $100 minimum order.

Williams-Sonoma
PO Box 7456
San Francisco, CA 94120
(415) 421-4242
Catalogue of kitchen and tableware and baking equipment. Copper bowls for KitchenAid mixers. Callebaut chocolate. Williams-Sonoma also has retail stores in many cities across the country.

YELLOW PAGES

Look in your local Yellow Pages under the following listings to find specialized tools and equipment, ingredients, and ideas.

Art supply stores
for artists brushes, books, ideas, and gold leaf.

Cake decorating shops
for anything to do with cake decorating.

Ceramics supply stores
for banding wheels, texturing tools, and ideas.

Gourmet food stores
for ingredients.

Indian groceries
for edible gold leaf called vark, for decorating.

Natural foods stores
for organic produce, bulk nuts and dried fruits, etc.

Restaurant supply stores
for pans, equipment, decorating turntables, etc.

Sheet metal shops
for custom-made dessert rings.

PARIS

Not to be missed! These two spots could be a high point of your trip to France. They are within walking distance of one another for your convenience.

Dehillerin
18 rue Coquillière
Paris 1
Everything for the chef.

M.O.R.A.
13 rue Montmartre
Paris 1
Everything for the pastry chef and chocolatier.

Index

Conversion Chart

LIQUID MEASURES

Fluid Ounces	U.S. Measures	Imperial Measures	Milliliters
	1 tsp.	1 tsp.	5
¼	2 tsp.	1 dessert spoon	7
½	1 T.	1 T.	15
1	2 T.	2 T.	28
2	¼ cup	4 T.	56
4	½ cup or ¼ pint		110
5		¼ pint or 1 gill	140
6	¾ cup		170
8	1 cup or ½ pint		225
9			250 (¼ liter)
10	1¼ cups	½ pint	280
12	1½ cups or ¾ pint		340
15		¾ pint	420
16	2 cups or 1 pint		450
18	2¼ cups		500 (½ liter)
20	2½ cups	1 pint	560
24	3 cups or 1½ pints		675
25		1¼ pints	700
27	3½ cups		750
30	3¾ cups	1½ pints	840
32	4 cups or 2 pints or 1 quart		900
35		1¾ pints	980
36	4½ cups		1000 (1 liter)

SOLID MEASURES

U.S. and Imperial Measures		Metric Measures	
Ounces	Pounds	Grams	Kilos
1		28	
2		56	
3½		100	
4	¼	112	
5		140	
6		168	
8	½	225	
9		250	¼
12	¾	340	
16	1	450	
18		500	½
20	1¼	560	
24	1½	675	
27		750	¾
28	1¾	780	
32	2	900	
36	2¼	1000	1
40	2½	1100	
48	3	1350	
54		1500	1½

OVEN TEMPERATURE EQUIVALENTS

Fahrenheit	Gas Mark	Celsius	Heat of Oven
225	¼	107	Very Cool
250	½	121	Very Cool
275	1	135	Cool
300	2	148	Cool
325	3	163	Moderate
350	4	177	Moderate
375	5	190	Fairly Hot
400	6	204	Fairly Hot
425	7	218	Hot
450	8	232	Very Hot
475	9	246	Very Hot